– Oracle –
of the
Dreamtime

CARDS ILLUSTRATED BY

Danny Eastwood
Jamie Eastwood
Francis Firebrace
Leah Dawn Prior
Rocky D. Savage
Ian Bundeluk Watson

Oracle
of the
Dreamtime

Aboriginal Dreamings
offer guidance for today

Donni Hakanson

Foreword by Pauline E. McLeod
ABORIGINAL STORYTELLER

CONNECTIONS
BOOK PUBLISHING

To the memory and spirit of a great man,
Burnum Burnum (1936–1997)

A Connections Book
This edition published in Great Britain in 1998 by
Connections Book Publishing Limited
St Chad's House
148 King's Cross Road
London WC1X 9DH

British Library Cataloguing-in-Publication data available on request

ISBN 1 85906 014 5

AN EDDISON • SADD EDITION
Edited, designed and produced by
Eddison Sadd Editions Limited
St Chad's House, 148 King's Cross Road
London WC1X 9DH

Phototypeset in Caxton MT and Birch MT using QuarkXPress on
Apple Macintosh.
Origination by Bright Arts, Singapore
Printed and bound by C & C Offset Printing Company Ltd, Hong Kong

Contents

PART ONE The Dreamings 11

NATURE

EARTH

AIR

WATER

HUMANKIND

PART TWO Using the Oracle

Foreword

The artwork and Dreamings of *Oracle of the Dreamtime* represent the oldest continuing culture on the earth. Since the beginning of time, the people of this culture lived according to their creator's laws. For millenniums, few changes occurred; everyone lived in peace and harmony with themselves, each other and nature. Then came the "change!" Time began, and was given a number: 26 January 1788, "Invasion Day."

For over 210 years, our people, land and creatures survived the genocidal practices of the Caucasian race, and so too did the knowledge of the Dreaming.

Today, there is an opportunity to be introduced to a small fragment of the culture and spirituality of Aboriginal Australia. Our culture has no religion. We do, however, have a very intricate spiritual belief system, according to our ancestors. This is so integrated into our culture that it is part of our existence, our everyday life.

To begin . . . The animals, plants, and creatures of our land are our ancestors, our brothers and sisters, mothers and fathers. We call them our totems, and we must never harm, kill, or eat our personal totems. They are to be looked after. In return, they will never harm us, and, when necessary, they will look after us. They connect us to the spiritual (for want of a better word), and can guide us during difficult moments.

The totems are the creatures of the earth; indeed, the earth itself is our mother. They have a very important message, and their connection with the spiritual is immense. You cannot choose your totem in traditional Aboriginal culture, nor can you change your totem, or exchange it for another. Everyone has their own totem, and one man's totem can be another man's staple diet. You can also have up to fifteen or more totems, from ant, snake, fish, dog, kangaroo, swan, and even eagle. You might like to draw a card from the oracle deck, and view it as your own personal totem, as a way of understanding this concept.

The *Oracle of the Dreamtime* will introduce you to Australian Aboriginal culture. We did not use or need cards to guide us, but I feel this set will help the uninitiated towards a far greater understanding.

Pauline E. McLeod
5 December 1997

Beholder Of Dreams

And there came from the red heart
a wise man with Dreamings to tell
and knowledge to share.

"Of Dreaming comes creation,
and of creation the manifestation
of creative Dreaming," he said.

He continued, "Make your Dreamings sweet
and let mother's arms embody you,
acknowledge her wisdom,
learn from all creatures upon her
for each has something to tell.

Hear what you listen to
and listen to yourself
then the knowledge born of wisdom
will be yours to share
with the Great Ones."

Lisa Reid, Wreck Bay Mission, New South Wales 1995

Introduction

The Dreaming is alive today. I know this is so because, every morning, the sun rises, and the morning birds welcome the day. There is the gentle movement of the wind in the trees, harmonizing with an occasional hum of traffic. I see, hear, smell, and sense the life flowing and moving around me. Consciousness shapes our world. The Dreaming is still alive, even if it appears to be buried under concrete pavements, roads, and buildings. It is even more alive out in the bush, where kangaroos graze and brolgas dance. Superimposed over the ancient Dreaming is a different Dreaming, that of modern Western society.

This oracle is based on the ancient Dreaming stories of the Australian Aboriginal people who believed the world was full of signs from Spirit. These Dreamings are as relevant today as they were thousands of years ago. The Dreaming still exists, and always will, as long as we care for this world and its creatures. *Oracle of the Dreamtime* acknowledges and honors the ancient wisdom of the Dreaming, in a modern form accessible to all.

This oracle seeks a moment in your life when you can take time out, and be with nature and your self. Through the ancient and modern Dreamings of Australia's original inhabitants, the Aboriginal people ("koories," or "murries"), you will discover a new way of attuning to nature and the forces which move and shape your life. These people valued highly the spiritual worth of other people. They magnified the value of life by making its conservation and renewal into a lifestyle. They acknowledged that the material domain was under a spiritual authority, and lived in harmony with that authority, without pollution, destruction, nor wanton violence.

Oracles have been around for centuries: coins, cards, stones, bones, shells, tea leaves, entrails . . . The Aboriginal people believed the world was a living oracle, including the creatures which crossed their paths, and the cloud patterns above. They constructed oracles using natural things from the world around them, then released those items back to the earth.

The presentation of the Dreaming through the medium of an oracle would seem extremely alien and radical to the traditional Aboriginal people of past and present. Their ancient culture did not have a written language. The people relied upon extraordinary feats of memory to relate their Dreaming, and the spiritual laws. The culture was passed on through "storytelling," chanting, song, music, dance, art, including sand drawing, and through daily life. Certain areas of land, rocks, geographical features, and the life forms which inhabited them, also played important roles.

Oracle of the Dreamtime is a reflection of a part of this world, as perceived by a modern white woman and several modern Aboriginal artists. Each card in this oracle contains the essential energy of the symbol it depicts. This energy exists on an "astral and etheric" level, referred to as "morphogenetic fields" by Rupert Sheldrake. We have all been able to sense, in a photograph, the energy of an angry person; or, on the other hand, the reverential atmosphere of a place of nature, or a church. Most "primitive" peoples knew and acknowledged that there existed, and still exists, an energy field for every conceivable object or thing.

A strand of hair or feather radiates the same energy as the entire creature from which it came. These fields can be tuned into, if you wish to attune yourself. Photographs and drawings, for example, radiate in the same vibration to the items they depict on a higher energetic level. As another example of this way of thinking and living, an Aboriginal person does not dance Brolga, he becomes Brolga. He steps into the energy field of that creature and unites with it.

The cards in this oracle are a tool for self-exploration and inspiration. They are a way of solving problems, because they encourage you to seek answers, solutions, and alternatives for yourself. As an oracle, they challenge you to look honestly at the reality you are creating in your life, and at the things you have learnt, and also where you are heading. In effect, *Oracle of the Dreamtime* can help you to find the answers you already have within yourself.

The cards were conceived in a dream in early 1993. I was on a boat in the Basin, Ku-ringai Chase National Park, just north of Sydney. The dream was extremely vivid, and the concept of the oracle was very exciting for me. I was given my first Tarot deck at thirteen and had been using oracles for many years, yet it had never occurred to me, until then, that there was no Australian oracle. I was amazed it had never crossed my mind before. Inspired, and with a strong sense of purpose, I wrote "Eerin the Gray Owl." Upon returning to shore, I found an owl's feather. Many synchronicities followed the writing of the oracle, in my life, and in the card readings I gave myself and others. I saw this as confirmation that I was on the right track.

I believe the dream came to me because I had asked the "universe" for something to write, compatible with parenting, which would have meaning for other people. I had been researching Aboriginal Dreamings and culture with Francis Firebrace for a year. His path led to storytelling and art, mine led to this project. Both are modern expressions of the Dreaming energy. Looking back, I can see the strong thread of guidance for this project going back to my childhood.

It has been very challenging, as a white person ("gubba" or "migloo"), to write about Aboriginal culture. The spiritual essence of Aboriginality is not about skin color or lifestyle; it's the color of your heart that matters, and your link to the land. There are cultural differences, but they are not insurmountable. Even urban "assimilated" kooris have a strong Aboriginal identity. (Of Australia's population, 1.0–0.05% are Aboriginal people. Most white Australians do not know, and many have not met, a koori.)

I grew up mainly in outback Queensland, with a love for the bush and mulga scrub (dense acacia bush). The people out that way are generally known as murries. I was lucky to discover some old bora rings (used for initiation ceremonies) whilst bushwalking.

When I was nineteen I lived in Redfern, a Sydney suburb stereotyped as an Aboriginal ghetto. After I had left, I returned for a visit, and experienced the pain of racism, for the first time. Racism is still out there, on both sides, and we can only hope that increasing awareness and understanding will cause it to die out. The Council for Aboriginal Reconciliation is doing wonderful work towards this goal.

The writing of this oracle has been a journey through a few tests and initiations. It has also been an inner exploration of the influences on my daily life. It has always been during a life crisis, when I feel too attached or emotional to be clear, that I have been drawn to using divination systems. They seem to cut through the fog and get to the point, as long as I am willing to look at myself truthfully. I have used the Dreaming cards through times of difficulty, as well as times of achievement and success. They are a powerful tool for confirmation, as well as for attaining a deeper understanding of one's life lessons.

I gave readings to other people, and these also applied to my life. I experienced the "connectedness" we have with each other. I reconnected more deeply with nature, as well as myself. I have no doubt that you will enhance your own connection with the energies of nature through the use of these cards. They are a form of spiritual communion, and they can be used in meditation, dream analysis, or as visual affirmations of the energies you seek to embrace.

The oracle was written mainly when I was living in a renovated garage in Avalon, north Sydney; a sole parent on "the pension" (social security), with two babies and little support. Initially, I didn't even have a computer, so I typed everything out in the old-fashioned way. I had a dream and followed it. You can do the same. The universe supported me in this; I manifested what I needed on a physical level, including the life lessons needed to grasp the essential meanings for each card.

One of the biggest lessons has been accepting my ability to interpret and write this oracle, not just as a white person, but as a human, with my own faults and imperfections. I would ask myself if I was good enough. Was my writing honoring these great Dreamings and their messages? Yet confirmation surrounded my progress, supporting my faith in myself. I trust that you will take what you need from these writings, and leave the rest. We all perceive life differently, and you may create your own totally different meanings for these cards.

I hope you will seek out the Dreaming, or "higher truth," evident in your life as you use the oracle. May the messages and insights possible through the "chance" occurrences of the symbols amaze you by their relevance to your life. Most of all, do have lots of fun!

After all, this is a fascinating way of communicating with your all-knowing self! You do have the answers for every challenge you encounter in life. The oracle is but a tool, and our brothers and sisters in the different kingdoms of life can be our teachers, if we wish to learn. We are all capable of doing readings without a deck of cards; oracles merely serve as intermediaries. *Oracle of the Dreamtime* will help you to focus on, and reconnect with, your higher self.

This first part of *Oracle of the Dreamtime* contains the Dreamings themselves. It describes the cards which relate to each Dreaming "story," and gives the interpretations of the cards, when they are drawn in a reading. Each Dreaming tells the story of a particular "character," which is often an animal, or a plant, though it is sometimes a more abstract concept, such as Ochre, or Southern Cross (a constellation). The "characters" in the modern Dreamings, such as Sydney Harbor Bridge, relate directly to our interaction with the environment. Each "character" has a card, with an artistic depiction of its image, and including various other images that are relevant to its Dreaming.

Part Two *(pages 147–165)* is a user's guide, presented as a straightforward question-and-answer session explaining how to read the oracle, and how to interpret the spreads.

Note: the word "Dreaming" is synonymous with "Dreamtime," the former being technically and politically correct, as it denotes the past, present, and future connotations of the Aboriginal person's concept of the spiritual realms. The word "Dreamtime" can suggest that these energies are from the past only.

PART ONE
The Dreamings

*T*he Dreamings that follow all have explanations of the imagery contained within the Dreamings and the cards. All the easy-to-understand symbols on the cards can influence any reading. There follows, in each case, a detailed interpretation of the meaning of the card when drawn in a reading. A card can be drawn in three different positions: upright, reversed, and kobong (see page 151). So, the interpretation is divided into three sections.

"Kobong" is an Aboriginal word. Its nearest meaning in English is "totem," though this does not fully explain the concept. A card becomes kobong by a particular placement in a reading, or a card can become a person's kobong if that person is particularly and consistently drawn to that card. The concept has similarities with the signs of the Zodiac in astrology. Your kobong applies to your own actions and personality, and how you directly influence the course of the situation you are querying in a reading.

A special feature of Oracle of the Dreamtime is the circular nature of the cards. Because they are circular, they can be drawn in many different ways, with different symbols at the "top." Also, creatures may appear to be moving towards, or away from, one another. These easy-to-read visual dynamics influence the reading directly, and the range of interpretations is virtually unlimited. Thus, each reading is as unique as each individual using the oracle.

The Dreaming cards are divided into five categories, each category representing the different kingdoms or levels in nature (see pages 154–5). The five sections are: Nature (plants, rocks, celestial bodies and constellations, natural forces and spiritual energies); Earth (creatures which live upon or burrow beneath the earth); Air (birds and insects); Water (fish and water creatures); and Humankind. The Humankind category includes a modern Dreaming, and energies which relate directly to our interaction with the environment. These categories, and the numbers on the cards, can be used to help you find the interpretations quickly during a reading.

1 · Gymea Lily

RESPONSIBILITY · SACRIFICE · HOPE

" *In the Dreaming, a certain tribe lived in the mountains. One day, during a fierce summer rainstorm, the people took refuge in a large cave. Unfortunately, the great deluge caused a massive landslide that blocked the entrance to the cave with very large boulders. The people were trapped. The young man, Bullana, the strongest and most courageous of the warriors, sought a way out. Risking great injury, he climbed the wall of rock, searching for a cavity large enough to allow him to escape. He pulled and squeezed himself through the boulders until he was free.*

Once outside, the young warrior discovered he was not strong enough to move even slightly any of the massive rocks blocking the cave entrance. He could not release his people. Bullana, however, was determined to do everything within his power to keep his tribe alive. Day after day, he hunted from dawn to dusk, in rain or shine. He wove a long rope with which to lower food into the cave. Many times a day,

he climbed the mountain to let food down to his tribe, who depended upon him totally.

At last, the demands of this heavy, constant work and responsibility had its effect on Bullana's strength. One day, he slipped, and fell into a deep ravine, breaking many bones. Still conscious and in great pain, he struggled to crawl out. His greatest anguish was not the physical pain, but the knowledge that now he was unable to provide for his beloved people. His efforts were hopeless. He collapsed and died.

As he died, he clutched a small plant in his hands, and, as his spirit left his body, this plant grew instantly into a mass of long broad leaves. The great white flowers that burst from the center became red with his blood. This plant, known today as the Gymea Lily, gained its strength from Bullana.

Many centuries later, some white men discovered a way into the huge cave, and found the floor covered with the tangled skeletons of Bullana's people. "

Imagery

In this, one of the most tragic of the Dreamings, qualities of strength, stamina, and courage are tested well beyond ordinary endurance. The warrior shows great dedication and perseverance, crossing the boundaries of personal limitation to provide for his tribe. He could have saved himself, but he continued to strive for his people, possibly aware that his efforts were doomed to failure. Faith and hope are key words here.

On the Gymea Lily card, we see the beautiful flower, standing tall and proud. In Western tradition, the color pink represents the heart and love, linking with one of the major themes of this Dreaming. The strong hand of the warrior clutches the stalk, as he clutched his heartfelt responsibilities. The hand may also represent the young warrior's attempts to change fate, and save his people. The dark, somber clouds around the edge of this card represent the clouds of life, which can transform events and outcomes. Yet these storm clouds, which caused the landslide and trapped the people, now bring rain to nourish the Gymea Lily.

Upright

The warrior showed faithfulness towards his people. To desert them would have resulted in eternal anguish and pain for him. Negatively, Gymea Lily can represent rescue attempts that will fail, or totally drain you in the process. This scenario may be a repeated pattern, a recent experience, or one that could be created if you are not willing to evaluate your actions. In its positive aspect, Gymea Lily can imply strong devotion and trust.

In most cases, this stately, beautiful flower represents something you love and have been responsible for. The bonds are very strong. They can be broken only by death itself. This responsibility has entailed, not only hard work, but also the sacrifice of personal needs or wants. Love may require the surrender of independence. Love in action calls for commitment and nurturing, to varying degrees. Gymea Lily represents responsibility, hard work, striving, and ultimately completion (Gymea Lily blossoms to signal the end of the struggle.)

If the blossom of this flower appears to be pointing towards another card, this second card may indicate the source of your sense of responsibility and commitment. This card may signify the origin, or cause, of your present situation. If Gymea Lily card is drawn pointing towards the left-hand side of your reading, your sense of responsibility derives from a past event; drawn pointing towards the right, Gymea Lily suggests that your situation will continue long into the future.

Bullana was faithful to his ideals and knew his course. Try to clarify your ideals, working towards them, with the devotion portrayed by this Dreaming.

If **Seven Sisters** also appears in your reading, remember that the Seven Sisters chose to endure tests and limitations, whereas Bullana was forced to do so by fate. You may find yourself underestimating your situation. However, your strong belief in yourself will overcome any limitations. **Waratah** and **Sturt's Desert Pea**, both tragic Dreamings, may represent the energies of love and devotion being tested to their utmost.

Reversed

If you have drawn Gymea Lily in the contrary position, you are avoiding responsibility on some level. The blossom is torn from its stalk and is lying discarded. Are you looking after yourself properly? Do you consider your own personal needs as opposed to the needs and demands of others? How balanced is your life in this respect? Perhaps you need to spend some time alone focusing on yourself and creating personal boundaries.

Sometimes we can give too much, or too little; as we can also receive too much, or reject too much.

Gymea Lily card in this position can teach us to say "no," and to take control of our personal power. In situations of emotional involvement, it can be difficult to be responsible for ourselves, and easier to say "yes," even though this may be an "untruth," which brings further problems in the long run.

Kobong

As kobong, Gymea Lily represents a strong sense of integrity, ethics, and responsibility. Your choices in life center around these ideals, regardless of personal sacrifice or hardship. Your choices almost always entail the consideration of others, for you are a very giving and generous person.

These qualities make you particularly sensitive to a lack of ideals in other people. You tend to expect others to live up to your own personal standards, and, when people fall short, you cannot understand how this can happen. This quality becomes more judgmental if Gymea Lily is drawn reversed. You could also be described as naive or gullible; you trust people easily, therefore are vulnerable.

Gymea Lily can be seen in those who struggle against the vicissitudes of life, yet do not give in under the pressure. They have a strong, courageous spirit, which elicits admiration. Negatively, this Dreaming can refer to those people who seem to "draw trouble," and delight in

regaling others with their tales of woe.

If this card is drawn with one of the storm clouds appearing at the top, you may find yourself caught in one of the great storms of life. Your issue is being tested, and you may be bowing under your sense of responsibility to other people. The challenge here is to recognize the difference between your needs and those of others. A sense of obligation is not enough to sacrifice the requirements of your issue; it may be time to stand tall and proclaim your own needs and individuality.

If you have Gymea Lily as your kobong, a strong sense of responsibility affects the issues underlying your situation. Outside circumstances may push you away from your focus or course, challenging you to remain true to yourself. Like Bullana the warrior, unless you take time for rest and recuperation, you may end up feeling drained and weary. Gymea Lily challenges you to seek your own needs, and to balance them with the needs of other people.

2 • Lightning Man

WARNING • IMPACTS • POWER

" According to the traditional Aboriginal people of the Northern Territory, the Lightning Man, Namarragon, lives above the world, in the skyworld. In each of his great hands, he holds a spear of lightning, and, on his knees, he has clubs that he bangs together to make the loudest, roaring sounds of thunder.

Most of the year, Lightning Man stays away from the earth and its inhabitants. No one sees or hears from him while the days are at their hottest and the cicadas are ringing out in the summer evenings. He spends most of his time basking in the golden warmth of Bila the Sun Woman, until he becomes as bright as her and appears as if he is shining like fire. But, when the wet season arrives, he leaves the presence of his companion, Bila the Sun Woman, for at this time he has a special duty to perform.

During the wet season, when the people spend their time talking and telling stories, and painting and weaving in their caves, and the skies are covered with billowing, gray clouds, and rain falls upon the thirsty land, Namarragon the Lightning Man comes down from the heavens to ride the clouds. The people know he is there by the sound of his great clubs making thunder, and the flashes of brilliant white lightning bolts. He watches the earth carefully for any sign that the people are doing wrong, or breaking tribal, or spiritual, law.

Sometimes the people forget, so Namarragon sends a warning to remind them. He strikes a tree, or even the ground nearby. When the people see this, they become frightened and are reminded to mend their wrong ways. Sometimes, if this warning is not enough to get the message through, and people continue to do wrong, Namarragon the Lightning Man will strike one of them dead. "

Imagery

Power is a keyword here. Namarragon, from the clouds, sees what is going wrong, and gives a warning. His volatile energy can destroy what is no longer useful—what is, in itself, destructive, or inflammable. This allows regeneration and new growth. Lightning Man energizes all living things, preparing them for the coming time of renewal, flowering, mating, and breeding. He represents the life-enhancing and the destructive aspects of the element of fire.

The Lightning Man comes with the wet season, which, in Aboriginal culture, heralds a more relaxed time of plentiful food and social activity. The days are spent mainly in cave or shelter talking, celebrating, storytelling, and painting.

Upright

Namarragon the Lightning Man's appearance is sure to strike your reading with an impact. You are being warned. Find another approach, a different route, go another way. Changes are certainly indicated. Indeed, they are necessary for the success of your query.

Witnessing lightning at close hand strikes the heart with terror, and makes us aware how close we were to being struck ourselves. Namarragon asks you to face your mortality, or the loss of something you cherish. This could be something physical, or it could be an ideal, a situation or a plan. This very confrontation could lead you to follow a totally different path. As your perspective changes, so will your direction. Another route will become clear. Lightning will flash, bringing insights and impacts along the way.

The Lightning Man asks you to harness this energy and to use its potential in times of radical change. The bolt of lightning flashes as a message. The warning prevents indiscriminate destruction, unless it is ignored. Observe the warning. Stop! Go another way!

When Lightning Man strikes your reading, where are his bolts of lightning pointing? Any card under a direct hit is a certain indicator of where you may need to change your route. A warning isn't the end of the world; it is a guide, a signpost, a gift that persuades you to examine your position more closely, in the issue you are querying. Where are you wrong? Can you acknowledge any sense of unease you may be carrying? If you are safe from any direct hits from Lightning Man's spears, enjoy the spectacular storm. You may find he brings the chance to focus on the more pleasurable aspects of life.

Whichever way it points, this card may indicate the end of an unpleasant or limiting situation, and the opening up of new opportunities. For, at the end of the wet season, comes a time of plenty. Whichever way your path twists and turns, it will always move through these times of regeneration and new growth.

Other cards featuring lightning bolts will emphasize the presence of electrical energy coursing through your issue. This energy may hit with an impact, or it may flow smoothly, propelling you towards a different course of action. The energy is influenced by the issues covered by the other cards present. **Ochre**, **Platypus** and **Rainbow Serpent** also highlight unseen currents.

2 · LIGHTNING MAN

Reversed

With the card reversed, Namarragon the Lightning Man is still above the clouds, not yet ready to come down. The image of the Lightning Man building up his energy, to be more brilliant than the sun before he descends to the clouds, is potent with spiritual significance. On a mundane level, you could be "up in the clouds," and about to face the inevitable "coming down to earth." Alternatively, this may be a time of building up your energy reserves, ready for a power-packed time ahead. Latent forces are certainly building up in your issue. Any uncertainties or doubts will be resolved with the influx of energy.

Lightning Man reversed encourages trust in the best possible outcome. This is not a time of planned action, more a time of impulsive action within the events around you. Whenever possible, build up and concentrate your energy for when the storm hits!

Where is this card pointing? Lightning Man strikes with an impact. He acts as a destructive force. He may represent a negative energy field, or a series of events that appears to halt any progress. It is as if the universe is conspiring against you. In fact, you are being guided to change direction, especially in the issues covered by the other cards the lightning bolts may be aimed at. Slow down. What are you doing "out in a thunderstorm," anyway?

Kobong

If Lightning Man appears as kobong, or if you are particularly drawn to this card, he brings strong energy, with the power to heal or destroy. In a reading, this is a teaching card. You may learn you have the power to finish what is no longer useful, and to channel energy into more constructive avenues in your life, like creating what you want.

Lightning Man reveals that you are in a position of power, from where you can alter the course of your life, or even the lives of others. You have the ability to see what is wrong, or out of harmony, within the "bigger picture," and you have the force to engender positive, fruitful alternatives. This card can also indicate the need to be more alert to omens and messages.

This card brings a sense of being propelled by the winds of change. You are powerless to do other than what the situation demands, and there are many synchronicities around. Lightning Man strikes your path. ZAP! The claps and roars of thunder echo his ire, pushing you in the right direction.

As kobong, Lightning Man charges your reading, and puts you on notice to examine your direction. Intense energies will propel your situation into new areas. As the clouds build up, be prepared for a storm. After the havoc, there will be a clarity and freshness which will reenergize your issue.

3 · Moon

CYCLES · CHANGES · GESTATION

" Gien the Moon was a very handsome, clever young man, a skilled thrower of the spear and boomerang. He traveled around the country, visiting many tribes. He liked fun, food, and the good life, and would stay longer in the camps where the women were attractive. Gien was much admired by the women, and envied by the men. He was an excellent hunter, and would share his skills with the men, so they would go off to hunt, and he could stay back at the camp with the women. Life was good for him—no work, and plenty of fun.

Then he fell in love with two women at one of the camps he visited. By law, he couldn't marry them because he was from an unknown place. Where he came from was a great mystery. (Another of his secrets was that he could not swim.) Eventually, he suggested to the two women that they should run away with him, and, one night, they left the camp. They came to a river. Gien the Moon put his arms around the women, but, halfway across the river, they began to tickle him. He warned them to stop, but they wouldn't. They then swam away from him, and Gien the Moon sank like a stone, disappearing into the murky waters.

After several days, he emerged from the water, covered in mud. He revived slowly, and found his powers were stronger than ever. He made plans to wreak his revenge. When he returned, no one recognized him. He began to sing and dance, and this inspired the people so much, they decided to hold a corroboree.

During the corroboree, the Moon Man dragged a sheet of bark close to the fire. In between two performances, he made all the people bow their heads. Then, using his magical powers, he quickly lifted the bark over their heads and jumped on top of it, trapping them beneath. All the people perished, except two men who escaped. They warned the other tribes, who then chased Gien. Gien the Moon Man escaped by going to the skyworld, where he remains to this day.

When you see a circle around the Moon, this is the bark sheet, now Gien's humpy (hut). The waning of the Moon is when Gien goes off to get more bark. "

Imagery

There are many Aboriginal myths and beliefs about the Moon. The most common is that the Moon decrees that everything must die. The Moon avoids this decree himself by dying for three days before being reborn. In the Dreaming retold here, he is depicted as a virile youth of great physical prowess and skill, but a womanizer.

In Aboriginal culture, it was generally believed that if a woman gazed at the moon for too long, she would become pregnant. In one Dreaming, the Moon Man is said to make the female babies, and Waan the Black Crow makes the boy babies. The red blossoms of mistletoe are said to be the blood of unborn spirit children.

In this Dreaming card, we see the Moon shining between hanging strands of crimson mistletoe, a sign of life, representing the earth and nature. The Moon casts his seductive light, symbolizing cycles, beginnings and endings. The Moon, who is masculine in the Dreaming, also embodies conception, gestation and growth. The cycle of the Moon appears around the edges of this card.

In Western folklore, mistletoe is traditionally associated with Christmas. Having no roots and being neither a tree nor shrub, mistletoe was thought to have a special relationship to the divine, representing the ability to go beyond earthly limitations. (It also symbolized femininity, as the oak tree it was attached to stood for masculinity. So, on this card, mistletoe balances out the masculine energies of the Moon.) In Australia, there are mistletoe birds that eat the fruit, thus helping the plant to propagate by excreting the seeds. So, mistletoe can also represent new beginnings with unexpected sources.

Upright

Moon appearing in a reading can indicate you are involved in some process that needs to be completed before you can start something new. The Moon also brings new energy into the situation queried, and is particularly relevant to conception, and the start of new projects. The phase of the Moon that lies at the twelve o'clock position can indicate what phase you are in, and may act as an indicator of where you are in the cyclic aspects of your issue. The full Moon symbolizes the actualization of goals, and indicates that your issue has reached its fullest potential.

Gien in your reading can call for an acknowledgment of personal weaknesses, especially if **Spider** appears.

The mistletoe in this card could represent available resources, or some spirit yet to be manifested. The process of manifestation has cycles, like the Moon: from spirit to conception, gestation, birth, growth, and finally death, and back to spirit.

The Moon and Sun are inextricably linked. The Moon represents cycles, and "capsules" of time, with a beginning and end. Modern science has learnt that the cause of the moon's cycles is the sun's light. So, the cyclical nature of the moon is linked to the sun's apparently perpetual motion. The source of cycles comes from a larger, constant origin. Moon and **Sun** appearing together in a reading can point to a larger pattern influencing your issue. If this is not clear initially, refer to your reading again, a few days later, as this could provide an important insight. Like the Moon and Sun, you may have to make your journey a few times to see the pattern.

Reversed

With the card reversed, the mistletoe appears to be growing upward, against all rules of nature. However, this is not a disadvantage, as it fits in with the larger scheme of things. Although growing upwards, the mistletoe is surviving and flowering. It succeeds against the natural forces which fashioned it to hang from a branch. Do not be alarmed. The supernatural could well be touching your life, but it will do no harm, if you can accept a different view of the way things should be.

The emphasis is on the darkest phase of the Moon, which symbolizes the genesis of new ideas and projects. If the card is oriented towards the waning phase, a previous project has reached its highest potential and is now finishing. If the Moon is beginning its waxing journey, then creative, productive energies bring an influx of positive development and growth.

Kobong

If you have Moon as kobong, or if his alluring, magical light draws you, there is a desire for change, for new energy and fresh beginnings. Moon requires patience, because the need to complete a cycle before starting the next can be frustrating. Just as the Moon dies and is reborn, your situation, or issue, will decrease and wane, or be infused with positive and life-enhancing energy, depending upon which phase of the Moon is at the top of the card as it was drawn.

As kobong, this card can indicate that you have the ability to find answers in tricky situations, and that your natural talents may elicit envy. You may also have a strong charisma, especially if **Ochre**, **Spider** or **Uluru** appear. These qualities are emphasized by the energies of magnetism, and there may be a tendency to be seduced by exciting projects that are not necessarily realistic or practical.

The Moon is associated with change, especially in the arena of the emotions. As life is in a state of flux, so too is your situation. What phase of the Moon is at the center top of the card? Moods can swing and tides can rise. Being aware of the lunar motions can keep us in touch with the changeable aspects of life, and their part in a larger pattern.

Conception and pregnancy are also under the influence of the Moon, especially if the cards **Crow** or **Dolphin** appear.

The mistletoe could also influence your reading, by making available a vast resource of energy that may be utilized for the growth of your issue. The mistletoe represents a "baby," perhaps a special goal or project, definitely something which will require time, tender care and nurturing. You are being given a gift, and it is now up to you to use it in the best possible way.

4 • Opal

JUSTICE • SPIRITUAL LAW • KARMA

In the Dreaming, when the world as we know it had just begun, all the people on the earth lived without law. There were no rules and regulations of any kind, nor were there any standards by which to live. The people were very confused. They did not know how to track and hunt the animals; and neither did they know which foods were edible and which were poisonous. The people even married within their own families, because, at that time, they knew no moral correctness. They did not know any sacred ceremonies, and the Great Spirit was neither recognized nor honored.

Eventually, the Great Spirit came down to the earth on a rainbow. He gathered all the different tribes together, and proceeded to instruct the people about the laws they were to follow, and the way they should live their lives. The Great Spirit also taught them their food-gathering and hunting skills, their kinship regu-lations, and their spiritual responsi-bilities. In this way, the people's way of life was understood and established.

The Great Spirit told the people that he would continue to watch over them to see how well they had learnt and followed his teachings. He also told them he would return one day, when he judged the people were wise enough to carry out his plan for endless peace on earth. He said they would know when this time had come, because a rainbow would appear in the sky, and this rainbow would be much brighter than the usual rainbows, and a different shape.

The rainbow bore the Great Spirit back into the sky. Where the end of the rainbow had rested on the ground, the people found that there was now an area of rocks and pebbles, which flashed and glittered with all the colors of the rainbow. These sacred stones were the first Opals.

Imagery

In this inspiring Dreaming, Opal represents spiritual law, faith, and hope, entwined with karma, justice and balance. It symbolizes the idea of "reaping what we have sown," and the desire for spiritual ideals.

The mystical association of Opal with the creator spirit brings a magical quality to this Dreaming. The most important message of Opal is one of hope and expectancy, with the promise of the Great Spirit's return.

Rainbows are a powerful image throughout many cultures. The Rainbow Serpent creates reality and delivers retribution if the law is disobeyed. In the Hindu and Buddhist tantric traditions, the human body dissolves into rainbow light when the highest meditative state is achieved, revealing the world and "reality" as insubstantial. For the ancient Greeks, the rainbow represented a winged goddess, Iris, who carried messages from the gods to mortals. Many other cultures viewed the rainbow as a celestial bridge for deities to travel to earth and back again. In Christianity, it is a symbol of God's forgiveness after the great flood of Noah and his ark. In many cultures, the rainbow was evidence of divine activity. And many children today seek the elusive crock of gold at the end of the rainbow!

A rainbow makes an arc across the card, its bright colors reflected in the opal that it embraces. The two images symbolize the Great Spirit's journey from the spiritual to the material world, as well as the divine directive for mankind to practice spirituality in daily life. The rainbow bridges the two realms, uniting the spiritual and material dimensions.

Upright

Wherever Opal appears, you are on the right track. Peace is possible. Its equivalent in the Tarot is Justice. Searching may be a key word with the rainbow, and, with Opal, the spiritual quest is on. Opal asks you to examine your life. Physical circumstances could well be overwhelming your will. Now is the time to evaluate, judge, and act from a more focused and directed perspective. Being totally "in the now," with an awareness of forward direction, is a challenge of this card.

Opal can also indicate healing, on any level. The colors of Opal correspond to the seven chakras, so, as a meditative focus, Opal can facilitate a balancing of one's personal energy field (visualize the colors, or place a piece of opal upon your body). You may also like to try wearing opal as jewelry, or taking it as a gem elixir. Spiritual energies will be highlighted, as this stone draws and reflects the colors of life.

Opal reminds you to wait for your good—it is coming! The rainbow bridge is beginning its arc, bringing color and hope towards, and into, your situation. Opal is the card of faith.

On a mundane level, Opal can indicate self-discipline and working towards something which is rewarding. Studying, and learning new skills, may also be a part of this process. Or you could be awaiting the results of a past endeavor or achievement.

If **Rainbow Serpent** also appears, there is an emphasis on the correct course of action and ethical behavior. These two cards reveal you have the ability to actualize any results you may be seeking to achieve in your issue.

Reversed

With this card reversed, the rainbow is turned upwards, perhaps reflected in a still, outback billabong. Why are you looking downwards when the rainbow is above? Or perhaps you are able to acknowledge that you are enjoying the beauty of the rippling image. Reflections, as they are mirrored in the natural world, and in the actions of other people with whom you interact, can show you your own best and worst qualities. What do you admire and dislike in others? Can you acknowledge these qualities within yourself?

Traditionally, Opal is said to be unlucky. Any lack of harmony will be intensified by Opal appearing reversed.

The gemstone black opal is particularly sought and treasured. So, perhaps this card reminds you that, although your current experiences may seem black, they are valuable for your spiritual growth. The dark experiences you have drawn into your life may ultimately constitute treasure, although this may not emerge until later.

Opal reversed can also indicate an intensive time of giving up previous habits, and releasing negativity. It indicates increasing clarity, and an increase in one's personal value. There may be a lot of chaos and unrest in your situation, but persevere—there will be a rainbow for you!

Kobong

Opal is a very spiritual card as kobong, or if you are drawn to its ethereal beauty. It indicates that you are influencing your situation through expectations which inevitably act as limitations, even if your ultimate purpose is spiritual in its focus. You know what you want to achieve and, when this is frustrated, you may give up easily. Remembering your source of inspiration may be the antidote. Apply some creativity to your issue; break out of stereotypes. It is possible to stick by the rules, and still have fun.

Opal people believe strongly in karma, and in "doing the best" in every situation they encounter. They tend to be rather conservative, in that they follow society's rules and conventions, forgetting that these rules were made by fellow brothers and sisters, and are therefore fallible. They also need to remember that breaking away from those rules can enable intuition to flow, and better alternatives to emerge. In contrast with their outward conventionality, Opal people may possess some surprising interests: perhaps a passion for UFOs, astrology, Egyptology, or past lives.

Lawyers, teachers, people who work with facts and figures, mechanics, and scientists have Opal-oriented work. These people would benefit from a good dose of the rainbow colors of Opal, to enable them to rise above material distractions, to reconnect with the beauty and unpredictability of nature. This can be achieved by "going bush," and taking the time out to "look for rainbows." Alternatively, these people may be drawn to higher causes; they may be spiritualists, psychics or working towards a vision which improves the quality of life and the environment.

5 · Rainbow Serpent

CREATION · TRANSFORMATION · SPIRITUALITY

" *In the beginning, the land was flat, and the Rainbow Serpent lay in a deep sleep in the center of the earth. For a long time she slept. Then she woke, and crawled up through the earth, breaking through the surface in a shower of ochre dust. She traveled across the flat empty land. So powerful was her magic that, as she went, she caused it to rain heavily. The tracks made by her body were filled with water, thus creating the rivers, lakes and billabongs. Wherever she traveled, milk from her breasts soaked into the earth. This made the land fertile, and rain forests grew. She created the mountain ranges, and the valleys, but she left some parts of the land flat—these we now call deserts.*

She woke all land dwellers, and brought them to the surface: animals that carried their young in a pouch, or lived in trees, or burrowed under the ground. The bird tribes were woken. The sky was filled with birds of different sizes, shapes and colors; and there were flightless birds that walked upon the land.

Next, she woke the water creatures, placing them in the rivers, lakes and vast oceans: fish that darted in the shallow streams, frogs that sang in the shadows of night, eels and turtles.

Then, she brought from the womb of the earth man and woman. They learned from the Rainbow Serpent how to live in peace and harmony with all these creatures who were their spiritual cousins. She taught them tribal ways, and how to share with one another, to take only what they needed, to honor and respect the earth; and to pass this knowledge onto their children.

And man and woman were then the caretakers of this land. The Rainbow Serpent went into a waterhole, where she continues to guard the water creatures. When people go fishing, they know they must take only as much as they need for food. If anyone is greedy enough to take more than they need, the great Rainbow Serpent will come out of her hiding place to punish the person who broke this tribal law. "

Imagery

The Rainbow Serpent, in her many forms, is the most widely featured ancestral deity in Aboriginal culture. Many Dreamings attribute the creation of the landscape and all life to Rainbow Serpents. The feminine aspects of the Rainbow Serpent remind us of the powers of creation, and the essence of life. Most representations depict her "painted up" in vibrant ochres, again reflecting the energies of creation. There is a strong link with water, as denoted by the rainbow. The earth awaits water to release its potential.

On the card, the "mother" Serpent is depicted moving across a sand painting of the Sun. The Sun and the Serpent represent feminine life-giving energy. The red earth symbolizes latent potential. The Rainbow Serpent can shed its skin, symbolizing change, transformation, and regeneration. The Sun remains constant and unchanging, regardless of how this card is drawn.

If one were to draw a vertical line halfway through this card, the Serpent would cross it seven times. Each crossing point represents one of the chakras, or energy centers, in the human body. (The Serpent has been linked with the ancient yogic *kundalini,* the life force that is believed to lie coiled at the base of the spine until it is aroused and sent to the head to trigger enlightenment.) Its energy heals, cleanses and enlightens, but, when misused, it destroys. Aboriginal elders of great spiritual discipline recognized that the Serpent energy lay coiled in the body as "rainbow fires." By raising this energy, they could access knowledge and healing, and project themselves to other locations.

With this symbolism in mind, the five sections of this Serpent can, in turn, represent the five senses, five fingers, or the abilities and tools we have to perceive and shape reality. The four elements are represented in the four bands and, as a whole, the art symbolizes spirit descending into matter.

Upright

A river does not move in a straight line, and the Serpent follows a similar course. The message is to focus on the source of your strength, in the midst of change and movement. This card says you are on the right path.

The Rainbow Serpent can create a sense of "there's no turning back," and "the only way is forward." However, it is not external forces that are dictating your path. In another Dreaming, a young boy clings to the back of a Rainbow Serpent as they journey across the land. This potent image acknowledges your powers of co-creation with life's spiritual energy. As you ride the Serpent, you direct it. Yet, if you break the law, there will be severe repercussions. Take notice if the Serpent appears to be moving towards another card. If it does so, prepare to embrace or face the issues introduced by the new cards. A card near the tail of the Serpent can indicate the origins or causes of your present issue.

The appearance of **Uluru** can refer to an important goal or project. This is an auspicious placement, of spiritual import. Take notice of any cards between or near them; these will represent the energies influencing your situation. One Dreaming states that Uluru was a great egg dropped from the sky by the Rainbow Serpent. In another Dreaming, the Serpent emerges from the rock.

Reversed

In this position, the Serpent appears to be moving downwards, symbolizing a plunge into the past. This indicates that anachronistic echoes are strongly influencing your life. Is there something your thoughts keep returning to: the "good old days," or a time you wish to avoid and forget? If the Serpent appears to be moving towards another card, take special note of this card's issues, for they are tied up with your present circumstances. They prevent any change of direction, or forward movement.

The Rainbow Serpent is going backwards, where he has been. This may indicate the need to reevaluate your past. A new perspective may be all that is required. Emotions of guilt, embarrassment, anger, hatred, or regret may need to be released.

On another level, this position could refer to something in the past that is incomplete, holding you back, though not necessarily linked with negative emotions. Unfinished business can prevent you from fully experiencing the present. Having "no strings attached" means cutting those invisible ties through completion. Thus, the Rainbow Serpent is seen moving backwards to free himself. Then, and only then, can this powerful being move forward creatively into new territory.

Kobong

The Rainbow Serpent as kobong is a very important and auspicious placement, representing desire and will, combined with vision, the kind of vision which propels you into action and achievement. No doubt you are already tapping into the Rainbow Serpent's power of creation. Its presence is an affirmation of divine support, enforced by your own constructive action. (This energy is useless if it is not utilized.) The direction of the Serpent can point to other issues which may need to be dealt with along the way.

Medicine men and artists are closely connected with this symbol. Wisdom is another association. Rainbow Serpent people are very strong-willed, forthright, thorough, and dedicated. They have the ability to create something of lasting and permanent good in the world. Their personal epic can be retold by the landmarks they leave behind. Having strong values, they seek to influence their environment positively. However, when made angry by perceived wrongs, their vengeance can strike with thunderous impact. They need to remember that their power can easily frighten people who are less aware. The lesson here is temperance.

As kobong, the Rainbow Serpent reversed can point to the concept of past lives, or patterns that travel through the generations. The knowledge of one's ancestors, the history held within one's genetic structure, may be a strong influence on a current situation. Tapping into this storehouse of wisdom can improve your knowledge of who you are today. Honoring the past, its mistakes and lessons, will assist you in integrating the very powerful energies of the Rainbow Serpent. By going back, the way forward is made clearer.

6 · Seven Sisters

INITIATION • TESTS • CONVICTION

" *In the Dreaming, seven girls decided they wanted to go through initiation, just as the boys did, to mark the reaching of adulthood. They went to the elders of the tribe and made their request.*

"We will make new tests," the men told them. "Girls could never stand the ordeals that the boys must endure." The young women stood firm. They believed that women were able to overcome fear and pain as well as men. "Very well," said the elders. "We would never willingly make you suffer, but, if you can endure to the end, you will have our respect, and we will think more of our women."

The elders took the girls to a secret place to teach them the law of the tribe. The girls were given only small portions of food, and their bodies became lean. They learned to control their appetites.

Then they underwent the first test. The girls were taken on a long and difficult journey, and they were not permitted to eat. Finally, they were given food, and allowed to eat as much as they wanted. To the relief of the elders, the girls ate only enough to satisfy their hunger. If they had obeyed their instincts, they would have eaten too much, thus making them ill after the long fast.

They returned to camp for the second test. One by one, they were made to lie down. A wirrunun took a pointed stick and knocked a tooth from each girl's mouth. The girls endured the agony without a murmur. They had passed the test of pain. "It is almost over," the elders said, at last. "There now remains one last test, the conquering of fear."

That night, the elders told the girls terrifying tales before they left them to sleep. Later in the night, the elders stole back, and awoke the girls with horrible screams. The men enjoyed themselves as they keened and howled, trying to fill the girls' hearts with fear.

Morning came, and the whole tribe greeted the girls, who were now women. In the midst of the celebration, the women were snatched away, and taken up into the sky. They became the Seven Sisters constellation, shining down on every new generation, encouraging the young people to follow their example. "

Imagery

The Seven Sisters exemplify courage, endurance, strength and discipline. They had such faith in themselves that they were able to persevere, even though they were tested to the limit.

Traditionally, Aboriginal women did not go through the same initiation rituals as men. Women had their own secret, sacred ceremonies, and magic. Much of this has not been recorded because anthropologists were predominantly male, and excluded from knowledge of women's secrets. The initiation rituals for women were generally those of life and nature: menstruation, child-bearing and menopause. Menstrual blood symbolized life force and, in many areas, was regarded as sacred.

(The letting of blood in male initiations has been said to represent the blood of menstruation, in that it also symbolizes the release of life-giving and powerful energy.) Some tribes also included rituals, such as the ritual incision during grief, the removal of a tooth, or (a practical example from the Palm Beach area of Sydney), the removal of the end of the little finger to make it easier to use fishing nets.

This card depicts the Seven Sisters constellation as it appears in the heavens. The constellation has inspired many cultures, and its energies are often perceived as female. The stars shine brightly against the dark sky, as we too can "shine our light" against any darkness.

Upright

Seven Sisters in your reading shows a strong will, courage, and inner conviction. There is emphasis on the power of the mind over the physical body, and over challenging circumstances. The Seven Sisters were seeking to become whole, by experiencing the duality of their human experience, through the male initiation process. This card indicates you are going through some kind of personal initiation. You have chosen the more challenging path, which may require you to reflect qualities, or traits, associated with the opposite sex. Making the choice to take control of your personal power, and defining its boundaries by testing its limits, brings you into the celestial reaches of the Seven Sisters.

As the card of initiation, the Seven Sisters are a guiding force, and have the ability to share their qualities, if you allow them. Gaze upon them; absorb their energies

of courage and conviction. During times of stress and challenge, this card can be an affirmation of the qualities you possess, even if you cannot see them. These qualities are available to you through difficult times, indeed, the initiations of life. It is up to you whether you look up to the Seven Sisters to absorb their inspiring and courageous energy, or whether you continue to be focused on the earth and mundane reality, oblivious to the Sisters' shining example.

The Seven Sisters place a testing and strenuous focus upon whatever cards are nearest in a reading. If any of the stars appear to point towards another card; the issues contained within that card will be challenged. The presence of **Rainbow Lorikeet** emphasizes an aspect of self-sacrifice in your issue. **Sea Hawk** will further crystallize your strong focus and desires.

Reversed

If drawn reversed, Seven Sisters appears as it would if reflected on a still body of water, perhaps a billabong or protected cove. The water perfectly mirrors the shining brilliance of the Seven Sisters, but, if you gaze at the card long enough, small movements ripple the image, breaking its continuity and your focus.

The influence of the Seven Sisters reversed is that of the small ripples. This suggests you are getting caught up in things that disturb your vision and blur your focus. The movements around you are distracting. It is easy to float aimlessly on the relaxing currents, losing sight of your goal. Appearing in this way, The Seven Sisters are challenging you to persevere with the issue being queried. Do not give up. By remaining focused, you will achieve your objective.

Like a hunter or fisher, watching for the slightest movement of prey beneath the water, it is not wise to allow your attention to be diverted. Like the beams of light shining from the Seven Sisters down to the land below, remain true to your course, direct, and steadfast. Believe in yourself, and concentrate your energies more fully upon your goal.

Kobong

With Seven Sisters as kobong, or if you are drawn to this card, there is a spiritual, dedicated questing. You put everything to the test, particularly yourself. There is a need to prove yourself by crossing personal boundaries and achieving success. This can involve crossing the pain boundaries through extreme mental discipline and emotional control. There is a strong focus, which will greatly benefit the outcome of your query.

The word "initiation" is likely to contain a strong personal meaning for you, as your experience of life has tested you well. Generally, people feel a great deal of esteem and respect for those who have successfully crossed the boundaries of pain and fear. This card can signify accolade for your struggles and achievements.

Surgery and life-threatening illness are examples of modern initiations. They involve facing fear and pain, and learning to trust. Other modern day initiations include challenges that entail the acceptance of greater responsibility, or a test of the physical and/or mental endurance of the body. In Western society, the importance of ceremony has been greatly reduced. Growth, achievement and the crossing of boundaries are not generally celebrated (except in the sports arena). Humanity is no longer spiritually in touch with the stages and challenges of life, let alone the great step into adulthood. As kobong, Seven Sisters might bring a ceremony, or celebration, to mark your progress, and acknowledge your abilities.

Strength, confidence, conviction, initiative, and related qualities are all evident in this Dreaming. With the card in the position of kobong, these characteristics influence all other cards in your reading. It is time to prepare for an exciting challenge, one that will certainly test all your reserves of fortitude. However, the Seven Sisters continue to shine in the heavens above you, as a celestial affirmation that "you can do it!"

7 · Southern Cross

DEATH · ENDINGS · SPIRITUAL BELIEF

" In the beginning of the world and time, in the Dreaming, there were only three people on the earth: two men and a woman. The Great Spirit provided them with plenty of bush tucker and water, but he forbade them to eat meat, saying it was wrong. His word was law. The three people obeyed him, for there was more than enough food other than meat to eat. There were many new tastes to experiment with and savor. They enjoyed the nourishing food the Great Spirit had provided for them, and were grateful. They explored their world, and were amazed by the wondrous things they discovered.

After some time, the food gradually diminished until, finally, there was none left. In hunger and desperation, one of the men killed an animal, and the woman cooked it, against the protestations of the second man. This man insisted that the Great Spirit would surely not allow them to suffer for much longer without food, and that it was wrong to kill another living creature. But his protests fell upon deaf ears.

The two who were eating the animal argued that the Great Spirit had provided them with a meal, and they found it very tasty. They offered some to their brother, but, although he was hungry, and salivating at the aromatic smells of cooked meat, he remained strong. He stayed obedient to his creator. Their arguments had no effect upon him.

Disappointed and angry with his companions, the man walked away and lay under a tree. He prepared to die. His companions continued to try to persuade him. Suddenly, in a flash of light, Mowi, the Death Spirit descended. Mowi lifted the man into the tree under which he lay. Then Mowi lifted the tree into the sky. The tree's form grew smaller as he rose higher. It rests in the sky as the Southern Cross. The top star represents the eyes of Mowi, the bottom star symbolizes the eyes of the first man to die.

The stars at each side are two cockatoos who had made their home in the tree. When Mowi lifted it, they followed, squawking and screeching angrily. "

Imagery

Southern Cross is a Dreaming about the first death. It speaks of transformation, change, endings, and new beginnings, suggesting similarities with the Butterfly Dreaming. It speaks of a man (the first committed vegetarian!) who honored the word of the Great Spirit and died for his beliefs. He was transformed, and, through his obedience, attained eternal life. Those who disobeyed the law by eating flesh survived, but they, and all generations after them, were punished by death, without the transformation of eternal life. The bright stars of the Southern Cross are a shining celebration of the power of devotion, obedience, and will.

This Dreaming also has similarities with the Seven Sisters. Both convey strong beliefs, and mental and physical discipline. The difference is that Southern Cross emphasizes the spiritual dimension, while the Seven Sisters follow their belief in themselves.

In this card we see the constellation of the Southern Cross. The imagery focuses on results, and in this case, it is the lasting, eternal constellation which has come to symbolize the southern skies. The bottom star in the Southern Cross constellation has been used as a pointer for the direction of south. The stars on the left and right indicate the two cockatoos, and, as stated in the Dreaming, the other stars represent the eyes of death and the first man to die.

Upright

The Southern Cross is equivalent to the Death card in the Tarot. It strikes with great impact, and irreversible change. This change ends a cycle; it is not part of a continuous process. This card suggests testing forces in your life, requiring you to stand up for your beliefs.

If either of the cockatoos (the two stars on the left and right), are drawn at or near the top, they represent the desire to be at home; or to retain something which is lost. You haven't reached it, but you're chasing it. There could be a sense of urgency and panic in your pursuit.

You are being asked to examine your spiritual beliefs, particularly those around "God." You could have the opportunity to practice your beliefs in testing conditions. Like "gold through a smelter," the dross will be burned away, leaving the pure essence of your beliefs shining like a star in the Southern Cross.

Other people could try to lead you astray. The way will be challenging, and difficult. You may feel tempted to give up. You will need courage and fortitude. Changes may be irreversible and drastic, but your new conditions will far exceed anything you could have imagined. Welcome your symbolic death, because it heralds something lasting and meaningful.

Does the pointer star (the bottom star) point to another card? This could reveal where you may expect the strongest changes. If it points away from your reading, the changes will happen around you, in your environment, rather than directly to you.

The appearance of **Emu** has special significance. The outline of Emu's neck and head appears in the space between the stars of this card; and, according to Aboriginal lore, this Emu protects the world from harm. In the early hours of the evening, this shape looks like a boomerang, also symbolizing protection.

Reversed

With the card reversed, the pointer star faces towards the top, and the situation is being viewed from a different perspective. Like the Seven Sisters, the image now appears as if reflected. Doubt is the key word for Southern Cross reversed. You doubt what you see, there is uncertainty around you, and you may waver like the image before you. It looks familiar, but maybe not ...

"Sitting on the fence," and having "a foot in both camps" delays decision-making and making a commitment. You may have to undergo a time of uncertainty and lack of faith to strengthen your inner convictions. You could feel isolated, and there may be pressure to give up your ideals, to conform.

Being aware of this possibility can enable you to reaffirm your beliefs. Clarifying your position could make you more certain of your personal truths. This may require time out alone, away from distracting influences and pressure to be "one of the sheep." It is time to work on your inner doubts, to clarify the reflection which may be blurred by any movement on the water.

Kobong

If you have Southern Cross as kobong, or if you are attracted to this card, it can reveal a strong, spiritual focus, which goes beyond theory into practice. The strength of your convictions could make you act contrary to the beliefs of others, and this could make you isolated. Your values could alienate you from those people who cannot understand the strength of your convictions. Southern Cross as kobong indicates that your beliefs will certainly be tested.

Obedience is a key word for Southern Cross as kobong. Discipline and commitment are required for the successful outcome of your issue. The other cards in your reading could point to influences which may distract you from your planned course of action. With Southern Cross as kobong, you should follow through with your personal beliefs, without compromise.

Southern Cross augurs a spiritual focus influencing the course of your situation. What are your beliefs about a Great Spirit? Do they sustain you? How are they reflected in your daily life?

Look out for any of the creatures or issues represented in your reading to manifest in some way in your life over the next few days and weeks. Also, notice your dreams, as they provide an avenue of communication from "Spirit" that could bring a greater awareness of your purpose. Like the pointer in the Southern Cross, dreams emphasize the important underlying issues in your reading which should be regarded from a spiritual perspective.

Should you gaze into the heavens, you will be reminded of faith, obedience and constancy, in the shining brilliance of the Southern Cross. Your ultimate reward is eternal and lasting; like a star it shines on through generation after generation.

8 • Sturt's Desert Pea

INTUITION • TRAGEDY • LOSS

" *There were two young people who fell in love. The girl was promised to another, a wirrunun or magic man. So, the two young people ran away together, in the secrecy of night. This was against tribal law, and the couple risked severe retribution.*

They went to live with the young man's tribe, and the young woman bore a son. She had a special talent which delighted the people. She could sing beautifully, and was able to sing the songs of the spirits. One of these songs told how her son would live eternally, and be known as the most beautiful being on the plains. At one time, the song spirits spoke softly of misfortune, but her husband ignored these warnings, believing that he and his family were safe from the vengeful wirrunun.

Shortly after the sung warnings, the wirrunun and his men stole upon the tribe in the dark of night, and slaughtered everyone: men, women, and children, including the young couple and their child. The red of their blood stained the plains. The song spirits wept at this wanton destruction.

The next year, the wirrunun returned with his men. They found a lake full of salt, the dried tears of the song spirits. The men fled in fear, leaving behind the wirrunun, who wanted to gloat over the bones. Instead of bones, he found a great number of red flowers covering the scene of the massacre.

Suddenly, out of the heavens came a bolt of lightning, to strike down the wirrunun. The voice of the Great Spirit told him that he was being punished for the great wrong he had committed. The wirrunun was transformed into a large rock, which then shattered into a multitude of hard, tiny, lifeless pebbles. They remain there to this day. "

Imagery

In this Dreaming, intuition is ignored, and disaster results. Happiness is shattered by vengeful action, yet "cosmic justice" has the last say. From the tragedy of pain and death, beautiful flowers emerge, and for the child, there is the release from a mortal existence to an eternal life.

The red flowers of Sturt's Desert Pea symbolize the eternal life of the young couple's son. For many Aboriginal people, these "Flowers of Blood" also symbolize the blood spilt during the many massacres of Aborigines by white people.

Red predominates on this card, symbolizing the blood spilt on the desert sand. The white patches symbolize the tears of the song spirits, and the three flowers are the two young lovers and their son. The black dots represent the wirrunun's death and transformation into pebbles, and the lightning bolt delivers retribution. It may also represent divine law.

Upright

This card is difficult because it is so "negative." Our tendency is to recoil from any thought of tragedy, death and pain. The challenge is to suspend judgment. Eternal life in the form of a flower may offer more than anyone could imagine. On a practical level, this card could indicate a massive transformation in your situation.

Following your intuition is a major message of Sturt's Desert Pea. You must learn to be still and receptive, to listen intently. Perhaps, like the woman, you have ignored, or lost connection with, your inner knowledge. You may feel an uneasy discontentment. This feeling of uneasiness will continue to nudge at your awareness, until you take heed of that "still, small voice" within. Acting on impulses, instead of ignoring them, even if they seem irrelevant, will alter your situation or issue.

Spend some time being silent, concentrating on your breath, perhaps meditating before sleeping, or first thing in the morning. This focus of thought and energy brings freedom of expression to your intuition (and spiritual self). It will also influence other aspects of your life.

In this Dreaming, tragedy is the result of ignoring intuition and becoming too complacent. The focus of Sturt's Desert Pea is on acting upon your intuition and avoiding disaster. This Dreaming contains much more depth and meaning than outlined here, so you may find your own personal interpretation. (The Australian Bush Flower Essence, Sturt's Desert Pea, addresses the trauma of the tragedy within this Dreaming.)

With this card in your reading, you may find yourself in a situation where you have failed to act, and are experiencing the consequent effects of that failure. Difficulty, and even sorrow, may be evident in the issue you have queried. You may be challenged to perceive the lessons inherent in your situation, and to avoid blame.

If **Waratah** appears, this may indicate intense grief, emotional pain, and sorrow. This placement can refer to challenges, tests, separations and endings. The situation requires faith, and the inner strength to continue. Love and the emotions, particularly any concerns or fears, are under the spotlight. The surrounding cards could indicate the source or nature of this experience, and perhaps offer inspiration and encouragement.

Reversed

With this card reversed, Sturt's Desert Pea points to the earth, the eyes looking downward. This card appeals to your spirit, it begs to be acknowledged. Material distraction creates a life of looking earthward, and being unaware of the vivid expanse of sky above. When the card is reversed, heaven and earth are out of balance. With the heavens where the earth should be, the spiritual remains unacknowledged, under the ground.

This card can be the ultimate challenge to strong atheists to become explorers in the inner desert of their spiritual selves. They might be surprised to discover life in the apparent barrenness, and a vivid, red flower . . .

Should the tops of the flowers point to another card in your reading, this could indicate exactly where you are being distracted, to the exclusion of everything else. This could reveal the spiritual energies and purpose behind your current issue. The stems of the flowers may point to the root cause of your situation, so take notice if they appear to be growing from another card. Any warnings or uncertainties could appear in the issues of this second card, or, at least, indicate an area of weakness in the issue being questioned.

Kobong

This card asks you to examine your relationship with your spiritual nature. How do you express, repress, acknowledge or ignore that nature? Are you following your dreams and hunches, or are you ignoring them, treating them as wishful thinking and idle fancy?

The presence of this card as kobong is an encouragement to follow your dreams, so that they will grow and bloom as abundantly as the Sturt's Desert Pea in the arid outback of Australia. Work on the unseen in life, and bring your hopes down to earth through practical action. In this way, your spiritual life becomes a reality through achievement.

Flowers of Blood draws people of a sensitive, intuitive nature, even if this nature is unacknowledged. These people carry the blood-red vision held within the black eye of the Sturt's Desert Pea. This manifests through the imagination, dreams, spiritual beliefs (and their expression), creativity, and meditation. Flowers of Blood demands expression; if this energy isn't expressed there could be a tendency for depression, denial, insomnia, addictions and dependencies, or other forms of avoidance.

Appearing reversed, this card practically demands that you devote some time to developing and expressing your spiritual awareness.

This card influences the rest of your reading by asking you to seek the inner voice or sense regarding the other issues covered. There is certainly a message to take a deeper look at your query, and to take action, before it is too late.

In the seemingly barren desert, the startling vibrancy of the Flowers of Blood bloom, as if tended by unseen forces. This could represent an affirmation of your own inner potential.

9 · Sun

PERPETUAL MOTION · JOURNEYS · AWAKENING

Many Aboriginal people believed that Yhi the Sun was a woman who made a daily journey across the sky, carrying a large burning torch to illuminate the world and its inhabitants below. During the dark of night, she would travel through a long tunnel that went under the earth, to reach the beginning of another day. The life-giving power of a female Sun has been acknowledged universally, and throughout Aboriginal culture. In one beautiful Dreaming from the Nullarbor Plain (along the coast of southern Australia), she uses her warmth to wake every creature from its deep slumber beneath the fertile earth. The animals of the earth, air, and water emerge into her light, and, thus, the creatures of the day come to populate the world.

Another Dreaming attributes the creation of the Sun to a woman known as Bila, a wildly ferocious, cannibalistic woman, who found her match in Koodna the Lizard Man. Bila possessed the only fire in the world, and refused to share it with anyone. The others wished to use it for warmth and to cook their food, but Bila refused any terms of barter. The Lizard Man and his friend, Jitta Jitta the Willy Wagtail (or, in some Dreamings, Kabori the Robin Redbreast) made a plan to ambush Bila. They crept upon her, and threw her into the fire, which then rolled away, disappearing over the horizon. Koodna attempted to gain the fire for his people by throwing his four magic boomerangs after Bila, following the four directions of the compass. He threw one to the north, one to the south, and one to the west. The fourth boomerang was thrown towards the east, and it hit Bila's fire. They knew it had hit when, from this direction, a great ball of fire rose in the sky.

In some Dreamings about the Sun and the Moon, the Sun Woman is chased endlessly across the heavens by the Moon Man. He is in love with her, but his passion is unrequited. **"**

Imagery

Yhi the Sun has been making her journey since the beginning of time. The light of the Sun symbolizes perpetual motion. Yhi the Sun's journey is constant and predictable. She never rests from the cycle of carrying the fire across the sky and returning under the earth. In her travels, Yhi the Sun unites the two worlds of sky and underworld. This process can represent the passage of time, as well as wholeness, balance, and unity.

Compared to the Moon, the Sun is constant, it does not wax and wane, although it has its own patterns.

The Sun's basic cycle is night and day. This is unchanging, predictable, and reliable; as is the cycle from hot summer, to cool winter.

This Dreaming card illustrates Yhi the Sun's path across the heavens and through a dark tunnel under the earth. The sun symbolizes the timelessness of this ancestral being's journey. The contrast between day and night is also depicted, representing the contrasts within life, such as happiness and grief, the conscious and subconscious, and so on.

Upright

This card speaks of larger patterns, a broader perspective, and a substantial length of time. The Sun generally indicates a long-standing situation. This reaches into the past or the future, depending upon the placement of the card in the reading. The Sun may also represent a time-honored institution, family tradition, or practice.

When it appears upright, the Sun represents the conscious mind; that which can be seen and known. Her journey through the dark of night, beneath the ground, represents the subconscious mind. If this Dreaming card is drawn pointing closer to the underground part of the journey, be aware of the subconscious energies filtering into your issue. These may appear in the form of dreams, aspirations, or those events that are imbued with the magical essence of synchronicity, which propel you into the realms of the unbelievable. It is certainly a time for becoming more acquainted with your psyche, that is, your personal and spiritual needs.

As the Sun rises upon your issue, there will be a great awakening. The Sun has the ability to draw out the contrasting forces of life and nature, such as summer after winter, or the opposites drought and flood. These contrasts may be creating a sense of uncertainty in your issue.

In some Dreamings, the Moon Man chases the Sun Woman. If Moon appears in your reading, he can indicate a chase. The pursuit of your dream may be frustrating, so it is up to you whether you wish to pursue in the face of possible futility. If Sun appears with **Kookaburra** or **Magpies**, your situation is certainly being infused with a good dose of creative and spiritual energy. This will be accompanied by positive change, in the form of new beginnings—an inspiring new dawn for you!

If **Sea Eagle**, **Rainbow Serpent** or **Uluru** appear in your reading, strength is evident, but it could be too narrow or rigid. There is a need for adaptability and a relaxed attitude, to compensate for the potential flammability of the issue.

Reversed

With the card reversed, the Sun's emphasis is on latent possibilities that are threading their way through your issue. The Sun is underground, unseen. She is moving towards the sky to bring light. Subconscious issues are working below the level of your normal awareness, and you need to anticipate their "coming to light" in your life. The position of this card can indicate whether this is a new process, or one that is partly completed. If it is drawn at the beginning of the underground journey, that is, nearer to the nine o'clock position, we witness the beginnings of the night. Towards the three o'clock position, dawn is on the horizon, and night is drawing to a close, bringing with it the completion of your issue.

It is a good time to do some work on your subconscious mind. Take notice of any "slips of the tongue," fantasies, flights of imagination, and mental associations related to the aspects and events around the issue queried. Synchronicities will be making an impact in your life, so follow any feelings which are urging action. This is especially important if **Sturt's Desert Pea** or **Moon** also appear.

To bring the energy of this Dreaming further into your life, you could spend more time in the sun (bearing in mind health precautions). Meditate on the Sun shining onto you and filling you with light; sense her warmth waking every cell in your body. In this way, you will be acknowledging her power and life, and drawing in her energy. Sun reversed heralds a new dawn approaching. Her energies are "warming" you to the possibility that you might shine as brightly as she does.

Kobong

If Sun is drawn as kobong, or if you are drawn to her light, she indicates constancy, reliability, and a warmth of personality which draws others to you. You are outgoing, capable, stable, and faithful to your ideals and goals. In Western astrology, this card relates to the sign of Leo, and there are similarities to the Sun in the Tarot.

In this position, the Sun may bring light into your issue and allow you to see something new. That which is unconscious is made conscious. The darkness is dispelled by the light of understanding. With the appearance of this card, you will gain a deeper and clearer awareness of what is happening.

Sun as kobong in a reading can indicate that you need to look at recurring patterns in your life from a higher perspective, to see the wider picture. "Rising above the world" and enlarging your horizons can allow you to see your situation without any obscuring "clouds." The Sun Woman is oblivious to the ways of the world, whether they be petty or important. She knows, and focuses solely on, her duty. Each day, she makes the choice to continue with her known pattern. Do you know your unchanging personal patterns? This card brings routine and regularity to whatever issue you are questioning.

If Sun as kobong appears reversed, unconscious motives and desires are influencing the situation, and perhaps challenging you to question whether they are true and relevant, or in need of reevaluation.

10 • Uluru

POWER • CENTER • BALANCE

" *The Yankuntjatjara and Pitjan-tjatjara people have belonged to the place known as Uluru since the beginning of time. (In Aboriginal culture, people belong to places; places do not belong to people.) Today, Uluru, the Rock, enormous and monolithic, is a world-famous tourist spot. Its smooth, water- and wind-weathered surfaces bear testimony to eons of time. However, the Aboriginal people had a great struggle to gain legal "possession" of this place; to prove to bureaucrats that Uluru has great cultural significance.*

To prove this significance, the Australian legal system insisted on knowing details of the secret Aborigine rituals associated with Uluru, and this caused enormous difficulties. Such lack of understanding is typical of reactions to current claims for land rights throughout Australia. Uluru can be seen as a symbol of the Aboriginal people's victory in gaining acknowledgment for their human rights.

There are different Dreamings for the north, or sunny, side of Uluru and the south, or shady, side. One Dreaming describes two boys playing in the mud after rain. One of them tosses a rock, which is transformed into the massive monolith. Their bodies are transformed into large boulders.

Other Dreamings attribute the creation of Uluru to Rainbow Serpent, or even describe the Rock as the Serpent's egg. There are many other Dreamings about Uluru, attributing different formations and markings on the rocks to events and battles. The creation of Uluru is also said to mark the end of the creation energies of the Dreaming, and the beginning of present, modern time.

There are women's sacred sites at Uluru, including fertility and birthing sites, but women are forbidden by tribal law to climb the rock face. This is made known to tourists, but many ignore its message. Tribal law also forbids the removal of rocks from the site, but this is also ignored by the tourists. These are just two examples of how the wishes and spiritual rights of Aboriginal people have been ignored and violated. However, this powerful place, said to be one of the major energy centers of the world, remains as solid and permanent as the Aboriginal spirit. "

Imagery

Uluru represents power, one of the seven chakras of mother earth. It is an incredibly powerful place, with a special significance. Many of the ancient songlines, or Dreaming tracks (the journeys made by the Rainbow Serpent and ancestral beings) meet and cross at Uluru. It has become a place of pilgrimage for people from all over the world (nearby Katajuta, previously known as the Olgas, is also visited). Many visitors experience a sensation of timelessness at this spiritual site.

On the card, Uluru is central and powerful in the image, the Rock emerging from the desert sands. Although there is no sign of physical life, this Dreaming card is imbued with a radiating energy that has its own form and creative power.

This Dreaming card is predominantly red, an earthy, ochre red. Red relates to the base chakra in the human energy field, traditionally symbolizing personal power and connection with the earth.

Upright

Uluru represents finding your center, your inner source of personal power. It can indicate some time alone, and the chance to establish your sense of balance, and "groundedness." These potent energies are infusing your situation, and perhaps challenging the resolution of your issue.

Sexuality and the will to live are also covered by this card. As Uluru has a sunny side and a shady side, the tension between these two opposites may challenge you to seek a personal balance between the light and dark aspects of your psyche. There may be a sense of uneasiness until these two opposite qualities are resolved to your satisfaction.

Finding your personal center could require a "pilgrimage," an inner, or actual, journey, to the source of your situation, which could then draw you to the source of your power. There is a need to see the wider picture—the Rock, rather than a pebble.

Issues around personal strength are being tested, on all levels. Strength is something which can be gauged only through testing; until then, its limits can only be estimated. The tougher the test, the greater the testimony. Uluru stands as an inspiring testimony to the passage, and ravages, of time. Your own testimony will be a reminder of your spiritual and personal strength.

The appearance of Uluru can be a reminder of the need to create your own center, within the context of your query. Time moves around Uluru like hands on a clock, flowing, and changing. Whether your sense of time seems accelerated or slow, it is wise to focus on your center, rather than deadlines or projected outcomes. It is the inner spark of the soul, unchanging through time, which can provide a haven, or center amidst change.

It is a powerful meditation to focus on the Uluru card, or place it where it will often be seen. Its qualities include personal power, creating your dream, manifesting your spiritual purpose, or finding your path in life.

Reversed

With the card reversed, Uluru looks displaced and in a very unnatural position, as if being seen by someone plummeting towards the earth upside-down, or dreaming. This position indicates a loss of a sense of belonging. The surrounding cards could point to the precise nature of this loss. Does Uluru appear to be about to land on another card? The energies represented by this card could be downtrodden and repressed in your issue. In general, Uluru reversed can symbolize the "lost tribe," the "dispossessed," the "stolen generation" (the Aboriginal children who were forcibly removed from their parents as a result of the government's "White Australia" policy), or even the futility associated with the deaths of Aboriginal people in custody. Aboriginal people have had their land, culture, even their children, taken from them. The attempted genocide of their race has left an impact which is still felt today.

Uluru is displaced, and the world reflects this loss of balance. Many people ignore the spiritual law that only men should climb Uluru Rock. As long as this disrespect continues, the energies of Uluru will create lessons for such people. Perhaps they too will be "walked over."

This position speaks of a "dark night of the soul," a time of testing circumstances, which challenges the existence of a spiritual force operating for ultimate good. This darkness plunges one to the depths of depression. However, once "rock-bottom" has been reached, regardless of how things appear outwardly, the only way is up. Uluru here is a signal of difficulty, but also, with the sunrise, a sign of hope.

Kobong

This card can seem to be grounding the entire reading, especially if you are using the Southern Cross Spread *(see page 158)*. The base behind your issue is as solid and enduring as this symbol, so you may be assured of success, in a way that is more meaningful than any physical, outward manifestations. This Dreaming card urges you to focus on the unchanging, essential nature within you—the spiritual, eternal, wise aspect that knows the answer to every question.

As Uluru is the card of personal power, as kobong, or if you are drawn to this card, it indicates a strong, balanced, and stable personality, which is centered and willful. Uluru energies bring a spiritual focus to the earthly dimension. The two realms unite, and the result is a focused, clear vision. Uluru as kobong can indicate you are working through your emotional "excess baggage" to give yourself more space.

The Rock changes hue in the varying intensity of light at different times of day, yet it remains the same. Mirages shimmer and undulate along the Rock's contours, changing its shape and appearance, yet it remains the same. Uluru is unchanging as the world around shifts. Your situation will be influenced by these eternal energies. Whatever you seek in your issue is already rock solid in your life. You already know what you need to know!

11 · Waratah

GRIEF · DEVOTION · LOVE

“ *The Wonga Pigeon camped with her mate in a lush green, plentiful forest. Together, they grew fat on the rich food which grew there. They had more than enough to eat, and were very happy together, in their strong love for each other. There were plenty of ferns and undergrowth for cover, so they were reasonably safe from harm. They never flew above the trees, because they knew that their enemy, the Eaglehawk, hunted there.*

One day, the Wonga pigeon became so engrossed in feeding that she wandered away. Suddenly, she realized that she had lost her mate. Frightened at finding herself alone, she started to search for him, running around, and flying from tree to tree, searching their favorite places and feeding spots. She called his name as she flew through the undergrowth and trees, but there was no answer. She was in anguish, fearing the worst, envisioning a life bereft of her partner, without his love and companionship. Panic began to rise, her heart beat faster and faster. Risking her life, she flew high above the treetops, in a desperate bid to locate her mate.

She broke above the green canopy of the forest, gliding over the tops of the trees, calling in a voice filled with panic. At last, her mate answered, from far below, in the forest. Overwhelmed with joy and relief, she plunged downwards to return to him.

Alas! The Eaglehawk had heard her cries, and he spotted her as she flew down. He swooped upon her and clutched her with his sharp talons, tearing into her flesh. She struggled, managed to free herself, and fell down through the forest. She landed on some white Waratah flowers, which grew there profusely. Her blood stained the flowers crimson. She flew from one flower to the other, still searching for her beloved mate. Finally, she gasped her last breath and died. That is why you rarely see a white Waratah, they are mostly red. ”

Imagery

Waratah is strongly associated with pain and loss, but it also represents love and devotion. The blood-red color of the Waratah is an explicit reminder of pain, hurt, and death. Yet, within the heart of this stunning flower, lie the seeds of renewal and growth. Red is also the color of life force and energy.

Love, devotion, loss, and tragedy are highlighted in another well-known Dreaming about Waratah. A young woman loved a warrior. When he went out to hunt, she would await his return, watching from a high vantage point. When he was away, he would look forward with longing to his first sight of her red cloak, made from red kangaroo skins, and adorned with red cockatoo feathers. One day, he was killed in battle and did not return. The young woman waited and waited, until at last her spirit left her body, which was then transformed into the Waratah. The serrated leaves are said to represent the spears of the warrior, and the plant stands tall and proud like him. The red cloak of the woman is seen in the color of the blossom.

On the card, the Wonga Pigeon is partially enclosed beneath the safe canopy of the forest. She is draped over the Waratah, dripping tear-shaped blood, which symbolizes pain, sadness, and loss. This card is black, representing the "dark night of the soul" as experienced by the bereft bird. The petals point to new growth, from the experience of loss. The Waratah appears without a stem to ground it upon the earth, as the pigeon lost contact with her own grounding and common sense by allowing fear to overtake her.

Upright

Waratah symbolizes fear of loss, in this case, loss of someone you love. The card can also refer to any business, social, and health issue close to your heart. It refers as much to loss as to the fear of loss. It does not necessarily mean an "actual" loss. (Wonga Pigeon might have found her mate if she had not acted in panic.)

Waratah reminds you that the more you value something in your life, be it a relationship, situation, or goal, the more potential there is for pain. This Dreaming raises the well-known question: is it "better to have loved and lost than never to have loved at all?" There is a degree of risk involved, but, if we took no risks in life, we would remain static and become dissatisfied. And one of the greatest risks in life is the risk of love.

Waratah often appears for those who have experienced the pain of separation. It can also refer to the grief of bereavement. Such people need to work through their pain, so they can once again trust the world, and open their hearts, as the Waratah blossom opens its petals. With the appearance of Waratah, you may need to acknowledge the benefits, as well as the negatives, in your situation.

Situated in the recent past position *(see pages 157–8)*, Waratah can refer to patterns from childhood that are currently being replayed in your life. This could represent an actual experience of love that resulted in loss and pain. As a future indicator, it may refer to facing your fears of loss.

Reversed

When the card is reversed, the flower appears to have been torn from its stalk, cut off from its source of life. This indicates some past hurt that continues to influence your situation. Perhaps you are feeling "ungrounded" and bereft. The challenge is to pick up the torn and discarded blossom, take it home with you, and allow it to adorn a place you thought empty—your heart.

In this position, Waratah requires you to work through your emotions. It is time to acknowledge any pain, instead of hiding it or running away. It won't go away until you resolve it. Avoiding your intense feelings can cause them to override your will, to the extent that you become reactive rather than active, just like the Pigeon who reacted in panic at the loss of her mate. This could also manifest itself as depression, or an inability to cope with the demands of the issue you are querying.

Kobong

If you have Waratah as kobong, or if you are drawn to this card, you are a very loyal, loving, and devoted person. Your experiences with pain, hurt, and loss enable you to be compassionate and understanding with other people who encounter this in their lives. You can reach out with open arms to those who need your empathy.

Your experiences give you courage to move forward in life, with the confidence that every negative experience provides a lesson that will help you grow.

Waratah as kobong reveals the effects of a past hurt that could still be influencing and affecting your approach to life. This pain and, perhaps, a lack of trust have created a blockage that could prevent any new growth or development in your issue. It is often easier to be aware of and accept other people's pain, than to accept one's own. Acknowledging, and acting on, your need for resolution and healing will encourage you to move on, and wholeheartedly rejoin life. The sweetness of Waratah nectar has its Dreaming origins in the tears of repentance and forgiveness. Sip deeply, imbibe its essence.

Waratah Dreaming asks you to examine your fears of loss in the situation queried. There is no need to "fly above the canopy" like the Wonga Pigeon. If you are patient you will find what you are seeking nearby. The urge to escape is particularly compelling if there is open space, rather than a leaf, at the twelve o'clock position as the card is drawn.

If this card is drawn out of balance, facing towards the left side of your reading, your fears draw from a past event or influence. If it is drawn pointing towards the right, your fears are likely to be future projections and assumptions, and not in line with reality. Exaggerated emotions have a strong influence on your reading, and the challenge is to maintain a balanced perspective.

Waratah can be seen in those individuals who are true healers. They are excellent teachers, able to impart their wisdom gently and lovingly.

12 • Dingo

INDEPENDENCE • LESSONS • EMOTIONS

" A long time ago, back in the Dreaming of the Kalkadoon people who live around Mount Isa in central northern Queensland, a woman sat by a fire crying. The tears were running down her face in streams, and she was wracked with sobs. Her crying shattered the stillness of the day with its intense grief, drowning the humming of the cicadas. Up above, in the great blue sky, Jarlem the White Cloud was not unaffected by the woman's great sorrow. He said to Beegi the Sun, "Why is that woman so sad?" Beegi said, "She cries because she has lost her two children in a big bushfire."

Jarlem the White Cloud said, "You are the biggest Turwan (Great Man) in the sky. Give her back the children." Old Beegi said, "I cannot do that, but I will put their spirits into those two parrots sitting in Munguree, the old gum tree."

Straightway, the parrots started to chatter, just like the children used to, and Mirri the Dingo jumped up and started to bark. He barked loudly, gazing intently at the woman, seeking to draw her attention to the parrots who sounded just like her children. The woman became angry, not knowing what the fuss was all about, and caring only to return to her profound sorrow. She hit the dingo across the throat with a piece of burning wood from the fire. This hurt Mirri so much that he stopped barking immediately. The woman returned to her position by the campfire and stared into the flames, tears coursing down her face and drying in salty streaks. After a time, she stopped crying and felt a little happier because she thought she could hear the chattering of her children.

To this day, the Dingo does not bark and, if you listen carefully, some parrots can say a few words in voices that sound like the voices of little children. "

Imagery

This Dreaming highlights the relationship between man and beast. The woman was out of touch with her environment because of grief, so she was unaware of the great gift in her presence. Mirri the Dingo was aware of the changes and tried to alert her. Mirri's bark heralded the transformation of the children's spirits into parrots.

Jarlem the White Cloud can bring rain, providing a symbolic link with the woman's tears. Jarlem wished her sorrow to end, and acted as an unknown intermediary in her plight. Instead of being alert to Mirri's warning, the woman released more of her pain through striking him.

The dingo has borne the brunt of much blame since the colonization of Australia. Considered dangerous pests (except in the Northern Territory), dingoes are still poisoned and hunted, and there is now the serious problem of cross-breeding with feral domestic dogs.

On the card, we see Dingo and the campfire. Fire is an important symbol in the Dreaming and it may represent many things. In this Dreaming, the woman's children die in a fire and now she is crying beside one. It represents the cause and effects of grief, and it directly injures Dingo. Dingo represents the archetypal figure of watchfulness, loyalty and protection, acting as an alarm for the woman. The sun represents a creative, benevolent power who may intervene in a compassionate way. The clouds represent an intermediary, or a concerned party who tries to instigate improvements by recourse to a higher power.

In another Dreaming, Dingo is a much-loved, yet lazy and spoilt, son. His parents and tribespeople do all the hunting, and bring him food, yet he refuses to contribute. The tribespeople hold a corroboree and, while Dingo is distracted, they gradually sneak away, leaving behind hunting tools. Dingo now has to learn how to hunt, so he can feed himself. Dingo learns out of necessity, but resentment grows in his heart because of the way he was treated, and he becomes greedy, killing in excess of his food requirements.

Upright

This card warns you not to focus so much on your losses that you forget the present moment. Dingo alerts you to move out of the past and to be totally "in the now." Dingo also teaches there is no separation between loved ones. Be aware of the omens around you, especially if you are going through a difficult time emotionally.

Dingo appears in your reading to ask whether you are relying on others to do what you could do for yourself. Could you learn to be more self-reliant and independent in the situation you are questioning? Or could you accept the assistance offered, instead of considering it a nuisance, as the woman in the first Dreaming did?

Both Dreamings illustrate how becoming caught up in emotions results in loss and suffering. In the first Dreaming, Dingo gave warning but became victim of the woman's emotions and lost his bark. In the second, Dingo refused to help other people, took them for granted, and eventually was forced to fend for himself, with no support. By allowing resentment to direct his actions, and consequently killing beyond his requirements, Dingo lost his tribal family. This Dreaming is a reminder not to be overtaken by your emotions.

Reversed

Dingo reversed emphasizes wildness, slyness and stealth, in effect, your animal nature. Dingo appears here as if he is lying on his back. He needs to get up on all four legs, follow his instincts and join the hunt. Modern society has lost contact with the basic skills of gathering, hunting, and preparing food; we forage in supermarkets and light our campfires by the flick of a switch. Renewing contact with your animal nature, and allowing its expression, can balance your life, adding the spice of unpredictability and spontaneity. Attuned to the forces of nature and life, we can sense our direction as keenly as Dingo senses his prey.

There have been no authenticated reports of a wild dingo attacking a human. The bizarre case of a dingo stealing a baby at Uluru in 1980 hit worldwide news, but remains a mystery to this day. This event highlighted our relationship with wild animals—the dingo itself cannot be seen as guilty in our sense of the word. You may need to allow something freedom and the chance to fend for itself, with Dingo appearing reversed.

Kobong

Dingoes are intelligent, secretive animals. Often solitary, they forage alone for small game, though they will form packs to hunt larger game. Dingoes rarely fight, and they are not particularly vocal—they howl to keep contact with others while hunting, to avoid strangers, and to find a mate. They also have a howl-bark, which raises the alarm if anything is amiss. As kobong or if you are drawn to this card, you are generally a loner, although you will join forces with others when necessary. In your issue, you may well be asked to do just this.

You may be in a situation where the emotions of others are influencing you, or your issue. This may require the continued devotion of Mirri the Dingo, rather than the resentment revealed in the second Dingo Dreaming.

Dingo as kobong influences your reading through the energies of independence. Especially in the issues covered by the other cards, you may seek to strike out alone, and to achieve without the support of others, unless group cards such as **Kookaburra**, **Magpies** or **Rainbow Lorikeet** appear. There may also be a healthy sense of pride accompanying your accomplishments.

Dingoes are handsome creatures. Their sandy hues reflect the earth, reminding us of the beauty of nature. At the top of the food chain, they challenge us to accept what humans judge to be negative aspects. As kobong, this card could ask you to examine those inner places where you are wild at heart, and to release those aspects of yourself "in the play of Dingo frolicking."

13 · Echidna

SHARING • SELFISHNESS • IRRITATIONS

" *All the people of a certain tribe were camped near the Palmer River and they went into the bush to look for their favorite food, the sweet honey ("sugarbag") from the native bee. The Echidna Man was the first person to find some honey, in a hollow log, but he couldn't reach the honey because he didn't have a stone ax. Just then, the Cockatoo Man came along, so the Echidna Man asked if he could use the Cockatoo Man's ax. But the Cockatoo Man refused, saying he would not loan his ax to anyone.*

The Echidna Man asked all the people that came along—Kookaburra, Brolga, Emu, and Plains Turkey—but no one would lend him a stone ax. At that, Echidna became angry with the people. He went straight back to the camp waterhole, and drank as much water as he could hold in his body. There was only a small amount of water left that he was not able to drink. So, he sat on this last remaining water to cover it up.

When the people came back, they were very thirsty from eating all the sugarbag, and they went straight to the waterhole for a drink. They asked the Echidna Man to move, but he just grunted and refused to budge. The people talked amongst themselves, and decided the only way to get the water was to spear the stubborn man. They surrounded him, and threw spear after spear, until his body was covered with spears. Then they dragged him away, turned him over, and cut him open to let the water out.

After a while, the people felt bad about what they had done. They decided that, in future, water and sugarbag should belong to everyone, and that they would lend their stone axes to anyone who needed them. From that time on, they decided to share everything. "

Imagery

In Aboriginal culture, giving help to anyone who asked for it was a moral imperative. Assistance was automatically given, and expected. Giving, helping and sharing benefited the whole tribe, and the community could not survive without such ethics. This Dreaming about Echidna may well have been the first lesson in sharing.

Such cultural attitudes can seem incredibly alien to the modern Western mind. To adopt them in today's society would be to practice both random and premeditated acts of kindness whenever you can!

Upright

Echidna has an important message to share. He encourages you to consider your attitudes towards sharing, giving and receiving. It is also time to question your attitudes towards asking for assistance, and your reaction if assistance is not forthcoming.

Echidna changes an attitude or practice in the "give and take" of life, showing where you have made inappropriate or incorrect judgments. Are you being "used" as much as you profess? Do you offer your goodness to the world, or does it come with a price? When you do not want to give, are you unable to resist the pressure? Do you feel that you are not getting what you deserve?

Echidna brings the inevitable "prickles of life" into your issue, but, remember, the echidnas also feast on ants, the prickles of the insect kingdom. This image of Echidna eating ants has protective qualities in visualization; its subconscious affirmation aligning you with your ability to allow the irritations in life to sustain you. Things that do not go to plan are gifts for unlocking your own potential. Irritations in your issue may cause your "spines" to "stand on end," or, like Echidna, you may prefer to dig a hole in the earth and roll into a little ball. Echidna requires you take notice of any irritating circumstances, because they contain valuable lessons.

If Echidna is moving directly towards the position in the reading representing you, the querant, this could indicate where you will be asked for support. You may choose not to give support, even though you are able. If Echidna is moving away from you, you will be seeking support, and what you want may be represented by the card in Echidna's direction. You may need to ask for what you require, and to persevere if you receive rejection. Perhaps you could ask in another way, work out an equal exchange, or present yourself differently. Assistance could be obtained elsewhere, especially if Echidna is not moving directly towards another card.

Echidna brings valuable lessons around sharing, and will continue to "prickle away" in your life, until you resolve your stand on the issues discussed here.

If **Frog** also appears in your reading, remember that Frog also drinks all the water in his Dreaming, and this could indicate a tendency to wallow in the negative aspects of your issue. The appearance of **Koala**, who hides a water supply, can mean you may be hanging onto something you are very attached to, but it is time to let go. **Dingo** highlights independence as well, but, in this case, beware of any tendency to hold resentment, as this may obscure the success of the issue queried.

Reversed

In the reversed position, Echidna appears as if he is lying prone on his back, feet up in the air. Stubborn Echidna has died for his cause. The spears penetrating his body are a message for generations to come. Of course, he may be merely stuck, unable to turn himself upright; in which case, all he has to do is call out for assistance.

Echidna in this position could reveal an inability to ask for what you need, perhaps due to pride, or an inability to accept it when it is offered. Independence at the cost of effectiveness results in failure. Unless you can ask, you will remain as prone and as uncomfortably stuck as our brother. So, will you ask for help to regain your upright stance, or will you remain where you are, flat on your back?

With the ants now appearing towards the top, your emotions may have a strong influence on your approach, especially if there is stubbornness, resentment and an inability to admit you were wrong. This is where Echidna really needs to ask for assistance, otherwise he will forever remain immobile, his own prickles pinning him down.

Kobong

People who have Echidna as kobong, or who are drawn to this card, have a strong, forthright personality, unafraid to ask for what they need. Echidna people know what they want and how to get it. In a reading, this card may indicate you need to learn to accept rejection, and, instead of expressing resentment or revenge, take your cause elsewhere. As with a young child, the word "no" can result in some very loud tantrums.

This strong aspect of your personality could well be channeled into seeking other, more suitable avenues of support. Or, perhaps you could convey your needs in a way that is more appropriate to the situation. If Echidna had said that the honey he had discovered would be shared amongst everybody, he may have received what he needed to get it. This Dreaming teaches the lesson of "You scratch my back, and I'll scratch yours." Some type of cooperation, especially at a community level, is required for the success of your issue. And, if your requests are rejected, you may need to seek what you need elsewhere. Don't take it all to heart. There may well be an even better, and more fulfilling, option just around the corner.

Apply Echidna to the other cards in your reading, by asking what it is you must seek, request, or give, in the issues highlighted by each card. There are exchange rates and this reading may confront your preconceived ideas about what is really happening. The "give and take" of life is working for the positive outcome in your issue. You may well be surprised by what you discover in this reading. The answers it offers could reveal unexpected options which will help you to achieve your goals. Echidna will directly influence your reading by applying exchange rates or requirements in every aspect of your query.

14 • Emu

COMPETITION • STATUS • SELF-ESTEEM

" Two sisters, Waraji the Emu and Wildura the Wild Turkey, each had a large family of chicks. Each thought their brood the better. The Emu, being the younger, thought she was in an inferior position, and she wanted to be of superior status. Then she had an idea. Waraji the Emu hid all her chicks under her wings, except for two. "Where are your other chicks?" asked Wildura.

"I killed them," replied the Emu. "It is much easier finding food for only two chicks. They'll grow big and fat. Why don't you do the same?" Wildura was unwilling to kill her pretty chicks, but it was hard work feeding them. So she destroyed all but two.

Opening her wings and releasing the chicks, the Emu derided her sister. When Wildura realized she had been tricked, she told her husband how foolish she had been. The Wild Turkeys mourned for days over their loss. They also knew it would not be long before they had a chance for revenge. They bided their time.

A plan was devised. The Wild Turkeys found that they could tuck the points of their wings in close to their bodies, so that it looked as though their wings had been cut off. They practiced this, then, one hot day, they came dancing into the Emu's camp. "We've just cut off our wings so we can be cool. It is so comfortable and light. Better than having those heavy things flapping around. Besides, having no wings makes you look sleeker and more attractive. Why don't you do the same?"

The thought of how much more attractive she would look persuaded Waraji to cut off her wings. When she had cut them off, the Wild Turkeys shrieked derisively, opened their wings and flew around Waraji. "Now you'll never be able to fly! You'll have to stay on the ground where men and dingoes can run you down and kill you—but not us! We can still fly!"

Waraji the Emu still has her large family, and Wildura the Wild Turkey retains the power of flight. "

Imagery

In this Dreaming, actions and emotions are exaggerated to encourage discussion about our place in our environment, our personal relationships, and our role in society. Emu seeks to "fit in." She wants to be accepted, and to raise her status. Emu is so disconnected from her heart, and focused on her desires, she encourages Wild Turkey to kill her chicks, and inflicts pain upon herself by removing her own wings. She allows her emotions to take over.

We can be like our sister Emu, adapting to fit in socially, while compromising our integrity, and sacrificing something of personal value in the process. Or we can come from our heart, and risk being rejected, or feeling inadequate.

In this Dreaming card we see Waraji the Emu flightless upon the ground, while her sister, the Wild Turkey is in flight. Both have their young present, symbolizing the responsibilities of family.

Upright

Emu is all about what you think: what you think is best for you, what you think other people expect of you, and also what you expect of others. Analyzing, comparing, judging and evaluating are all characteristic Emu processes. This is the card of competition, and the attainment of status.

Emu is also about the emotions, about being sensitive, and prone to acting without thought. Emu is facing the shadow side of painful insecurities around the need to be accepted. Waraji the Emu compensates for her lack of esteem through dreams, not of equality, but of superiority. This can be seen in her competitive outlook, which compels her to prove herself better than others.

These issues could be propelling you towards finding the social status within you that you have been seeking outside. That is, until you're a winner from within, you'll continue to strive to be one without!

In a reading, this card could indicate it is not the right time to take action, or to attempt to prove yourself. It is a time for waiting and patience. Your situation or process cannot be hastened, and there is no need for personal sacrifice or manipulation. Everything has its time, and now is the time to focus more on your inner environment, rather than the outer.

If the card is drawn with Wild Turkey close to the top, this could indicate a sacrifice in the area of family commitments, or a lessening of responsibility. Emu closer to the top suggests a sacrifice in the way you move through life, perhaps on a social level, and in relation to your issue. Neither of these sacrifices is necessary; there is another way. Ask yourself what you feel you have to prove, and why it needs to be proved.

With the appearance of **Southern Cross** in your reading, spiritual issues are highlighted, as the form of Emu appears in the spaces between the stars. **Platypus** will bring reconciling energies towards your issue, and, with the acceptance of differences, rather than continued negative comparisons, things will proceed much more smoothly. You may have to forego your pride, and prove yourself, just to keep the peace.

Reversed

Wild Turkey is emphasized when the card is drawn reversed. This can indicate you are being manipulated in some way. Perhaps you are coming more from your feelings and are not seeing the true situation. Wild Turkey is a signal to look at issues from a less emotional perspective. What is really happening? Are you acting from your heart and personal integrity, or are you playing into another person's expectations? What do you really want?

In the Brush Turkey Dreaming (the names Brush Turkey and Wild Turkey are used for the same bird), the Brush Turkey carries resentment over her own drab appearance, and, in a fit of jealousy, creates a bushfire. Brush Turkey, singed by the fire, is left an even duller color. She carries red on her face as a reminder of her shameful actions.

You are asked to examine where you might have been changing your actions, to fit in with the expectations (real and assumed) of other people, and society. Wild Turkey can call for action which is contrary to these previous actions. Sometimes, "walking your talk," that is, being honest and true to yourself, can be a challenge. Be prepared to go against the norm and follow your personal truth.

Kobong

Emu as kobong indicates sensitivity to other people's thoughts, opinions and judgments. Your motives or actions, perhaps not immediately (or easily) recognized or accepted, are adapted to what you perceive is expected of you, and to achieve status or recognition. This may work to your benefit or detriment. The need to achieve social status ("stepping up the ladder") is influenced by the perceived expectations of other people.

What do you want for yourself? What is "following your excitement?" Emu people can evaluate their actions in accordance with their own needs, and achieve the status they desire, without hurting others.

As kobong, Emu influences the other cards in your reading by flavoring them with the need to be socially accepted. Personal standards are high with this card, and there may be a tendency to overcompensate for any perceived lacks in your issue.

Reversed, Wild Turkey can indicate the development of independent thought and action. Being aware of the possibility of being manipulated by outside conditions or people can enable you to perceive more clearly what it is you want.

Wild Turkey no longer gets "sucked into" games which require the sacrifice of herself in order to be accepted. Wild Turkey in this position has overcome the need to seek social acceptance; she is happy within and knows all else will follow. Her keen individuality positively influences the other cards in your reading.

15 · Frilled-neck Lizard

PERSONAL POWER · EGO · MAGIC

" *Back in the Dreaming, all the creatures bred successfully, and became so numerous, that food became very scarce. This caused fights and trouble between the creatures. A great drought came. The land became very dry. The little food that was left could not regenerate. Meetings were held to discuss the situation.*

All the animals, birds and reptiles debated the situation. They presented many ideas, some outrageous, most impractical. Someone suggested all the birds should leave, because they could fly, but the birds did not like this idea. Another put forward the proposal that they should seek another place to live, but there were arguments over who should search for that place. The debates went on for days and days, and nothing was resolved.

Kendi the Frilled-neck Lizard, who had been quietly observing the arguments, offered his services as a powerful rainmaker, believing he had the only solution that would satisfy everyone. The others ignored his offer, and Kendi was left to himself, forgotten in the excitement of other ideas.

In anger and frustration, Kendi decided to take matters into his own hands. He quietly left the meeting and climbed the tallest mountain nearby. He painted his body with the sacred ochre and fat, in the patterns of great magic. He chanted and danced, thumping the ground, and called up a great storm, the greatest storm ever. The power of the storm, and its vibrant energy, surged through him, overpowering his anger, to a point where the magic was beyond his control.

Lightning, thunder, hail, wind and rain assaulted the dry, parched land with a ferocity so mighty, that everyone ran for cover. It rained and rained. It rained so much that all the land was flooded, except for the highest mountain tops. In the course of this great storm, most living things died.

Since the days of the Dreaming, this has been the mightiest demonstration of magic ever performed. And to this day, Kendi the Frilled-neck Lizard is the most powerful rainmaker and has to be respected, otherwise his anger could again unleash massive destruction. "

Imagery

The Frilled-neck Lizard brings storms, but also represents cleansing. He symbolizes the unrelenting forces of nature that are unleashed against the land and its inhabitants. This cleansing appears destructive, although ultimately it achieves its purpose of solving a collective problem. Kendi the Frilled-neck Lizard symbolizes powerful magic.

Anger is a key word. Its overpowering force swept through the Frilled-neck Lizard. Dealing with frustration and anger is the lesson of Frilled-neck Lizard.

On an esoteric level, this Dreaming relates to the use and abuse of energy, and the powers of manifestation. This energy is best used for the benefit of others, and more importantly, in conjunction with those others.

On the card, Kendi is painted up in his special designs, standing upon the mountain, above the world; a position which represents his self-importance and power. The ochre brown of the mountain, the color of the earth in the Northern Territory, symbolizes power. The lightning flashes in an ominous sky.

Upright

Personal power is an issue here. The lizard's solution was right, but his emotional reaction to rejection resulted in destructive energy. This card could bring up issues around rejection and lack of recognition.

The gentle breeze has the potential for a gale. This card teaches you to practice control, and to balance thought and feeling. The Frilled-neck Lizard brings an important message: efficiency and purpose are affected by your state of mind. Deal with any negativity as soon as possible; it is not time to go off alone and act.

Perhaps, like the creatures in this Dreaming, the answer to your own personal dilemma is staring you right in the face, but you are being caught up in other, more exciting, (but less realistic) options. Sometimes, the way out seems so obvious, we need to evaluate every other option available in order to confirm that the simple, straightforward answer is the right one.

The Frilled-neck Lizard puts you on notice to observe just where you are using your personal power. Are you applying yourself in a positive, constructive manner, with the support of other people? Or are you acting as a destructive force, disregarding others, "playing God?"

Kendi was a great magic maker; what magic can you create in your life now? How can you influence your environment to bring "refreshing abundance?" Frilled-neck Lizard brings with him the power to create positive change in your life. However, it is important to remember this energy should only be wielded when one is in a clear and balanced state of mind.

Other cards with the symbol of lightning could exaggerate any feelings of insignificance, resulting in spontaneous emotional outbursts. **Bat**, in particular, relates to the expression of anger resulting from fixed ideas and a lack of control (whereas Frilled-neck Lizard's anger is motivated by a lack of acknowledgment.) **Rainbow Serpent** reversed would also highlight issues around anger.

If **Willy Wagtail** also appears, communication issues are especially important. Group cards such as **Kookaburra**, **Magpies** and **Platypus**, emphasize the need to work with others as a united group.

Reversed

With the card reversed, Kendi the Frilled-neck Lizard is looking down, perhaps into the depths of his being. He is alerting you to issues around your view of yourself, in particular, your self-esteem. Beware of developing an inflated, egotistical view. If this is the case, a superior outlook could very well be masking a lack of confidence. As a result of this, you could be misusing your energy, and reacting to circumstances emotionally. There may also be a tendency to justify existence through accomplishment.

Is your worth as a human being tied to your success?

Here, Kendi is asking you to evaluate your stance in the world, as well as your motives. Are you being true to yourself? And is being true to yourself an excuse to hurt or trample on other people's feelings? Do you feel you have to prove something, to push yourself? Kendi reversed challenges you to explore, honestly and without reservation, the issues around your ideas about yourself, and how they are reflected in the world around you.

Kobong

If Kendi the Frilled-neck Lizard is your totem, or if you are particularly drawn to this card, you have the capacity to create great good, or cause great harm. You are charismatic, but your energy may repel as strongly as it attracts. Others may find your forceful ways or strength of conviction intimidating, which may cause them to back away. This could create frustrations in your situation; you feel as though you know the answers, but perhaps others are not receptive. It may be worth considering changing your approach. A breakdown in communication may not be the result of unsuitable ideas. You may have "raised your hood," like our brother the Frilled-neck Lizard, and, instead of looking capable and strong, you have intimidated those you wish to impress.

It is important for you to share your ideas with your peers, otherwise you could lose your objectivity regarding the situations you encounter. There is the possibility of developing "tunnel vision," to the point of becoming dictatorial. Ego issues will challenge you to define your personal limitations and capabilities, especially when it comes to relating to, and working with, others.

Learning to deal with frustration and anger, particularly in the issue queried, is important. Achieving a balance between mind and emotions is the key. Communicating with others, and getting your point across, especially if it is contrary to the general opinion, could be a challenge. What alternatives could Kendi have chosen in his situation? This Dreaming shows how we often learn through our mistakes. Acknowledging errors provides alternative solutions and, ultimately, success without negative repercussions.

Frilled-neck Lizard influences your reading through strong convictions. The first card drawn may be a good indicator of where you may need to relax, and perhaps try another, softer approach. Powerful, magical energy infuses this reading, and the power is all wielded by you, unless you lose your focus and give in to the emotions.

16 • Kangaroo

KINDNESS • CONSIDERATION • GENTLENESS

" In the Dreaming, the Kangaroo mother did not have a pouch in which to keep her baby joey safe. She would leave her joey under a tree, or hidden in long grasses, while she looked for food and water. While she was away, the joey was in great danger from hungry dingoes or eagles.

This particular time, she left her joey in the shade of a large gum tree while she went for water. On the way to the waterhole, she met an old, partially blind, wombat ambling along. The Kangaroo mother saw that the wombat was moving in the wrong direction, so she offered to lead him to water. He accepted her offer, and she patiently guided him along. She even had to push and steer him along the path.

They finally arrived at the waterhole. When they had quenched their thirst, the wombat asked the Kangaroo to guide him to some grass, for he was hungry. The Kangaroo mother agreed, but, first, she bounded away to check her joey. When she had made sure that he was safe, she returned to help the wombat. She was very patient with the wombat's slow, stumbling pace, guiding him at every step.

While the wombat was feeding, a hunter came along. He was hungry and had not caught anything, so an old tough wombat was better than nothing. The Kangaroo, sensing the danger, leapt across the hunter's path to distract him from the wombat. The ruse worked and the hunter chased the Kangaroo. She led him away, then lost him. Kangaroo went to check her joey before returning again to the wombat. The wombat was gone!

Then, the Great Spirit of Biami spoke. The Great Spirit had pretended to be an old, thirsty, and hungry wombat, who needed assistance, to find out who, out of all the animals, was the kindest. Biami offered to give the Kangaroo a gift, as a reward for her consideration. She asked for a pouch, so that she could carry her joey with her at all times, instead of leaving him alone. She also requested pouches for her sisters, the other marsupials.

This is why so many Australian animals have pouches. "

Imagery

Compassionate Kangaroo helped those in need, without any expectation of reward. She also remembered her sisters, the other marsupials, asking Biami to share with them her reward of a pouch. She reminds us not to forget others and to practice true gratitude by sharing our blessings. In this Dreaming, giving from the heart, with no anticipated returns, is repaid many times over.

This Dreaming can bring home the message of tolerance and consideration. We are all living manifestations of the Great Spirit, able to acknowledge the divinity in others, even if they are weak, old, garrulous and testing of one's patience.

Kangaroos are very intelligent creatures and, being naturally wary, they pose a challenge for traditional Aboriginal hunters. The Koori people tracked and hunted them for their meat, organs, skin, sinew, and bone. They are held in as much value and esteem as is the buffalo by Native Americans. The kangaroo bone is also famous for its use in witchcraft: a medicine man could cause someone's death by "pointing the bone" at them. ("Pointing the bone" has become an Australian colloquialism.) Kangaroo always brings powerful magic.

On the card, Kangaroo is evidently carrying her little joey in her brand new pouch. The wombat prints represent Biami, the Great Spirit. (We see only the prints because Biami, in spirit form, is unknowable.) Also shown is the gum tree, where the mother left her joey. This represents a necessary risk, and the element of trust. The tree has many branches, offering excellent protection from the sun and elements. The billabong and green grasses are also depicted, reminding us of how the Kangaroo mother helped the wombat, as well as the need to nourish ourselves. The spear of the hunter indicates the presence of a threat.

Upright

The gentle energies of kindness bound into your life in the form of the patient, helpful Kangaroo. She brings power, many blessings, and gifts. Grace is the quality of Kangaroo. She reminds us to be thankful for the gifts she brings. If you allow her to, she can nurture you, and bring softness into your life. "Climb into her warm pouch and embark on a rhythmic journey, bounding across the plains, secure and protected."

Kangaroo can bring into focus your relationship with your mother (or a mother figure in your life), or your relationships with your sisters. It may highlight your ability to nurture others. Working with older, or less able, people may be indicated. This is a teaching card; the lesson of kindness radiates from Kangaroo's eyes.

If the hunter's spear appears at the top, you may need to change your plans, or diversions may cause you to move in another direction.

Kangaroos are group animals, so, if this card appears with **Kookaburra**, **Magpies** or **Rainbow Lorikeet**, your good fortune will be connected with the efforts of others. If **Echidna** appears, you may feel you are giving without receiving. If so, practice Kangaroo's patience, and give without expectation of reward, or even acknowledgment. **Dingo**, the main predator of Kangaroo, may indicate pressing concerns in your issue, maybe even a need to restrain your generosity.

Reversed

With the card reversed, the mother Kangaroo appears to be lying on the ground, dead or perhaps mortally injured. Her joey is vulnerable, powerless to live without its mother's support and protection. This highlights qualities that are the very opposite of kindness.

The bodies of the Kangaroos will return to the earth. There is no further action except decay. There is no wastage. The crows will pick the bones, and what is left will enrich the soil. Everything has its place in the cycle of life, including unfairness and cruelty. Is there something in your issue that is being wasted, which could be put to use? How are you being cruel to yourself; have you cut something short which had promise? Where do the energies of unkindness, lack of consideration, and victimization play in your issue?

Or, like the joey, are you waiting for the end of something that had promise? Do you feel as if your support system is gone? The mother Kangaroo thought of others, yet, with this card reversed, she and her joey are alone. Issues around abandonment, fear and loneliness may be influencing your issue. It may be time to "climb out of the pouch," and throw yourself into life.

This card reversed can indicate an unprovoked attack on some level, and a loss. The wombat prints now appear at the top, so the great mystery of life may be testing you, as Biami did the Kangaroo. Surrounding positive cards may suggest a merely temporary setback; otherwise a total change in direction is indicated. Kangaroo returns to her source, the Dreaming, and new beginnings unfold.

Kobong

With Kangaroo as kobong, you share Kangaroo's qualities of kindness and gentleness. Compassion and the avoidance of aggression can influence any situation positively. Kangaroo also showed consideration by sharing her reward with the other marsupials. She acted as a spokesperson. Like Kangaroo, you have the ability to help those in need, and can actively seek assistance on their behalf.

In a reading, Kangaroo reveals that your compassionate qualities are affecting the situation positively. If you are being tested in any way, do not be surprised if the Great Spirit brings rewards for your patience. Kangaroos cannot move backward, so, with this card as kobong,

there is every indication of moving forward in your issue. Purpose and direction, balanced against the needs of others, are Kangaroo energies.

Kangaroo is the dedicated parent who cares diligently for her young, without ignoring her own needs. The archetypal mother, Kangaroo brings steady growth and maturation to something that (like a child) needs time, patience, dedication, guidance, and great care before it is capable of functioning independently.

Kangaroo people make excellent health practitioners, child-care workers, nurses, social workers, charity volunteers, and spokespeople for disadvantaged people and the environment.

17 · Koala

SECRETS · RESTRAINT · RESPECT

" *Back in the Dreaming, there was a great drought upon the land. There was no water to be found anywhere; every waterhole and stream was dry. All the creatures were very thirsty, but they noticed that Gula the Koala was the only one amongst them who was not suffering. They suspected he had a secret water supply.*

Buln-buln the Lyrebird was the best tracker, so he was persuaded by the other creatures to track Gula the Koala. He followed the Koala, quietly, keeping a safe distance between them, so Gula's suspicions would not be aroused. Finally, the Koala stopped. The Lyrebird hid in the low bushes, where he was well camouflaged, and watched Gula climb a large gum tree. In those days, Koala had a long tail. Buln-buln the Lyrebird saw the Koala balance on a tree limb, then, hanging by his tail, swing down to reach a large hollow below the branch. He greedily drank water from the depths of this hole. The thirsty Lyrebird could hear the sound of the water splashing.

Buln-buln felt even thirstier, hearing the sounds of Gula drinking, and became angry. The thought of the Koala secretly enjoying a water source, while he and the others suffered a great thirst, enraged him. Eager to get the water, and to punish the Koala, he quickly and quietly emerged from his hiding place, and rubbed together two sticks to start a fire. The noise he made was drowned by the Koala's greedy gulping, and the splashing of the water. The Lyrebird then set fire to the large gum tree which, being dry and highly inflammable in the drought conditions, burned quickly. The fire raced to the top of the tree, hungrily devouring the dry wood and leaves. As Lyrebird hoped, in the process, the water was dispersed. In his haste to escape, Gula the Koala left behind his tail.

To this day, the Koala has no tail, and, if he is angered, he can cause a great drought by keeping all the water to himself. This is why he deserves the greatest respect. "

Imagery

This Dreaming explains the mystery which has bemused scientists and biologists for decades—why a tree-dwelling animal has no tail! The koala poses many questions (and has many secrets) for science to discover, but, for most people, he is an endearing creature, and a symbol of Australia.

In many Aboriginal tribes, especially in the south-eastern parts of Australia, the Koala was held in great esteem. A popular source of meat, certain rituals surrounded its cooking and division amongst the tribespeople. Koala was always cooked unskinned, as a sign of respect; and, although koala fur is the most insulating of all marsupial furs, using it was a commonly held tribal taboo. Any disrespect for, or ignorance of, these laws would cause the spirit of this creature to bring a great drought upon the land and the people. Koala was capable of taking and hiding all the water, and still is.

The name "Koala" is said to mean "no water" in an Aboriginal dialect, referring to the fact that koalas live exclusively on eucalyptus leaves, without apparently needing to drink. Some water, however, is ingested from the morning dew and during rain. Koalas are endangered because vast numbers were previously killed for their fur, because forests are being clearfelled for timber and woodchips, and because of introduced diseases.

On the card, Koala sits in his tree. We can see the hollow where he hid the water. Vibrant flames lick the base of the trunk, signifying Lyrebird's actions, justice and irreversible change. The predominant brown and red colors suggest the drought conditions, and the wavy patterns seem to shimmer and rise, like heat waves in the arid outback.

Upright

Koala has climbed into your reading and entices you to discover his secrets. Gula hoarded the water, his secret for healthy survival. He was selfish, yet there was enough water for everyone. This Dreaming could indicate you have an asset, and are keeping it to yourself; or perhaps you are stuck in a state of "poverty consciousness" and fear, so you are grasping onto everything, just in case. The warning implicit in Koala Dreaming is not to be selfish, and to realize there is plenty to go around. Your time of drought, on whatever level this manifests itself, can be broken by an awareness of your assets. And by giving, you will not have less. Issues around abundance and scarcity could be influencing your situation.

Gula the Koala wanted to keep the water a secret from the others. What secrets do you have in your life, jealously protected and guarded? Are you hanging onto something, perhaps out of an imagined need for concealment? Can you share, and give, and risk loss? Or would you prefer to wait until the fates reveal your treasure? Koala asks you to examine your secrets and reevaluate the need for their concealment.

If **Lyrebird** also appears in your reading, be warned—someone else could discover or utilize your secrets before you do. Surrounding cards could indicate the issues you may need to delve into more deeply, to discover your unique secrets. Or, the secret to the final success of your query may be entwined within the issues covered by any surrounding cards.

Reversed

With the card reversed, Koala climbs out of his tree and onto the earth. He is going against his natural inclinations by climbing head first. Does he reach the ground safely?

Appearing in the contrary position, our brother Koala indicates you are in unfamiliar territory, lost, and unable to find your hidden source of replenishment. This could indicate the effects of illness, or a setback; you are literally "out of your tree." This Dreaming card calls for you to find your inner sense of well-being and balance, to seek out some "bush medicine," and to reorientate yourself. Then you can "climb back up your favorite eucalyptus tree," safe and sound.

Perhaps the water hidden in the hollow of the gum tree is stagnant and contaminated, and this is why Koala is climbing down. The fire now appears at the top of the card, and it can refer to the secrets which you are trying to keep hidden. Using another analogy, Koala can call for an airing of any skeletons in your closet. See them as old bones, no longer useful in your life. Unless you examine your secrets, the winds of life could well push the closet doors wide open, fueling a great fire from any spark of curiosity!

Kobong

As kobong, Koala brings the energies of mysteriousness, secrets and intrigue. As a creature who elicits great respect, Koala indicates that you are in a position of power, and are able to affect your situation positively through giving. There is no need for restraint.

Koala appearing as kobong can indicate you are hiding something, and your need to maintain secrecy influences your actions. Why is this secrecy necessary? And why do you restrain yourself, holding yourself back in some way? As kobong, Gula the Koala demands you give, especially of yourself.

The message to Koala people is: stop hiding your secrets—you have a special gift which could help those around you, if you were to share it. By sharing your humanity, even pain and shame, you make healing possible, for yourself and other people who share your journey.

In an oyster, an "irritation" transforms into a treasured pearl. Similar potential is evident in your situation. Koala as kobong asks you to find the "pearl." You may even be surprised by its value and perfection. The surrounding cards could indicate how you could best work with your secrets.

When Koalas are approached by people, the Koalas do not respond; they stare straight ahead, seeming to ignore the people. Koala people are usually uncomfortable meeting others, and this makes them appear inaccessible and aloof. This facade hides a loving and warm-hearted nature. They can keep secrets (unlike Jitta Jitta the Willy Wagtail), and are very discreet, quiet and passive. Koala people generally stick to familiar territory, and they are not known for noticing small details. They also tend to command respect.

18 · Spider

ILLUSIONS • SEDUCTION • CHARISMA

" *There was a woman, Jitai, who attracted men like a flower draws honey bees. Her husband had been killed, and she hungered for men. Jitai slept with some of the men, and pleased them greatly. Others she rejected. The rejected men began to murmur amongst themselves. They believed that she had been told to reject them by the men she slept with. The wives began to talk among themselves. They complained to their husbands: "The Ancestor Spirits will be angered, and they will destroy us."*

The men who liked Jitai spoke in her favor, the rejected men complained. Soon fights broke out. A spear flew, then another. Finally, the men who favored Jitai drove the others away, forcing them and their families to leave camp.

From that time on, the two groups traveled the country separately. Whenever they encountered one another, spears flew. Each group tried to sneak upon the other one. The men who were with Jitai suffered the most, so they decided to use their powers of magic. They called up poisonous snakes to kill their opponents. The other group made magic also; they killed the snakes, and sent up a great cloud of stinging bees. But the men with Jitai changed themselves into rocks. And so it went on.

Finally, Jitai's men made a mountain higher than any ever seen before. Its top reached the skyworld. One morning, they saw their enemies approaching, so they decided to climb to the top of the mountain and stay, forever safe, in the skyworld. They began to climb the mountain, but, the higher they climbed, the more they gasped and struggled for breath. Jitai suffered the most. "You must leave me," she said, then fell to the ground.

The men refused to leave Jitai. They carried her back down the mountain. They came to a cave, where they changed themselves into spiders, so they would not be discovered. They crawled into holes in the dark. When their enemies appeared, they found nothing.

The spiders spread to other caves. As time passed, they also made their homes on the riverbanks and among the rocks. There they are found to this day. "

Imagery

The main focus of this Dreaming is seduction and sexuality, or illusion and physical pleasure. Jitai the Spider is an enchantress of excessive charisma. Her vitality, stamina, and lust are magnificent. However, the results of her overpowering desires have significant personal, and social, repercussions. Her community is drastically affected by her actions. Jitai and her lovers follow their desires selfishly, breaking society's conventions, and causing hurt and pain to others.

On the card, Jitai the Spider is clinging to the sides of the cave entrance, waiting for the danger to pass. The entrance and cavity symbolize male and female sexuality.

Upright

This card tingles seductively with attractive energies to be dealt with in the issue queried. Spider can reveal the results of an overindulgence in sexuality, or being judgmental, manipulative, or discriminatory. All of these actions show a lack of consideration towards other people, and they are all against tribal law. Were Jitai and her lovers entirely powerless against their drives? They were certainly aware of the social consequences of their actions.

Just as real-life spiders can be threatening, something is threatening in your issue. On another level, Spider is "the other woman." She can emphasize issues around divided loyalties, moral dilemmas, and jealousy. Escape (and hence caution) is a key word for this card. There is a need to seek fulfillment.

This card is similar to the Devil in the Tarot. It can indicate temptation; something exciting, but possibly dangerous, or not acceptable to society. Spider can point to something spontaneous and passionate, that opens up new areas of life to explore. Take care not to get too caught up in the passion that you forget where you're going! Jitai the Spider indicates a time when physical gratification is important, or, at least, is compelling you into action. You may need to consider carefully the positive and negative consequences of your actions, from an objective, rational point of view. It may be time to practice some self-discipline and moderation, and to overcome physical desires.

Spider weaves the surrounding cards together with her sticky web from which it is difficult to escape. Spider with **Barramundi** can represent the achievement of a deep, heartfelt desire; the uniting of passion with enduring love. The presence of **Moon** emphasizes the sexual aspects of the reading. In the Moon Dreaming, Gien the Moon was beguiling and charismatic, the male version of Jitai. The presence of these two cards together may indicate a perfect match, if the reading concerns love and a relationship.

Whenever Spider appears in a reading, notice is being given to step cautiously. The Australian funnel-web and redback spiders are deadly, so caution is not only indicated, but necessary. The appearance of **Gray Owl** or **Kookaburra**, both natural predators of Spider, would be a very positive sign in this case.

Reversed

The spider is a symbol of feminine power in many cultures. As a dream symbol, it can represent unconscious fears. When reversed, this card can represent fear, rejection of one's desires, or fear of rejection. It could also symbolize generalized fears, if you are frightened of spiders.

Spider in this position can also indicate you are resisting whatever is tempting you. You may be turning down an offer or opportunity, as Spider appears to be moving downwards and away from the entrance to her cave. Spider is now saying it is not time for distracting sensuality and pleasure; it is time for more serious, mental activities.

Jitai is learning self-control and discipline. She is, whether by choice or circumstance, celibate and non-productive. Yet, there is still an urge for creativity that seeks to touch upon the divine in a way which is "real." This energy can be channeled into creative expression, or the learning of something new and interesting.

Kobong

Jitai the Spider as kobong points to a strong, even overpowering, emotional desire influencing your situation. It also indicates that you have the ability to draw your desire to you. This may express itself as sexuality, a strong charisma, and/or an ability to get what you want. There could be, however, some sort of dilemma around the situation or issue queried. You are certainly aware of your "prey," on whatever level. But is it the right prey? Will it sustain you, or cause "indigestion?"

The lesson for Spider is to balance desire and emotion with rational, practical action, in line with personal and social morals. The other cards in your reading could indicate the issues affecting your situation, especially what attracts you and, conversely, distracts you from the main focus.

As kobong, Spider indicates the achievement of goals. However, beguiling energies could seduce you away from your path, and they will continue to haunt you, unless they are resolved. The challenge is to practice self-discipline and the rational evaluation of priorities.

Spider can represent seduction by the media, money, drugs, cults, and magnetic ideas; or the quest for eternal youth, and the pursuance of unrealistic dreams. As Spider's intricate web attracts and traps her prey, beware you do not become entwined in some equally attractive web. Avoiding an alluring trap requires attention, and an awareness of where you are heading in your issue.

If **Ochre** also appears in your reading, there is a great chance of success in creating the exact conditions you desire. Spider's charisma and Ochre's magnetism draw your desire to you in a way which may seem overpowering. The warning here is to evaluate carefully the importance of your objectives.

If Spider as kobong appears reversed, this can indicate the resistance of temptation. It is not time for sensuality; it is time for more mental energies, or putting other people before your own pleasure. Service to others, and the delay of personal gratification, are indicated here, especially if **Gymea Lily**, **Bat** reversed, or **Bogong Moth** reversed also appear in the spread.

19 · Wombat

HOME · SECURITY · BOUNDARIES

" Warreen the Wombat and Mirram the Kangaroo were good friends. They lived together and, although they agreed upon almost everything, they each had their own way of doing things. Warreen built a gunyah (bush hut) to protect himself from the wind and rain. He offered to build one for Mirram, who only laughed. Mirram lived under the stars, in the open. He said that this was the best way.

During the summer months, they were happy together. It was different in winter. One night, there was a bitterly cold wind. The Kangaroo huddled against a gum tree, proud that he could face the weather while Warreen was crouched in his tiny, stuffy gunyah.

Then rain started to fall in icy sheets, and the gunyah suddenly seemed quite attractive. He thought about it, then, fighting the wind, he made his way to the Wombat's home. He asked to be let in, but Warreen laughed and refused. "Isn't yours the best way to live?" he jeered. Mirram forced his way in, but Wombat told him to stay in the corner, as he was wet.

As the night drew on, Mirram became very angry because he couldn't sleep, as there was a draught where he was huddled. He became bitter, resenting the comfort of his companion, who was snoring loudly. Morning came. Impulsively, Mirram picked up a large stone and threw it at Wombat. The impact flattened Wombat's skull. "That'll teach you to neglect a friend," cried Mirram the Kangaroo. "You will always have a flat forehead to remind you of your unkindness. And you will always live in that damp, dark hole you call a home!"

From that day on they never spoke, but Wareen the Wombat planned his revenge. He cut a spear and made a woomera (a notched stick, which would help him throw the spear further). He had to wait a long time for his chance because Kangaroos are vigilant creatures, but his opportunity finally came. He threw the spear, and it landed on the Kangaroo's rump. Mirram pulled at the spear, but it was stuck. "That'll teach you to knock me about. From now on, you'll have a tail and always live out in the open!" cried Warreen the Wombat. "

Imagery

This Dreaming teaches us to consider the best environment for our home. Wombat's home, although airless and damp, protected him from cold, wind and rain. Kangaroo's airy home enabled him to enjoy the panorama of night skies and stars, but his home was the least practical in inclement weather.

Aboriginal people were nomadic. They followed the change of seasons, searching for fruits and other bush tucker. They traveled to maintain their spiritual obligation as caretakers to the earth. Their homes were simply constructed humpies (huts), or they slept under the stars. They were like Kangaroo, whereas Western man is more like Wombat.

On the card, we see Wombat emerging from the comfort of his home. Wombats are nocturnal creatures, so we also see the dark night sky.

Upright

Wombat is all about the home environment, and the structures we build around ourselves for protection from the elements. It represents our sense of security, our personal space, and how we feel about sharing them. The issue of boundaries may be present. Like Wombat, you may have unwelcome guests, or you may feel that your personal space has been violated or invaded.

This card emphasizes the balance between logical thought and personal preference, in the choice of a home. With the appearance of Wombat, home-oriented issues will certainly be in the air.

Wombat is shown emerging from his home. Is he moving towards another card? This could indicate your direction, and the energies that are presently influencing your home environment. This card may also bring up plans regarding your home environment, or subconscious desires for it, or even dissatisfaction with your home.

The home relates to the first chakra, according to eastern lore. It is the place that gives you your feeling of being "grounded," the place of family, and the Western ideal of security. It is your own personal space in the world, and in some ways it defines who you are.

Your living space has a direct influence upon your well-being, and, with Wombat making an appearance, a reevaluation is required. Many things influence this space: location, living space, sound, color. Are you willing to make changes in some way? If you are living with another person, can you accept their different preferences, and reach a compromise? Where do you feel most at home, and how can you create a more nurturing, sustaining home space? Your home is linked with your will to live. Are you happy? If not, why stay? Are your personal boundaries intact, or have you chosen your home from a perspective other than what is in your heart?

If Wombat appears with **Waratah**, this could refer to your childhood home, experiences undergone there, and the subconscious patterns formed then. With **Opal**, Wombat urges you to examine how you have created your present reality. With **Emu**, the emphasis is on how you judge your home. If **Kangaroo** appears, expect visitors! Kangaroo can also signify learning to live with others, while maintaining your need for personal space.

Reversed

If Wombat appears reversed, it is time to dig a new burrow, or start renovations! Perhaps your attitudes need to be reevaluated, or perhaps you need a change of wardrobe or image. Something about your personal space is in need of an overhaul! This position could also indicate moving to another house or location, or some form of transience in your situation.

Issues around your home environment could well be highlighted through disharmony, dissatisfaction, or being forced, by outside conditions, to move or change. The challenge here is to view your situation as the catalyst for creating greater harmony and happiness in your life.

This position can indicate dealing with anger, whether you are feeling it, or at the receiving end. This meaning is emphasized if **Bat, Dingo** or **Whale & Starfish** appear. If **Kangaroo** appears, then disharmony is indicated, though a positive resolution is available in the energies covered by any surrounding cards.

Kobong

If Wombat has dug his way into your reading as kobong, issues around your home environment are under the spotlight. Perhaps you wish to spend more time than you do at home, or perhaps you need to get out more. Identifying your requirements, attitudes and personal preferences regarding personal space, will help you to attain the kind of environment you require.

In this position, Wombat can indicate your home life is influencing other issues related to your query. It can also point to where you feel most comfortable, and "at home." The surrounding cards could indicate where this is likely to be. Because Wombat is a nocturnal creature, and night symbolizes dreams and the subconscious, the undercurrents in your issue may well be flavored by unseen and unknown desires.

What issues do the other cards in your reading highlight? Do they represent issues you feel at home with, or do they make you feel uncomfortable? Wombat seeks to be in his little hole, but, are you like Kangaroo, prefer-

ring to be unrestrained and in the open? Is personal freedom and change more important than security and putting down roots? This is a time for choices. Decisions will need to be made. Personal comfort and needs are the criteria for optimum satisfaction!

Wombat's need to feel comfortable will affect your reading strongly. Like our brother, you may have a tendency to feel superior. Wombat was quite competitive with Kangaroo in this respect, yet he resented his friend's intrusion when he was finally proved right. The need to prove yourself right might be hindering the success of your issue.

On a personality level, Wombat is the homebody, the person who is happiest in his or her own burrow. Such people may seem to have lived "sheltered lives," and could have a sense of innocence. Wombat people enjoy entertaining at home. They could be interior decorators, architects, builders or they could work from home. In astrology, Wombat relates to the astrological sign Cancer.

20 · Bat

CHAUVINISM • FIXED VIEWPOINTS • ANGER

" *In the Dreaming, there was a man called Narahadarn who was very selfish and didn't care about the feelings of others. His totem was the Bat. When Narahadarn the Bat Man was searching for honey ("sugarbag"), he found a hive high up in a big hollow gum tree. He returned to camp and sent one of his two wives to the gum tree to cut out the hive with a stone ax and bring back the honey. But when the woman pushed her arm into the hole, her feet accidentally slipped and she could not remove her arm. She was left hanging, and unable to move.*

Narahadarn was more interested in the honey than in his wife's plight, and he became angry. He cut off his wife's arm and she bled so much that she died. Narahadarn then told his second wife to get the honey. Her arm too became caught in the tree, and she met the same unfortunate fate as the first wife.

The Bat Man realized his actions were wrong and became ashamed of himself. On returning to camp he refused to answer any questions about his missing wives and avoided his people, remaining alone. The mother of the two wives became concerned, and secretly sent out some young men to track the women's movements and find out what had happened.

When the men returned with the gruesome story, the tribesmen were so horrified and angered they built a huge fire, overpowered Narahadarn, and threw him into it. As the flames rose high into the darkness of the night, the people saw a dim figure emerge from the flames, rise above them and vanish into the heavens.

Narahadarn, now a bat, is so ashamed of his behavior that he sleeps during the day and hunts for his food at night, to avoid being seen by his tribespeople. "

Imagery

The energies of cooperation and understanding are lacking in this Dreaming, and so form a main part of its message or lesson. Bat also teaches an important lesson about anger. Had Bat thought before he acted, or allowed himself to view the situation from his wives' perspective, the whole episode could have been dealt with in a more satisfactory way. Bat's "excessive devotion to a cause" (chauvinism) resulted in his very limited vision or one-sided focus; at the time, he was so certain he was right he gave in to self-righteous anger. In a modern sense, Bat was expecting his wives to do all the work while he contributed nothing. He was a "user" and didn't consider others. Narahadarn the Bat now has a different perspective on life; his whole vision has been turned upside-down—literally!

On the card, Narahadarn the Bat hangs in the tree where he found the honey. You can see the hollow which held the honey, and the blood of his wives which is evidence of his dreadful actions. The fire which transformed Bat is burning vigorously in the foreground. It is a dark night, yet the flames and the moon illuminate Bat's shame.

Upright

By flying into your cards, Bat brings a message which requires your active participation. Bat asks you to examine your life and to work consciously on those issues you have been trying to avoid. These issues are related to the subject of the reading and to the surrounding cards.

It is important that you find the appropriate action to take, especially in situations related to the issue of the reading. It is time to examine your personal motivation closely—in doing so, you could release a long-held, subconscious pattern or thought process. Any anger or even shame could be the result of a fixed mind-set which could be limiting your situation. In times of frustration, remember Narahadarn the Bat; there's a chance to get some delicious honey, but think first, how will you go about it?

When Bat appears with **Dingo**, this may signify the presence of a close companion. Alternatively, the elements of favoritism may be influencing your actions.

Another Dreaming about Bat portrays him treating his dog with more love and compassion than his wives. In this second Dreaming, his wives reach breaking point as a result of his selfish demands. They overpower him, push him into a hollow tree, and block the entrance with mud which hardens and traps him. They also put his beloved dingo in the tree with him, and, as the days go by, the Bat Man allows the hungry dog to eat his flesh (which is why the Bat has tattered-looking wings to this day).

The presence of **Frilled-neck Lizard** or **Rainbow Serpent**, especially if negatively aspected, can emphasize the destructive potential of fixed views or anger, related in some way to your issue. These cards also indicate an equally strong possibility that this energy can be transformed into something more constructive, especially with positive spiritual cards like **Kookaburra**, **Magpies**, **Opal**, or **Rainbow Lorikeet**.

Reversed

Bat reversed puts Bat upright, to our way of looking at the world. This card is similar to the Hanged Man, perhaps the most mysterious image of the Tarot. Look at things upside-down, and a new perspective may emerge. You could try to "brainstorm" the situation queried—concentrate on your question or issue and write down all the ideas and thoughts which come to you, no matter how outrageous. In this way, you may access new possibilities and avenues which could lead to a successful conclusion of your issue.

On a mundane level, Bat in this position could indicate reversals in your situation, or your approach to it. Other people in your life could also reflect this aspect of changeability.

Or, are there important, unresolved life issues which seem to be suspended? Like Bat, could you be unable to let go and move on? This would be emphasized by the presence of **Bogong Moth**. Bat appears to be balanced or suspended in such a way that he could fall backwards or take flight. Which is it for you?

Kobong

People who have Bat as kobong, or are drawn to this card, exhibit the strong energy of this creature, which can be seen by others as plain stubbornness. Even if wrong, Bat people will stick to their beliefs. They should try to look at the situations they encounter through the eyes and hearts of others. Empathy is a quality they could learn to develop, especially when feeling wronged. Bat's response to this would be: "How dare you! You don't know what I've been going through!"

Bat people can be very moody and easily irritated at times. As kobong, Bat can indicate a tendency to overreact emotionally in any situation that causes feelings of powerlessness or being out of control. This is often the result of avoiding the main issue, and this avoidance can result in a cathartic release and further lack of control, unless the value of compromise is accepted, along with its broader view. In this way, we can overcome our emotional reactions, and function from a more balanced, open and loving perspective. Bat may swoop from the superficial to the underlying cause, as kobong.

Bat influences your reading through his narrow viewpoints. In such a position, you will not "get your own way" unless you change your approach and expand your vision! Can you see how your current focus "burns you up" (or contains this potential), or limits your situation? Narahadarn the Bat left his wives to perish "out on a limb." What aspects of your issue are in the same predicament?

Bat people have great reserves of strength. They are good at acting upon their decisions and seeing them through to completion. Objectivity and perseverance are keywords here. Bat people need to balance their innate wisdom with their emotions when deciding how best to get their honey.

21 · Black Swan

VICTIMIZATION · ASSISTANCE · MIRACLES

" *Way back in the Dreaming, the Wibalu women were very good craftspeople, and they made the only boomerangs in the world. The Wibalu were very possessive of the boomerangs, and refused to share the secret of making them. They were prepared to barter this secret, but the price was so high that few tribes could raise the necessary goods. This created resentment and jealousy amongst the other tribes, and, one day, the men of a nearby tribe decided to steal the boomerangs from the Wibalu women. As the women were very powerful, the men planned to trick them.*

Two tribesmen changed themselves into white swans, and flew to a waterhole near the women's camp. The men felt sure the Wibalu women would rush to see these strange birds, and forget to guard their boomerangs in the excitement. The scheme worked perfectly. As the women rushed to see the strange new birds, the men, who had hidden themselves nearby, raced into the camp, seized the boomerangs and ran away. When the women returned to camp and discovered their loss, they screamed with rage, and rushed to punish the thieves, who by this time had escaped. So, the women turned their rage on the swans.

But the swans had flown to a lagoon that, unknown to them, was the territory of the eagles. Angry at the intrusion, the eagles picked up the swans, tore out their feathers, and carried them to a desert. The victims were left almost naked, and bleeding. Their white feathers were transformed into the beautiful flannel flower. On seeing what had happened, a large flock of crows plucked feathers from their own bodies, and let them fall to the swans. "The eagles are our enemies too," they cried, "our feathers will keep you warm!"

Today, Black Swans still have their black feathers, except for the white tips of their wings, and the blood remains on their beaks. And the Wibalu women? They rose into the skyworld, arguing over who was to blame for not guarding the boomerangs. The red tinges of sunset show them fighting to this very day. "

Imagery

In this Dreaming, although the men were wrong to steal, this was their only apparent recourse, and they did not intend to cause bloodshed. As victims, they attempted to change the situation they were in (by stealing the boomerangs, which represent power), and they were given assistance. Although the Wibalu women also became victims, they can be accused of not sharing their secrets and skills. Also, they continued to argue over who was to blame for their loss.

The second part of this Dreaming continues the theme of victimization. The white swans are stripped naked. Protection against the elements is gone; they are in a life-threatening situation. However, the crows assist them (to spite their enemies rather than out of true compassion), and the swans are saved.

On the card, a Black Swan clutches a boomerang, the symbol of greed and power. The black feathers represent timely assistance, and the flannel flowers symbolize loss, though they also remind us that, out of pain and suffering, can come something beautiful.

An interesting fact about the Black Swan: before its discovery by European man, all swans were thought to be white. There was an expression referring to a black swan as something fantastically impossible!

Upright

The presence of this card reveals a situation that makes you feel powerless and even a victim. Like the Black Swan, you may have "overstepped the mark" and, as a result, you may be "stripped of your covering," which was just a disguise anyhow. You may feel you are in an emotional desert, alone, and separated from your own kind.

Where people feel victimized, their personal boundaries have been overpowered, violated, ignored. Yet they can be held partially responsible for their situation if they have not asserted their own integrity and personal rights. If you were to acknowledge personal responsibility for your position, you would then empower yourself to move through it, by gaining awareness of its dynamics. Like the plucked Swans, you would be able to redress your situation, accept help where it is offered, and take flight again.

Know that feeling naked and stripped bare, and experiencing pain and fear, are part of the process of getting clear about yourself, about what you want, how to get it, and the events you create around yourself. Once again, this process requires a willingness to move beyond the victim state. Unless a victim is willing to accept any assistance offered, that assistance will not be useful to growth.

So, expect a miracle. Out of victimization can come assistance. Some feathers of the past will remain as a reminder, and your new color can serve as a visual affirmation of the new freedom gained.

As the boomerang is a symbol of greed and power, if it is positioned near another card, it could indicate something coveted.

On a mundane level, Black Swan may symbolize a life crisis that, when faced, will change you forever. This card can suggest any situation in which you may feel powerless, but everything will work out perfectly in the end, with Black Swan taking flight.

Reversed

Black Swan reversed is prone and apparently lifeless. The black feathers show help was given, yet he remains stuck; there is no moving on, he is still flightless.

If you have drawn Black Swan in the contrary-position, you are asked to become aware of the invisible weight holding you back from flight. What is holding you back? Can you throw off any limiting beliefs and attitudes to see the gifts that are already in your life? You are no longer a victim, there is nothing to prevent you moving on, except your own attitudes. You need not remain stuck in the past. Look at your feathers, brother or sister swan. You can fly! It is certainly time to stretch your wings, and take off.

Black Swan indicates that opportunities may present themselves, perhaps unexpectedly, bringing a change of circumstances, especially if the flannel flowers appear at the top of the card. This will allow you to break any negative cycle, and improve your situation or issue.

Kobong

Black Swan as kobong reveals that you are operating from a level of unawareness, and you are blaming outside conditions for your circumstances. The position of victim is one of weakness, fear, or perhaps resentment. Black Swan people need to take responsibility for their situation, and become informed of the options available to them. Only from a position of understanding and awareness can they take their steps to freedom.

Black Swans are beautiful birds; they embody the qualities and energies of grace, freedom, and serenity. As kobong, this card can represent emotional growth and new patterns of behavior, with an accompanying improvement in your situation. This card highlights the possibility of small miracles gracing your journey; those synchronous events or occurrences that change your destiny. It's an exciting time, Black Swan, so remember, there can be light, even when you are in the dark.

Black Swan influences your reading in profound ways. Appearing as kobong, there is an indication you may be feeling trapped and powerless in your situation, and the energies of this card are propelling you towards resolution. The choice facing you is whether to accept any assistance offered, or to continue fighting, like the Wibalu women. Apply the message of Black Swan by asking how you feel trapped, as well as assisted, by the issues highlighted in the reading. A major key may be revealed in the first card drawn.

The Serenity Prayer, an affirmation used in Alcoholics Anonymous, could be a useful tool in your situation: "God grant me the serenity to accept the things I cannot change, courage to change the things I can, and the wisdom to know the difference."

22 • Bogong Moth

CURIOSITY • JOURNEYS • ADVICE

" *Way back in the Dreaming, in a tranquil and serene place amongst the river grasses of the Snowy Mountains, there lived a beautiful, brightly colored moth called Myee. Her wings were every color of the rainbow.*

Myee was very curious by nature, and she yearned to discover why the tops of the distant mountains were a sparkling white color, instead of the vivid green of her home. She would ask everyone she encountered whether they knew the answer to her question, but no one did. She wanted to journey there to discover the reason firsthand, though her partner, Bogong, warned her not to seek the answer to the mystery. He said that she should stay in the safety of their home.

One day, however, curiosity got the better of her. Myee left secretly in the stillness of dawn, and flew towards the mountains. It was a very long journey for a little moth. If it wasn't for her curiosity, she would have succumbed to weariness, and returned home. When sunset graced the horizon, snow began to fall, beating her to the ground. She was quickly covered by snow, and trapped. She was unable to move. The snow fell thickly for many weeks, yet Myee did not perish. She lay under the icy blanket for the entire duration of winter.

When spring arrived, the heat of the sun melted the snow, and Myee was finally released. As she stretched her wings and took flight, the beautiful bright colors of her wings remained in what was left of the snow. Before her amazed eyes, the vibrant colors blended and dissolved into the earth, until they were no longer seen. And that spring, for the first time, beautiful, bright, new flowers emerged from the earth.

Myee returned home. To this day, Myee's wings are a dull brown-gray, but in the Snowy Mountains the flowers of spring and summer display her splendor. "

Imagery

Each image in this Dreaming is a step in a voyage of discovery. The white mountain looms, a symbol of mystery and challenge. The snow falls, a symbol of hibernation, a state of suspension. The beautiful, colorful flowers emerge as Myee returns to the green grass of home, forever changed, and with a story to tell.

The grass represents familiarity, safety, and the voice of reason, which advocates caution. This voice dislikes change, especially something as dangerous as Myee's quest. The mountain symbolizes her dreams, and her urge to find answers, and the snow teaches the lesson of trust and patience while awaiting results. Myee was warned not to attempt to satisfy her curiosity. She chose to ignore this advice, and paid the price with the loss of her colors, but the flowers of renewal and change were her reward for facing a challenge.

The Bogong (or Bugong) moth is one of the more unusual food sources of the Australian Aboriginal people, who dwelt in the south-eastern highlands. Nutty in flavor and very high in protein, the Bogong Moths were so prized that, every summer, the people ventured hundreds of kilometers into the mountains to collect them. Social and ceremonial celebrations were held in conjunction with this annual pilgrimage.

Upright

Appearing in your reading, the Bogong Moth will certainly indicate a time of sustenance, nourishment, and celebration. Myee advises you not to have preconceived ideas on outcomes, just the faith to know things will improve. Myee's vivid hues bring color, movement, and zest. However, curiosity could propel you into a situation that may "snow you under." If this is the case, it may be wise to await the thaw patiently. An attempt to dig yourself out could drain your energy and valuable resources, which could be expended more constructively.

Patience is called for—practice it and you will fly free. Myee may have felt powerless during her enforced hibernation, at the mercy of natural forces beyond her control. You too may be feeling lifeless and trapped, as a result of your current situation, but the flowers of renewal and change will bloom as spring comes.

There is no indication in this Dreaming of the effect Myee's adventures had on her personally. If an issue is being questioned, the direction you take is ultimately up to you, even if those around you disagree. The issue may be one of heart versus head. Try to evaluate for yourself what is actually being risked, and what the potential gains might be. Or, like the Bogong Moth, follow your heart, and be prepared for a challenge!

In your journey, you may sacrifice something which is no longer necessary, although you may not see this perspective initially. In exchange, spiritual growth, learning, and wisdom will form another ring on the tree of your soul.

If any of the symbols appears against another card, the symbol will influence the meaning of that card. For example, if the mountain appears next to **Barramundi**, the energies of mystery and challenge will influence the issue of love.

Reversed

If you have drawn Myee reversed, she appears as if she is about to land on the green grass. While on land, there is no flight. You may be in a situation where a loss of some sort is the direct result of a risk, or action, taken (or, maybe, not taken). This could be on a spiritual, mental, emotional, or physical level. A key point to remember is that the learning and wisdom gained far outweighs any sacrifice.

With the green grasses of Myee's home appearing at the top of this card, there is an emphasis on sticking to the familiar. Whether this is by choice or circumstance, there may still be an inner urge to explore new territory, and face the great unknown.

Throughout life, advice surrounds your every choice. Live your life the way you choose. Make your decisions for yourself, as you will have to live with the results.

Myee's bright colors drained away, and were replaced by drab brown. However, brown is the color of the earth, and the earth is full of potential. Perhaps your potential is of a different color to the one you had expected.

Kobong

Myee the Bogong Moth appearing as kobong brings the urge to explore, especially regarding the issue you have queried. This card brings with it a sense of excitement, an eagerness to move forward, even against the "better judgment" of your peers.

If you are drawn to Myee, then you are indeed inquisitive! Perhaps you are not obviously adventurous, but, underneath, the multicolored zest and energy of life simmers and bubbles, emerging now and again when you least expect it. You inadvertently bring color with you, a vibrancy others perceive with joy.

It is wise to expend your energy on your interests, researching or studying, engaging and inquiring. Otherwise, this energy could be used where it shouldn't—prying and spying for instance!

Myee affects surrounding cards by highlighting areas of indecision, or a waiting period. Our sister will emphasize what is in suspension, awaiting outside circumstances for change. Curiosity will also be strong; your inquisitiveness may be propelling you towards something new and exciting. On a mundane level, a journey of some sort is indicated, either physically or inwardly.

Like Myee, you cannot resist breaking free of restrictions in society, such as conventional thought and dress. If this doesn't manifest itself outwardly, you could be a dreamer with a strong fantasy life, or a rebel fighting against everything that crosses your belief system. Take care not to be too impressionable, or too dogmatic and headstrong. Look closely at other points of view, judge the facts at hand, and act rather than react.

23 · Brolga

CREATIVITY • DANCE • EXPRESSION

" *Way back in the Dreaming, in a certain tribe, there was a tall, graceful girl called Brolga. She loved to dance, and spent every moment she could out on the claypans dancing. She was so good at dancing, she was permitted to practice while the women were gathering food and working. Also, the men allowed her to join them in corroboree—this was a sign of great esteem, as women were not normally permitted to participate in, or even watch, the sacred ceremonies.*

Brolga was dearly loved by all her people, and not just for her ability to dance and entertain. She was sweet-natured and cheerful. Many of the young men wished to have her for their wife, but she refused them all, wishing to concentrate solely on her dancing. A powerful wirrunun, who possessed the powers of magic, also wanted Brolga for his wife, but she refused his offer. The wirrunun man became resentful, and plotted his revenge. Brolga's people, concerned the wirrunun would cause trouble, warned her to remain in the camp because they feared for her safety. One day, while Brolga was out on the plains digging for yams, and dancing on the claypan, she forgot the warning and drifted away from the camp. The wirrunun, who had been patiently awaiting the right opportunity, saw his chance. He quietly left the camp, quickly painted himself, and began to chant and sing his magic, turning himself into a giant whirlywind. In this form, he stole upon the girl.

Brolga, sensing danger, turned, but too late! The whirlywind quickly caught up with her, engulfing her in clouds of swirling red dust. Gone was the girl. In her place stood a tall, gray bird.

Her people, seeing the great whirlywind and fearing the worst, came running, panic filling their hearts. They called her name, "Brolga! Brolga!" but there was no answer. Instead, a tall graceful bird came to them, bowed her head and began to dance. "

Imagery

In this card, we see the graceful Brolga dancing on the plain, her wings reaching out to embrace and fill the space around her with, not only movement, but also herself. Her personality fills this card with her unique energies, her joy of dance infuses the image with the enthusiasm created by following the heart. The evil whirlywind, which transformed her, is in the background, suggesting the feeling of being swept up by the winds of change, its spiral representing the endless processes of change as well as the processes of life.

If Brolga has danced her way into your reading, enjoy the freedom of movement and creative self-expression she is offering to you. Brolga's graceful dance is an elegant reminder that, as we move through life, we can take pleasure in our creativity and, in the process, have all our needs met. Social birds by nature, brolgas perform in a troupe, so the presence of others is also indicated. Enjoy and share your dance!

Upright

Brolga brings focus and energy for all creative endeavors, particularly the arts (dance, theater, drama, music, and so on), and, more generally, daily activities that require creative thought (such as, interpersonal relationships, problem-solving for business, parenting, personal and domestic issues).

Our sister Brolga typifies the ambitious, focused career person. Her strong focus excluded all except her love of dance. This same strength of commitment can be applied to every task of life, particularly if that task is a labor of love. In this situation, though, it is possible to become obsessive if we pursue exclusively what we love, without the support of others. It is here one must learn to practice discipline through moderation, unless, like our sister Brolga, you find external circumstances favor the expression of your dance, and all your physical needs are met, so you may be exclusive in your focus. The presence of this card certainly indicates support for any endeavor which generates personal enthusiasm.

The appearance of the whirlywind at the top of the card may indicate changes in your physical world. You may feel as if you have been engulfed in a maelstrom of change which is literally "spinning you out." Although, in this Dreaming, the whirlywind was the result of an evil man's actions, its presence in a reading can be an acknowledgment of talents and support for their expression. It may have seemed to Brolga that her life as she knew it had ended, yet divine intervention created the perfect circumstances for her to continue her dance. The energies of renewal will be swept into your life through the whirlywind—see Brolga dance!

Dancing was Brolga's goal, and nothing was allowed to distract her from this. You may find yourself in a situation where the many demands of life are pulling you away from your own unique form of self-expression, especially if **Gymea Lily** or **Wombat** also appear.

Reversed

Brolga reversed indicates that you haven't found your path in life, there is a degree of uncertainty. Your focus is diffused, and you are seeking the right avenue for your creativity. The surrounding cards could indicate where, or how, you are hindering your process, or how to facilitate it. If the whirlywind appears near another card, its issues could point to the distractive forces that may be absorbing your time, energy, and focus.

Another pitfall is procrastination. Following through dreams, creating them, and actively pursuing them will generate an influx of new energy which will propel you back to the right direction. Is there any unfinished business in your life that is locking you into the past? If so, do what is necessary to finish it, and then you will be emotionally clear to rejoin Brolga's dance. By following her example, each step you take (again, with that conscious intention for completion) will become as effortless and stately as that of our sister. Go on, dance it up!

Kobong

If Brolga is your kobong, she represents talent, creative energy and drive. Our sister focused on what she loved, to the exclusion of all else. Brolga is an example of love in action, and her society supported her. If you are following through with your dreams, this card reveals support for your commitment. However, there is an inherent warning to practice caution, and to take note of any advice given regarding your security (on whatever level). Don't forget the practicalities when you are caught up in the excitement of self-expression. The fine line between enthusiasm and obsession may be crossed if you lose sight of the realities of the material world.

In Aboriginal culture, one of the spiritual purposes of dance was to re-create the Dreamings in a "performance" known as a corroboree. It was believed that the ceremony made possible the continued breeding of the different species of animals and plants, without which they would eventually die out. In a modern form, visualizing previous successes re-creates those energy patterns in the present. This continues the theme of personal power and spiritual responsibility. Are your thoughts and mental reenactments in alignment with the energies of integrity; are they life-enhancing? Or have the dreams that you hold close to your heart become diminished, forgotten in the mundane realities of modern society? Brolga as kobong will infect you with the excitement of corroboree, and of being a co-creator within the great dance of life.

Brolga as kobong represents talents and their development, and the need to express them in your issue. Brolga's work was her love. If you too could focus on what you love, you would have the same capacity for fulfillment and success. Join the dance—Brolga is center stage, and the audience is waiting!

24 • Brush Turkey

RESENTMENT • COMPARISONS • INTROSPECTION

Back in the Dreaming, there was a lush, green rain forest in central Australia, where there is now desert. It was the home of all the birds of this great land, birds of every size and color.

Amongst these birds was the Brush Turkey. She wasn't very happy with herself. She couldn't fly as high as the other birds, nor was she very colorful. Everyday, when she went to the billabong to drink, she would see her mirrored reflection and feel unhappy. She was jealous of the other birds, and wanted to be like them.

A great storm came. The Lightning Man sent down bolts of lightning and one of them struck a tree. The tree fell and the stump smoldered. This fire was magic because it came from the Lightning Man.

When the Brush Turkey saw the fire, she half flew and half ran to the smoldering stump, then placed a dry stick into the fire to set the stick alight. She then took the burning stick to the largest tree in the rain forest, and set the tree alight. The fire raced up the tree and spread rapidly because it was magic.

Eerin the Gray Owl, the only one awake, flew from tree to tree to warn his brothers and sisters. As the fire spread, the birds escaped. Some flew to the north, others to the south, east, and west—this is how Australia became populated with birds.

Some of the birds flew so high to escape the smoke, they ended up over the ocean. They grew tired and plummeted into the cool depths of the ocean. Their feathers turned to scales and their wings to fins—they became fish. This is how the waters became populated.

However, the Brush Turkey didn't escape. Though once she had gray plumage, she now has a black coat where the fire burnt her, and gray flecks from the ash. Her head and neck became wrinkled, burnt, and red from the fire, to remind us of her shameful action. Today there is only desert in central Australia.

Imagery

This Dreaming teaches us to be content with ourselves, and not to take revenge for seemingly unfair circumstances beyond our control. Brush Turkey is all about issues of self-esteem. She was not happy with her appearance and carried resentment. Had she realized she was the cause of her own unhappiness, she could have been enjoying whatever beauty she did have.

Brush Turkey's card shows her running to escape from the fire that she created from the lightning-strike. She wears her red badge of shame. The billabong where she would look at herself is also depicted; it represents resentment. The lightning symbolizes revenge.

The brush turkey *(Alectura lathami)* belongs to the worldwide order of Galliformes, though our vain friend is the only one of this order not brilliantly colored. And it is only in Australia that the Galliformes build leaf mounds in which to incubate their young. In this respect, the brush turkey is a most unusual bird. Dreaming legend has it that the female Brush Turkey saw Turtle laying eggs in the riverbank. Brush Turkey thought this was a better idea than sitting for weeks upon her eggs, so she laid her eggs on the ground and covered them with leaves (she laid them away from the river for fear of flood). In the modern Dreaming, we know it is the male who builds the mound, and regulates its temperature by removing or adding leaf matter until the chicks are hatched. His heat-sensitive beak detects the temperature of the mound.

Upright

The billabong represents a time of carrying resentment in your heart, or of comparing yourself with others. The lightning represents acting in revenge, seeking justice from an emotional rather than rational perspective. The fire points to something which is inflammable in your issue, perhaps it is "burning you up."

Brush Turkey goes beyond physical appearances, seeking the spiritual light and love within every life form. It is time for you to evaluate your attitudes about yourself. Are you stagnating by concentrating on "what could have been," or are you acting in revenge? Focusing on, and developing, your positive attributes will encourage new opportunities. The challenge is to release any resentment, and achieve self-acceptance. Are your standards too high? How is your criticism permeating every level of your life, as well as the most obvious? Can you give praise and acknowledgment as easily and more often than criticism?

On a mundane level, if Brush Turkey appears with **Turtle**, Turtle could represent a role model, something or someone you wish to emulate. If **Lyrebird** appears, you may be searching for (or have found) a teacher, guide, someone who can give you answers. If **Uluru** is drawn, this can indicate the development of confidence as a result of crossing boundaries and believing in yourself. This strength of conviction gives a strong charisma; power becomes "owned" through the dark journey of resolving personal pain and resentment.

Reversed

In this position, Brush Turkey can refer to resentment, and its effects on your life. Carrying this negative attitude can literally "eat away" at your self-esteem. It keeps you chained to the past by re-creating past emotions. Your actions will inevitably reflect this bitterness. Others will tune in subconsciously and veer away from you, perhaps creating further resentment as a result of feelings of abandonment, or of not being good enough, etc. Positive change emerges when you can break the negative cycle by moving from the position of victim to a direct confrontation with your situation.

This can be achieved in a number of ways. As each of us are individuals, our ways of tackling situations are different. Resentment is an important issue, one that can affect the whole approach to life. Meditation, visualization, writing, the use of essences, and counseling are all effective techniques. There are many good books (in the realms of dependency, addiction and self-help) describing various methods that could be tried. If resentment is a current issue, it is important to work through it actively. You will be drawn to what you need, for Brush Turkey reversed indicates emotional cleansing.

Kobong

A typical Brush Turkey person is a "people-pleaser," influenced by peer-group pressure, and conforming even when there is disagreement. This need to comply has its roots in a lack of confidence and need for approval.

Are you in some way sacrificing your ideals in the situation you are questioning? Do you have the courage to take a stand, and affirm your own inner truth, even if, by doing this, you risk rejection, or being different? Learn from Brush Turkey's Dreaming, and work through your feelings of inadequacy, or engage in open and honest communication to find a compromise. This means being totally honest with yourself, as well as communicating with others.

You can apply the message of Brush Turkey in your life—by being true to yourself, you are true to others, as long as you are motivated by love rather than feelings of "I'll show them." Convey honestly your feelings and thoughts around the issue queried, without reservation. Sometimes we can become obsessed with how others should behave or think, and we expect them to read our minds. Also, if you feel you aren't getting the acknowledgment you deserve, ask yourself when you last gave praise to yourself, and others.

Brush Turkey is obvious in people who draw their inspiration from the world around them. They develop their ideas using already existing models as springboards. They could also be people who help others to be happier with their lives, especially with their inner feelings—from beauty therapists, mental health professionals, and counselors to environmental planners!

25 · Butterfly

TRANSFORMATION · SPIRITUALITY · EMERGENCE

" *Back in the Dreamtime, death had never been known. All the creatures would regularly meet to talk about their adventures. One time, while they were talking, an old cockatoo slipped and fell. Before he could spread his wings, he hit the earth. Thud! For the first time, death had come.*

The creatures tried to raise their brother, but, whatever they did, he would not respond. So, they came to the conclusion that the cockatoo's spirit had left his body.

"But where has it gone?" they asked.

Bunjil the Wedge-tailed Eagle said, "Allow me to show you what I think has happened to our brother's spirit." He took a stone from the banks of the river and dropped it into the water. The creatures all leant forward as the stone sank out of sight. Bunjil said, "As the stone has disappeared, so too has our brother's spirit. There is no more."

For a while there was silence. Then Waan the Black Crow spoke. "Allow me to show you what I think has happened. Brother Water Rat, go to the bottom of the river and fetch me that stone, because I believe that it is still down there somewhere."

The Water Rat disappeared. He returned with the wet stone. Waan said, "What was once an earth stone has now become a water stone. Just because you can't see something, doesn't mean it doesn't exist."

For a while there was silence. "There must be more to this," someone muttered.

Waan replied, "Before we meet again, let's see if we can find out more about this spiritual thing. If there is anyone who wants to devote their time to this, speak out now."

"I will," replied a small voice.

"You are just a caterpillar," Waan answered. "What would you know about spirituality?"

The Caterpillar replied, "I would like to try nonetheless." So Waan agreed.

At the next meeting, Waan asked the gathered creatures, "What have you learnt about spirituality?"

Nobody spoke, except Butterfly. "Waan, I have learnt much!"

Waan looked intently at Butterfly and said, "I know you not, who are you?"

"You do know me," she answered. "I am the green Caterpillar!" "

Imagery

From the small beginnings of a humble green caterpillar, easily camouflaged against the trees, a bright and glorious Butterfly emerges—from the unnoticed to the noticed, from the mundane to the special. Butterfly is a great teacher. She brings change and growth, she is a spiritual emblem embodying the principles of transformation.

The tiny Caterpillar took on a task so great it emphasized her smallness. Yet the task was no greater than her belief in her ability to achieve; she felt equal to the challenge, so physical size was irrelevant. Caterpillar was courageous, and prepared to risk all.

In another version of this Dreaming, she builds a cocoon to protect herself from predators and the weather, then dies so she may experience this new phenomenon of death. When she returns from the world of the dead, she is transformed into the glorious Butterfly. And the result is a greater understanding of life as well as death; and for the group, as well as for her personally.

Upright and Reversed

In gracing your cards, Butterfly brings a loving and positive affirmation of the transformation which is happening within you and without you. The message our sister Butterfly brings is to have faith and to trust. Courage is a key to freedom, for, without courage, we cannot move and grow. The Caterpillar clings to a leaf, the Butterfly is drawn further afield to the bright blossoms. Why don't you move towards your chosen destination, with the faith and determination Butterfly displayed? Allow change to flow by releasing the old and accepting the new.

The Dreaming card of Butterfly utilizes the circular aspects of the oracle in a unique way. Here we see six stages of the life cycle of the butterfly, as it moves through its transformations. There is no separate reversed interpretation for this card because each individual symbol has its own special meaning in your reading.

What cycle of life appears at the top? The symbol drawn at the top gives the meaning, as follows.

BUTTERFLY: Maturation * full glory * beauty * symbol of the soul * understanding * spiritual growth

MATING: Force of creation, renewal * union, sexuality * conception, procreation

EGGS: Potential * the future * genetics * time preceding manifestation * abundance, legacy, inheritance

CATERPILLAR: Growth, development * learning, seeking nourishment * sustenance

COCOON: Dormancy preceding the emergence of something new, waiting * fate, destiny, inevitability * appearances, things are not what they seem * hidden potential

EMERGENCE: Release * new beginnings, a new stage in life, gateway, turning point * taking flight * life from apparent death

Move from a leaf to a flower, into the next stage of your growth. As you grow and change, so will your environment. All aspects of life are closely linked. Change in one will precipitate change in another, and so it flows.

Take heed of Butterfly's message. Do not resist change. Seek it out, allow it, embrace it and challenge it! Then you too can emerge from your cocoon a beautiful butterfly.

Kobong

If Butterfly is your kobong, or if you are particularly drawn to this card, the wheels of change turn and spin in your life! Those axles are well-oiled, especially on spiritual levels, largely due to your eagerness to explore and investigate.

The life stage represented at the center top of this card indicates where you are in your process. Can you welcome the next step in your journey, or are you hanging onto the situation as it is, not wanting to move on? Butterfly as kobong strongly emphasizes the energies of transformation and change.

One of Butterfly's lessons is to have faith in yourself, and to support this with positive, affirmative action. If you can keep and nurture this trust, you will have a very powerful key which will unlock fulfillment, growth, and learning in your journey of life. Bon voyage, Butterfly!

The different stages of growth for Butterfly strongly influence your reading. Their meanings are outlined below.

BUTTERFLY: Butterfly in all her glory brings the energies of maturation and completion, although the ultimate cycle has not ended. She brings beauty and the joyful freedom of flight. Butterfly seeks the nectar in the vibrant world of flowers, she is drawn to the sweetness of life. Butterfly indicates positive, beneficial change in your life and brings these qualities to the issues covered by the other cards in your reading.

MATING: With the Butterflies mating, the energies of creation and desire for regeneration are influencing your reading. Before the Butterflies mate, their intricate dance is a visual metaphor of the dance of life, as they weave around each other in never-ending spirals. On every level, and especially relating to an issue of the heart, this is a great omen!

EGGS: Eggs represent the future, and potential. As kobong, they indicate you have planted the seeds, and are awaiting results. It is a time of patience. The eggs are fertile and, in their own time, they will hatch and begin the journey of life.

CATERPILLAR: Hungrily devouring life, Caterpillar is aware change is around the corner, but perhaps is uncertain of where or how. Even if you do not know where your path is leading you, follow through your appetites for greater knowledge and learning. Growth and nourishment support your reading.

COCOON: A time of stasis and inner transformation is present, though you may not be aware of anything different externally. Deep and lasting transformational energies are moving through your life. With Caterpillar here, prepare for a miracle!

EMERGENCE: The energies of birth are moving through your issue, as the Butterfly emerges from the cocoon. It is an exciting time, though Butterfly is vulnerable to predators and strong winds while her wings are drying out. This energy of vulnerability, and a temporary inability to fly, may encourage a greater sense of trust. Control is relinquished at this time, but, with patience, and a little time, you will make your maiden voyage!

26 • Crow

TRICKERY • DISTRACTIONS • THE MIND

" Back in the Dreaming, the secret of fire was known only to Seven Sisters who were known as the Karikarik women. They would not reveal to anyone how their fire was made, although many people approached them to seek this important knowledge. Waan, the Crow M**an, was determined to discover their secret, so he became friends with them. He won their confidence by helping them with their hunting and food gathering. He soon discovered that they carried the fire in the end of their digging sticks. He also discovered that the women were very fond of termites and terrified of snakes.

He soon came up with a plan. He buried a number of snakes in a big termite mound in which he had dug a hole, then covered all evidence of his work. He told the Seven Sisters that he had found a large nest of termites, and led them to it. As the women broke open the mound, the snakes attacked them. The terrified women hit the snakes with their digging sticks, and, as they did so, the fire fell out of the sticks. Waan quickly picked up the fire between two pieces of bark, fled to his camp, and started his own fire. The Karikarik women were furious about losing their exclusive ownership of fire. They rose into the sky and became the constellation of the Seven Sisters, the Pleiades.

This left Waan as the sole owner of fire. When his people approached him, and asked for fire to cook their food and to keep them warm, the Crow Man called out in a mocking voice, "Waan! Waan! I cannot give you fire, I must protect it. But I will cook your food if you bring it to me."

So the people brought their food to Waan, and he cooked it for them. They soon discovered he kept the choicest pieces for himself. The people were angered and held a meeting. They decided to take the fire from Waan. In the process, they began a grass fire that surrounded Waan and burnt him to death. And before their eyes, Waan was transformed into a Black Crow, and rose high above the fire and smoke, calling, "Waan! Waan! "

Imagery

Waan the Black Crow is the trickster, whose tricks often backfire. He can be found in different forms worldwide, in legends and mythology, the Tarot, and modern novels and movies. The Crow represents that aspect of the human psyche that will go to any measure to get what it wants. In many of the Dreamings in which he features, Waan's physical appetites dominate his behavior.

However, he isn't always greedy, selfish and sly—it is the Crows who assist (and create) the first Black Swans *(see Black Swan)*. In his way, Waan has contributed greatly to the world through the release of fire. Also, he teaches, by example, the effects of greed, covetousness and treachery.

On the card, Waan the Black Crow appears beside the fire of his desire and destruction. The snakes are part of the flames, representing his deception and also his betrayal. The Seven Sisters appear as stars in the sky behind him.

Upright

In Aboriginal culture, the human soul is made up of three parts, one of which is the trickster or ego soul. This part of the spirit is bound to the material planes of responsibilities, relationships and leisure. It also tries to maintain the illusion of earthly immortality and strives to make the temporal permanent. (The other two parts of the human soul are: the totemic soul, linked to the spirits of nature that provide nourishment in life, and the ancestral soul, which returns to the Dreaming or spirit world at the time of death.) The trickster soul has been related to the modern idea of the ego that, for some, manifests after death as a ghost.

In context within a reading, Waan, personifying the trickster within the self, forsakes the spiritual and truly everlasting for gratification of changeable personal needs. This material distraction could well be a running undercurrent in your situation. Crow asks you to separate the intellect and emotions, or the objective and subjective, so you can uncover the fantasy and reveal the situation as it really is.

Take heed of Waan's Dreaming, the Dreaming of fire. It cooks and warms as it can also overpower and destroy. Crow's action with the Seven Sisters was replayed between him and the tribespeople, so beware patterns are not played out in reversed roles. Crow certainly teaches the law of karma here; he and the Seven Sisters received what they deserved.

Crow brings ultimate judgment and balance; teaching how negative emotions may affect our lives. Had Crow shared his prize of fire, this Dreaming would have had a very different outcome. And had the Seven Sisters shared the fire at the beginning, we would not have learnt the lesson of greed. If the Seven Sisters appear at the top of your card, you may have something another covets; how can you share your good position without creating resentment and jealousy?

If **Bat**, or **Koala**, appears, remember that both die by fire. This important placement can signify "going through the fires" to achieve awareness of the dynamics within the situation.

Reversed

With the card reversed, Crow is upside-down, looking upwards. Like Bat, his views have been totally reversed. He sees the heavens and another dimension instead of the ground, where the fire of his desire burns. The fire he sees now is a spiritual fire, it is floating in mid-air. Is Crow peering at another card? If so, this could indicate inspiring energies benefiting your query.

In this position, Crow manifests the opposite quality to selfishness. He has learnt from his mistakes and his sight is clearer. Altruism enables Waan to utilize his keen perception for the benefit of himself, and others.

This card reversed is a very positive sign in a reading; it can indicate a spiritual experience, especially if the **Rainbow Serpent** also appears.

With the fire now appearing at the top, we are reminded that fire warms all, without distinguishing between the more or less deserving. Unqualified, open acceptance for all, without preconceived expectations or judgments, now motivates Waan the Black Crow. As a symbol, this fire may represent purification, especially of those earthly desires that waft clouds of obscuring smoke before one's true spiritual worth and path.

Kobong

With Crow as kobong, or if you are drawn to this impressive bird, he brings the practical energies of the mind into focus. The art of discernment is a challenge, as Waan will push you towards identifying the origins of your thoughts. The mind can play some clever tricks, like Crow, and you may need to examine your motivation. Are your goals for the good of self and all? Or are you following your desires and using your capable mind for achieving something transient and material?

Crow people always seem to get their own way. They maneuver situations to their own advantage, using effectively any resources that may be at hand. To learn the lesson of fire, crow people need to overcome their innate selfishness. If they can do so, they have the potential of becoming a powerful force for good in the world around them.

Crow is one of the most intelligent birds. (Crows have been known to use tools, for example, a stick, to pry prey from a crevice.) Crow has the ability to see what is in his immediate environment and to put it to good use. As kobong, this card is a good indicator that what you need is at close hand.

As kobong, Crow asks what you want from, and what you have to give to, your issue and each of the cards in your reading. What are the "exchange rates?" Are they fair, or is there something there which could backfire? Remember Crow the trickster—his tricks often trick himself, leaving him worse off than before.

Crow people are brilliant at pinpointing the weaknesses and strengths of other people, yet can remain blind to their own. Using this acute perception to help others, rather than for personal reasons, enables them to make a real difference in the world, in effect, to "share their fire."

27 · Gray Owl

PROTECTION • HONOR • SPECIAL TALENTS

" A long time ago, back in the Dreaming, and the beginning of time, there once lived a man named Eerin. He was not a hunter because he was not very strong, and had a gentle nature. He did not have the heart to wield a spear to harm a living creature. Nor was he able to fight battles to defend his people. He had no talent for tracking, storytelling, or any work necessary for the survival of the tribe. He did, however, have one very special quality. He had extremely keen hearing. With this talent, he could protect his tribe at night, while they slept. If any danger threatened, he would cry out "Mil, Mil!" (Beware, Beware!)

Eerin lived to a great age. He retained his acute hearing, which helped him to protect his beloved people faithfully. He was highly respected, valued and loved by his tribe. Finally, Eerin died, and a deep sorrow afflicted the people. He was greatly missed. As traditional law decreed, a great corroboree was held at night, to honor him, and the passage of his spirit.

The men painted up with their sacred ochres, and performed rites around the flickering fire. In one rite, performed only when the deceased was held in the highest of esteem, they slashed their wrists and allowed their life-giving blood to flow over their dead brother, honoring him with their own lives.

During the course of the ceremony, the neighboring Emu tribe, long-standing enemies, crept upon Eerin's people, with the evil intention of attacking them while they were preoccupied with their sorrow. Once more, the familiar cry "Mil, Mil!" alerted the tribe to the intruders. The people sought the origins of the call, then realized it came from above. They looked up. In the billowing smoke of the corroboree's fire, they saw the spirit of Eerin, in the form of a Gray Owl.

Even to this day, Eerin sleeps by day. When the sun has sunk in the western sky, he flies over his sleeping kinsmen, ready to warn them if danger approaches. "

Imagery

Eerin the Gray Owl represents protection in a dangerous world. In many cultures throughout the world, the owl is associated with the night, dreams, omens, sorcery, and wisdom. The owl is a powerful hunter, silent in flight and deadly. He is helped by his keen night sight and acute hearing. The Native Americans see the owl as a night eagle, a bird of power. This Dreaming highlights the need to listen and be receptive to the environment.

The Owl is often linked to women, and is a kobong of women in many tribes. The Australian Aboriginal people are the only indigenous people in the world who have totems for the sexes as a whole.

On the card, Eerin the Gray Owl flies into the night, wings outstretched. He appears to be hovering over the corroboree fire held in his honor, his beak open to call out his warning.

Upright

The appearance of Eerin in your reading means that you are protected, but there is some danger. Gray Owl is alerting you to wake, to be aware, to seek out the source of this threat, and to take action.

Examine closely those areas of your life about which you feel uneasy. Eerin offers protection, but, first, you must act on the signal of danger. Don't feel that you are powerless and cannot change your life. Acknowledge your gifts. You can make a difference.

On a mundane level, Gray Owl asks you to examine the issue of protection in your life. What do you protect yourself from, and how? Where do you take risks? What have your past experiences taught you about protection or lack of it? How did these experiences affect you and your actions? How are they influencing you now? How can you bring the energies of Gray Owl into your life?

Eerin the Gray Owl asks you to go within and explore the night-time places of your inner self. This is one of your pathways to illumination, be it for a particular issue you are seeking an answer to, or as a means of exploring those inner landscapes of thought and emotion. By allowing Eerin to accompany you on your journey, you will be free to discover aspects of yourself you were unaware even existed.

As the Gray Owl, Eerin's gift of keen hearing enabled him to become a very good hunter, even though this was an ability he lacked, and had no desire for, on the earthly plane. Be open to the possibility of a new talent emerging, possibly as the result of some catalyst, or life-changing event. This could be especially evident if the fire appears towards the top .

If Eerin keeps reappearing in readings, or, if you feel particularly drawn to this card, you may find it useful to visualize a Gray Owl sitting on your left shoulder (over your heart), protecting you.

Should **Lightning Man** also appear in your reading, you may need to evaluate carefully every risk in the issue you are querying. This close examination may help you to avoid a potential downfall, as there could be some aspect you have missed, ignored, or even forgotten. If this remains unconsidered, there is a strong possibility you will find your entire issue totally turned around. Change is especially indicated with these two cards, though much of it could be averted by deeper introspection.

Reversed

If you draw Eerin the Gray Owl in the reversed position, you are being alerted: "Mil, Mil!" The danger is well hidden. You may look and listen, but notice nothing extraordinary. This complacency could be your downfall.

The source of threat could be within yourself. Take the time to listen, to really hear what you are saying, about yourself and your environment. Are you threatening your own happiness and well-being? Do your own thoughts and words intrude upon your sense of peace and balance, causing distress? Look within, and listen. You may learn something, thanks to Gray Owl's timely signal.

This eagle of the night guides you to discovery. He wakes you up from the sleep of complacency. Seek out, and let go of, outmoded habits and patterns. By removing the old and obsolete, you can make room for the new and exciting. Your interests, dreams, and fantasies will reflect where this is to be.

Kobong

If Eerin is your kobong, or you are drawn to this card, he bestows keen sensitivity and perceptiveness. You have the ability to discern the truth from illusion, if you are willing to "sit in the dark" and listen.

Eerin can guide you to your strengths, as well as your weaknesses and inconsistencies. One of Eerin's ways of doing this is through your dreams and flights of imagination. What do you think most about? What occupies your mind? What issues are your dreams reflecting? Be aware of these, take notice of them. They reveal a great deal about you. As guides or signposts, they can point you in the right direction.

In your reading, Gray Owl as kobong can indicate the development, or use of, qualities associated with women. Traditionally, these would be food gathering; nurturing children, old people and the sick; and certain spiritual tribal obligations. Feminine energies could have some impact or influence in your query.

Although Eerin is male, as kobong he represents the female aspect. (He remains in the home camp.) He saves the tribe many times over. He is valued for his contribution, and earns great respect. Your own contribution to the issue queried may not consist of courage and action, like Gray Owl's, but it may have as valuable an impact.

The element of protection, however it relates to your issue, influences every other card in your reading. The protection and guidance Gray Owl brings towards your situation depends upon whether you act before it is too late. There is also the opportunity to gain recognition for your talents.

28 · Kookaburra

RELIABILITY • WORK • SATISFACTION

" *In the beginning, Emu and Brolga had a fight, and this created the first day. Emu was angry with Brolga, and Emu threw Brolga's egg up into the skyworld, where it hit a large pile of wood. The egg shattered and the yolk caught fire. The sky spirits enjoyed the effect of this fire so much, they decided to make their own fires. Every night, they gathered wood, and, every morning, they lit another fire. The fire always began as a few tiny flames, then grew into a large fire before, finally, dying away. The remaining embers were tucked away in some fleecy clouds, until morning, when the process would begin again.*

The glorious colors of the very first sunrise filled the people of the land with wonder, and they very much appreciated the warmth of the sun. But, after a time, the people stopped being amazed by the miracle of dawn, and they would often sleep through the sunrise. By the time they woke, most of the day had passed. The sky spirits created the morning star to wake them, but the people still slept.

Then, one day, the sky spirits heard Kookaburra laughing. His voice was ringing over the plains, waking all those who were still asleep. They told the bird that he must call out every morning, so that the people would know it was time to wake and greet the new day.

Kookaburra questioned the sky spirits. What if he didn't want to do it? They replied, in that case, the sun's fire would not be lit, and everyone would experience endless darkness again. Kookaburra agreed to do as they asked, because it would benefit everyone, and besides, he liked the sound of his own laughter.

From then on, when morning came, the Kookaburra woke the people with his laugh. The sky spirits were pleased, especially when the people again appreciated the gift of light, and the beauty of their brightly-lit world. It was like a new awakening for them. "

Imagery

Our brother the Kookaburra represents reliability, responsibility and work. Laughter rings out in the early dawn, welcoming the light of day. There is an awakening, a feeling of excitement at a new start, and the satisfaction of an enjoyable and worthwhile task, which will help other people. The people in this Dreaming lost their sense of wonder at the daily miracle of dawn, but Kookaburra helped them to find it again.

In this Dreaming card, we see Kookaburra, his beak open with laughter, as the first rays of dawn light the horizon. The compact yellow blossoms are wattle flowers, which have a special significance in the Dreaming. Wattle is a very bright, cheery flower; its unique fragrance is associated with the onset of summer by many Australians. The early settlers used wattle branches to make their wattle-and-daub homes, by mixing the wattle with clay, lime, and sometimes dung and chopped straw. The seeds were used in breadmaking, and the leaves produced a dye for fabric.

In one Dreaming, wattle symbolizes happiness. Wattle conveys the idea that we are never alone. Its flowers do not grow singly; they are tiny, compact balls joined together on one branch.

Kookaburra reinforces the domestic aspects of wattle. The Kookaburra is a very territorial bird, who generally remains within a home range. The young remain with the family group for four years, contributing food for successive generations.

Upright

Kookaburra has flown into your cards to greet the dawn within you. There is an awakening, and new energy is being infused into your situation. The light of clear-sighted understanding is well within your grasp. This is also a time of inspiration and guidance. You have a task; now is the time to complete it.

On the mundane level, Kookaburra is the work-oriented card. Kookaburra gets the job, and so do you. Kookaburra brings promotion, progress, and success in any endeavor. Work issues are especially highlighted. Improvements are likely in any situation. Life in general "chortles," with the newness of dawn, and its accompanying feelings of vitality and excitement. The focus is on the potential that each day can bring.

The challenge is to keep your enthusiasm, and not become caught up in the mundane realities of daily existence. Follow Kookaburra, enjoy the freedom of flight, do what excites you, and connect with something that stimulates your sense of adventure. If things have been boring lately, novelty is about to infuse your issue.

Wattle brings new understanding, which rises over any sorrow and hurt produced by manipulation, pride, or jealousy. If the wattle appears near the top, responsibilities center around the home.

The appearance of **Wombat** in your reading will emphasize the home or domestic aspects of your issue. Work is highlighted with the appearance of **Lyrebird**, **Gymea Lily** or **Magpies**. **Brolga** and **Emu** could indicate confrontation, but, as in this Dreaming, something wonderful will result!

Reversed

If the card is reversed, Kookaburra can highlight delays and frustrations in the work sphere. Other people could be unreliable, deadlines may be postponed or not met, and one's territory could be inundated with outsiders. Kookaburra in this position teaches patience and steadfastness. Keep your objective in view, persevere, and your goal will be reached.

Other people can reflect aspects of ourselves that have been repressed or ignored. Until we consciously "own" these aspects, by acknowledging them as part of ourselves, life will remain static. Now may be the perfect time to look within, to discover how you are preventing progress, and why you won't allow ease in your life.

Every situation in life has the potential to be a gift. To obtain the full benefit, we need to "unwrap" each one carefully, by asking ourselves: "What can I learn from this? How does this reflect an attitude I have about myself, or my environment, that I can now release? How does this teach me to move on, and create the situations I really want?"

Kobong

With Kookaburra as kobong, or if you are drawn to this card, you have the qualities of reliability, responsibility and dedication. You are able to enthuse others with your excitement, particularly in the issue of this reading.

This aspect shows itself in your personality, through a strong sense of loyalty and devotion, to family, friends and co-workers. You make the effort to help those who need, or ask for, your assistance, and you do this with a sense of satisfaction. This aspect also leaves you vulnerable to being "used" by people less scrupulous, who may take advantage of your generous nature. Establishing personal boundaries (what is, and what isn't, acceptable) will enable you to function more effectively, for your own sake.

As kobong, Kookaburra will highlight issues of responsibility, bringing enthusiasm where things are routine. Kookaburra people can be found in any area where the welfare of others is concerned, as well as in positions of responsibility. They tend to be the "nine-to-fivers," whose work hours are regulated. Kookaburra just wouldn't dream of sleeping in, so Kookaburra people are early risers.

If the wattle appears towards the top as the card is drawn, this is a symbol of sympathy in loss, and glory for those who have overcome pride and jealousy. It is also a symbol of release from emotional pain, but through the experience of a spiritual death, rather than healing. Are you allowing grief to rule your actions? This would influence the reading through the energies of depression, and being too negative. The yellow cheer of wattle can change your attitudes. You may seem to be "at the end of the road," but wattle represents the beginning of a new life. It points to release, and the dawn that makes Kookaburra laugh.

29 · Lyrebird

IMITATION • LEARNING • PRIDE

" A little stream in the mountains sang its way under the cool trees and ferns. All streams have bubbles, but this stream contained live bubbles. Within each bubble lived a tiny water spirit, and each bubble danced to the song of the stream. One bubble wished to be able to play with the floating twigs and dancing sunbeams. He wished so intensely, he almost became solid.

One evening, Lyrebird went to the stream to drink. He was used to seeing the bubbles, but, this particular evening, he noticed one was bouncing higher than the others. There seemed to be something inside this bubble; it was not clear like the others.

As he watched, Lyrebird sang the songs of other birds, to see how the bubble responded. After a while, he grew tired and decided to leave. Just then, a spirit voice sounded. The Great Spirit had taken pity on the tiny water spirit. He told Lyrebird to continue singing, because his song was bringing the water spirit to life, and soon the bubble would shatter and release the spirit as a living creature.

So Lyrebird sang until he felt his throat would burst. At last, the bubble burst, and a tiny green frog emerged, Son of the Clear-running Stream. His mouth opened and shut, but he made not a sound.

The Great Spirit told Lyrebird to teach the creature to sing. Day after day, Lyrebird returned to the stream to teach Son of the Clear-running Stream to sing. He learnt quickly and began to sing very well.

The Great Spirit again took pity on the little creature, and sent him a wife. Son of the Clear-running Stream boasted to his wife: "I am the best singer—I could charm the Moon down from the sky."

"Let's see you do it," she replied.

So Son of the Clear-running Stream sang. The Moon crossed the sky and took no notice. So he sang even more loudly, and then, suddenly, his voice broke and all that could be heard was a harsh croak.

To this day, frogs can throw their voices, but no one listens to their croaking. Instead, they listen to Lyrebird, the patient teacher. "

Imagery

Lyrebird represents ability and knowledge that can be passed on, or taught. Lyrebird is a gentle and patient teacher; lessons are a pleasure and so positively encourage learning. However, Son of the Clear-running Stream, allowed pride to overcome him, and gave himself a difficult lesson. In the end, Lyrebird is rewarded and Son of the Clear-running Stream is punished.

The Great Spirit intervened and granted the little spirit's wish to become real. The great, eternal spirit of life is capable of embracing the universe, or of noticing an unimportant bubble in a stream. Nothing is too small.

The stately, beautiful Lyrebird can teach us to sing! On the card we see him in the process of teaching Son of the Clear-running Stream, who is still in a bubble awaiting materialization. The other bubbles dance around him, content with their own world, and therefore transparent; they are not filled with desire. The Moon shines above, reminding us of the lesson of pride. The water represents the strong desires that propelled Son of the Clear-running Stream into physical manifestation.

Upright

Learning in this case is through imitation and practice rather than academic study or predominantly mental processes—Son of the Clear-running Stream particularly represents this aspect.

If the frog appears towards the top, you may be asked to be humble. Enjoy the process of learning, rather than focusing competitively on achievement.

Learning for the joy of it (Brolga exemplifies this; she loved to dance and was a very good dancer), rather than for the sake of it, can develop into teaching, and sharing with, other people. This card indicates practical, rather than intellectual, knowledge. As Lyrebird's song encompasses the tunes of many songbirds, this knowledge could cover a range of fields, linked by a common factor.

Lyrebird had a spiritual mission, a directive from the Great Spirit, to help the birth of Son of the Clear-running Stream and teach him to sing. Something in, or about, the issue you are querying is propelling you to the completion of something—perhaps an ideal, vision or dream. The source originates from an outside request or catalyst, and you are inspired to continue with a compelling sense of destiny. In this case, tuition is inspired by intuition. There is a definite short-term goal seeking completion, and fueling the desire for achievement, on some level. Spiritual guidance is also very strong, so, follow that inner voice with practical action.

Take notice of any cards surrounding Lyrebird, especially if he seems to be facing one of them. The issues covered will bring lessons for you to grasp or impart.

Should **Frog** also appear, his energies bring a touch of humor to your situation. You may realize you have been on the wrong course in some way and, in retrospect, laugh at your own follies. Perhaps you have been taught, or are teaching, something irrelevant or outdated. Your new wisdom may allow a different perspective to emerge, turning lessons around, so that they suddenly seem obsolete, or different from how you originally saw them.

Reversed

The reversed aspect of this card focuses on Son of the Clear-running Stream. These tiny frogs are delightful—the idea of them being beautiful singers is exquisite. Son of the Clear-running Stream represents those who have learnt the lesson of pride, perhaps to the point of loss and sacrifice. Yet he does not seem to be too unhappy—he can still be heard croaking away today. He moves from past negative experiences and lives for today, especially the joy of welcoming needed rain.

Son of the Clear-running Stream is a very good learner; he has the ability to imitate. Lyrebird learnt to sing by imitating other birds' songs, as the frog learns to imitate Lyrebird. Open your eyes, and notice what excites you in your environment. Son of the Clear-running Stream is a good omen for learning from others, in a physical, hands-on way. What are you learning? And, in turn, what are you teaching?

Learning from others, and taking notice of their knowledge, are all bubbles in the little frog's experience. Something revitalizes you. It could be other people, situations or something to do with the issue being queried. You accomplish things easily and enjoy learning. Personal improvement and advancement are assured, as long as you do not become self-important.

Kobong

Lyrebird's mission is to teach you to sing! With Lyrebird as kobong, or if you are drawn to this card, you have, or are seeking, a cause, a spiritual mission, something to do which is relevant and useful.

Patience, gentleness, commitment, perseverance and dedication are qualities found in Lyrebird. He encourages others positively. He is an admirable role model, and these qualities influence your reading positively.

Lyrebird as kobong represents learning from others before you can begin teaching. This meaning is stronger if this card is drawn pointing near **Frog**. Something from your surrounding environment will act as a catalyst and propel you into the role of teacher.

As a teacher, you are able to generate excitement and enthusiasm in your students. Like ripples in a pond, the effects of what you have learnt from your teachers will spread to others in a positive way. So, what are you teaching? How do others imitate you, and what do they admire in you?

If Lyrebird as kobong appears reversed, this indicates the importance of learning from another person's example. It also indicates the presence of a teacher who is willing and eager to impart knowledge. This learning requires the skills of imitation rather than developing new mental processes. The message here is to avoid an inflated opinion of one's own skill. Pride could be your downfall, unless humility is practiced. Be thankful for your gifts, rejoice, express them, and share them!

30 · Magpies

INSPIRATION · SOLUTIONS · LIGHT

" *In the Dreaming, way back in the beginning of time, when the world was first created, and everything was new and young, the sky was very close to the earth. The light was shut out by the sky, which blocked everything, and the world was dark. Also, there was no room at all to stand up, for the sky lay too close to the earth. All the people had to crawl around on their bellies in the dark, collecting any food they could find with their bare hands. All the animals, too, even the birds, walked upon the land, and many were easy prey for their predators. There were no tall trees to make safe nests in, so the young birds were defenseless. Life was very difficult. No one knew what light was. They had only ever experienced total darkness.*

Everyone complained about the situation, but no one realized there could be an alternative. The Magpies, some of the more intelligent birds, thought about the situation, trying to find a way to change it. Together, they discussed many ideas, tossing proposals around, weighing up the pros and cons, and dismissing those they considered too unrealistic. Finally, they came up with a solution they all agreed had potential. They decided that, if they worked together as a group, with their combined strength, they just might be able to raise the sky.

So, all the Magpies got together and began searching the ground for long sticks. They searched until every Magpie carried a stick. Holding the sticks in their strong beaks, the Magpies pushed with all their might, thrusting the sticks upwards, trying to push the sky up and away from the earth. Slowly, so slowly it was difficult to perceive, the sky moved. It was very heavy, but, with the concerted effort of all the Magpies, it lifted a small distance. The Magpies struggled to lift it higher, then, suddenly, the sky split open and revealed the beauty of the first sunrise. Overjoyed with the light and warmth, the Magpies burst into song.

To this day, Magpies welcome the sunrise. "

Imagery

As the light graces the horizon, the joy of the Magpies' song clears the morning air. The crisp coolness of night, the time of dark, dissolves with the Magpies' glorious singing, into the warmth and light of Yhi the Sun. Magpies conduct a ringing, joyful chorus at dawn, welcoming each new day with as much enthusiasm as if it were the very first morning. Their lightness of heart reflects appropriately the miracle of each new sunrise.

The Magpies lift the darkness, revealing light in the form of the beautiful colors of the first dawn. They combine their strength and work together towards a common goal. Because they are all equal, they form the shape of part of a circle on the card. The Magpies represent group effort and single-mindedness.

Upright

Magpies symbolize success and breakthroughs, bringing with them inspiration and the energies of birth.

The vibrant colors of sunrise correspond to three of the human chakras, or energy points. Red relates to the energies of life, sexuality and the will to live (the root or base chakra). Orange is the color of passion, reflecting the motivating appetites for personal power, love and sustenance (the solar plexus chakra). The soft color pink touches the heart chakra directly, and refers to love. These hues of red, orange and pink are a comfort for those who are feeling physically or emotionally depleted and "in the dark."

With the appearance of Magpies in your reading, you may need to integrate these colors into your life. You could, perhaps, wear garnet jewelry or a red shirt, eat oranges, or cuddle a pink teddy bear! Be inventive with this, and have fun!

Magpies lift your reading by casting light upon your situation. Whatever is around this card will certainly be illuminated by Magpies' light. This is the card of inspiration. New ideas, a change of circumstances for the better, and working in the company of other people, are all embraced by this symbol. Magpies bring light and joy. The dark, seemingly endless night is over, but only because these birds thought about their situation, came up with a possible solution and put it to the test. If you have drawn Magpies, now is the time for action.

If the dark area is pointing towards another card, this may indicate an area of your issue that is "in the dark," and requires creative thinking for it to be cleared. The tools you need are nearby, if you are prepared to look.

In your current situation, you would do well to sound your voice with other people to whom you feel drawn, especially if **Kookaburra, Rainbow Lorikeet** or **Platypus** appear. "Lifting the darkness" as a group effort is a shortcut to understanding. The knowledge that you most need is mirrored in the lives of other people.

The presence of **Rainbow Serpent** or **Sea Eagle** can indicate a solo journey, a time to be alone and keep to yourself. **Gray Owl, Southern Cross, Sturt's Desert Pea,** or **Uluru** indicate that you are in the company of spirit guides, or protective energies.

Reversed

With the card reversed, the Magpies appear to be pushing the darkness down, using the power of light. Magpies in this position can indicate a "dark night of the soul" situation. Despair and disillusionment are key words here.

It takes only one small candle to bring enough light to break the darkness. You have the power to overcome your situation. Your light will emerge, as does the penetrating warmth of the midday sun. As Yhi the Sun crosses the sky, its message is, "this too shall pass."

The Magpies seem very aggressive and protective in this position. During nesting season, these birds will swoop down to protect their nests. By nature, magpies are very territorial, and their attacks can be quite frightening. Are you being too defensive, or is there a degree of overreaction in your issue?

On a physical level, spend some time basking in the early morning rays of the sun. Its therapeutic energy will do much for your spirit. As the day awakens, so too will your situation.

Kobong

Having Magpies for kobong indicates a drive to understand life, a search for enlightenment. This search propels you into many situations in which you can practice what you have learnt, and by so doing lighten other people's loads. Like the Magpies, you seek to cast light upon the landscape around you.

Magpies represents anyone who works towards bettering the environment, or improving certain living conditions. Magpie people could also be "light workers," whose energy uplifts and inspires others. Their light automatically draws people, like moths to a candle.

Magpie people need to remember that, the more light they create, the stronger is the contrast with the dark (the white in a magpie's feathers seems to push through the black). These people need to protect themselves from those who would inadvertently, or intentionally, drain their energy. Uniting with people of a like mind, combined with periods of retreat for recharging, will enable

Magpie people to keep their light steady and bright.

Magpies influences every other card, by bringing light and creative solutions to any difficulty.

Magpies as kobong, appearing in the reversed position, can indicate the need to be more grounded. There may be a tendency to be too cosmic and "up in the air." Perhaps, like the Magpies, you are trying to push away or avoid something negative. This influences your reading; denial surrounds anything that you perceive as "dark" relating to your query.

To turn this situation around, "shine your light." Focusing on the light within will dispel the darkness around you, and give you courage enough to walk through. Seek your "source," Magpie. Contact your spirituality, but do not allow it to take you into the realms of fantasy. The challenge presented by Magpies as kobong is to be realistic, as well as spiritual, and to face the unpleasant as well as the sublime.

31 · Rainbow Lorikeet

OVERCOMING DISABILITY • LIMITATIONS • RELEASE

" Once there was a wise and powerful elder, who had many wives and several children. His sons were good hunters and his daughters were beautiful. This man should have been happy, but his heart was saddened because the youngest of his daughters, Meelia, whom he loved even more than the others, was born with twisted limbs. Her arms were useless, and her face was distorted with the pain of her crippling deformities.

The other children of the tribe teased her whenever the adults were not around. When this became too much for her, Meelia would seek out her beloved father. His warm, understanding heart would fill with sorrow and anguish, as he tried to explain to her that the other children did not understand her pain, nor how much they had hurt her feelings.

And, as he listened, the girl would share her deepest thoughts. She told him of her secret wish to become a beautiful, colored bird, so she could fly away from the children of the camp when they teased her. Her longing for freedom lit up her eyes, as she described her vivid fantasy. Her father listened without interrupting. He later thought about her dream and realized that, if she became a bird, this would indeed end her suffering.

So, that night, the elders met and decided that they would ask the Great Spirit to help with Meelia's transformation. All through the night, they danced and sang their magic, until Bila the Sun Woman lit her torch, and the first of its rays began to penetrate the darkness. The twisted body of the young girl, who was standing in a circle of the elders, began to change as the sky lightened. She was transformed into a bird of many colors.

As she stretched her wings and took to the air, her father cried, "Be happy my daughter! As a beautiful bird, you will no longer suffer! "

Imagery

This Dreaming is about the creation of a beautiful new species, which is brought about by the Great Spirit, working with mankind. In the Dreamings, animals and birds are often created by the Great Spirit alone, so this is unusual. The rainbow lorikeet is one of the most vibrant of Australia's native birds, a vivid rainbow amongst the flowers and leaves, and a symbol of the ability to create beauty through spiritual energy. Rainbow lorikeets live in pairs or groups, and are very noisy. They seem like children at play, enjoying life.

This Dreaming is unusual in other respects. The story features a child; the only other child is in the Sea Eagle Dreaming, and both children seek to become birds. It is also unusual because it is about deformity, a very rare circumstance in Aboriginal culture, as a result of the practice of killing weak or deformed babies at birth.

On the card, we see the beautiful Rainbow Lorikeet flying upwards, released from her deformities. The sun rises in the background, symbolizing a new dawn, new beginnings. The upward motion of this card highlights the card's basic meaning of overcoming disability. It visually reflects "rising above" personal limitations.

Upright

Meelia the Rainbow Lorikeet has brought a burst of vivid color and vibrant life to your reading. Meelia showed courage and faith in her decision to leave her loved ones and face a new world. She was prepared to leave the pain and suffering of the known behind her, and fly into the freedom of the unknown, where she would face new challenges. Was she solving her dilemma creatively, or running away from her problems?

The Rainbow Lorikeet has appeared in your reading to challenge you to follow her example of letting go of disabilities, and flying into the unknown. Generally, we are creatures of habit and routine. Meelia calls us to break through personal boundaries of predictability, and find a new means of expression. As Meelia flies from bottlebrush to fruiting mango tree, follow her colorful example and explore some new territory!

Facing the new and unknown is frightening, if exciting. We cling to the familiar, even if we are unhappy with it. Meelia thought about her problems, and found a creative alternative. You too can use your powers of deduction to release the unnecessary and painful in your life, and allow yourself to soar to new heights. By letting go of the past, you can fly into the future.

This card may symbolize pain or separation. The surrounding cards could indicate whether this is personal (as for Meelia), or as an empathic witness (as for her father). In your reading, Meelia brings positive transformation, indicating that wishes will come true.

If Rainbow Lorikeet and **Sea Eagle** appear together, especially side-by-side, this is an auspicious placement, showing that you will achieve your dream. Meelia's femininity, creativity, and desire empower Sea Eagle's masculinity and drive. Meelia creates what she wants; Sea Eagle finds it. On a spiritual level, they call for the union of your feminine and masculine aspects, and they can represent a strong sense of guidance and direction.

Reversed

With the card reversed, Rainbow Lorikeet's disability has become a liability; she appears as if she is flying down, down, down. Will she fly up in time, before she plummets into the earth? Or, is her momentum driving her to disaster?

Meelia reversed calls for profound understanding. You need to plummet into the depths of your failings and problems. You can make positive change through taking the initiative. It is possible to overcome disability, according to our sister, the Rainbow Lorikeet.

This card urges you to work through your liabilities, to free yourself from them. Are you prepared to let them go? Do you have the courage? Face the shadow side of yourself, and examine your fears and pain. Communicate with someone you trust, as Meelia did her father. By working through your pain and hurt (which takes courage), you will be clearer, and better able to avoid "plummeting to the earth."

Kobong

With Meelia the Rainbow Lorikeet as kobong, or if you are drawn to her, there could be something different about you, something that other people do not understand. In some ways you perceive this difference to be a disability or liability. Strengthening your belief in yourself will turn this around. (An old pattern may be to run away or avoid the issue.) The surrounding cards may indicate just where or how you can strengthen your sense of individuality.

Meelia people are very creative, and innovative thinkers. Yet they can appear to be timid and lacking in confidence. Or, in striving to be outgoing, they can overcompensate to hide their personal sense of being different. These people all have a special gift to share.

The Rainbow Lorikeet card will shadow your reading with the energies of dissatisfaction and unhappiness, which will then propel you to seek creative solutions.

Innovative thought, trust, faith, and the belief that anything is possible will encourage the emergence of a "dream come true."

Remember too, that, to achieve her goal, Meelia was totally receptive. She was very clear about what she wanted, and sought to realize her dream. Her guides were the elders and the Great Spirit. You may need to seek support from people who are in a position to help.

Should this card appear reversed, you may find it too easy to plummet down into the negative aspects of your situation, seeking an end to them, rather than a satisfactory resolution or creative alternatives. The challenge is to break away from this force of gravity, to use your God-given wings, and take flight. Move upwards by focusing on what inspires you, and this will give you the potential to shift any disabling energies and manifest a dream.

32 • Sea Eagle

MANIFESTATION • FOCUS • WILL

" *A young boy of the Sea Eagle totem lived with his family. His father told him his ancestor spirit was greedy and selfish, stealing food from others. The boy, like his ancestor, didn't like sharing his food, so he would hide and eat it secretly.*

Once, when he and his father and brothers were out fishing, they saw a Sea Eagle diving from the skies and catching fish. "I shall be an Eagle one day," thought the boy, flapping his arms like wings.

Seeing a barramundi, the boy picked up a spear and threw it at the fish. The spear struck its mark. When they returned to shore, the boy snatched the fish and ran away from his father and brothers. He returned empty-handed.

"Where is the fish?" his father asked.

"I caught the fish, so it is mine. Only I shall eat it," replied the boy.

His father said angrily, "Food is to be shared. Bad spirit comes to those who do not share. Bring the fish back, so it can be cooked." But the boy was stubborn and refused, and so the family ate only lily bulbs.

The next day, the father took the boy fishing. They speared many fish. When the canoe was full they returned to shore. By this time, the boy was hungry, so the father suggested they start a fire to cook one of the fish. When it was cooked, his father cut it apart. "It smells good," said the boy, clutching his empty stomach. He watched as his father gave a portion to each of his brothers. "Where's my share?" he asked.

"You did not share your barramundi, so we will not share with you," said his father.

Then, the boy noticed a Sea Eagle overhead. "Take me with you brother," called the boy. His voice carried on the wind.

After the family had eaten, they noticed the young boy had disappeared. They searched, and soon saw him on a rocky outcrop, his arms outstretched. They watched as feathers covered his body and limbs. His arms became wings, his mouth became a beak, and, with a shrill cry, the boy hurled himself into the air. His family watched in amazement as he flew above them and out over the shining sea. "

Imagery

Sea Eagle's family suffered hunger because of him, but this was of no apparent concern to the young boy. It appears that our brother was actually rewarded for his selfish actions; or was he rewarded for his ability to focus his desires and live his dream? Did he miss his family after his magical transformation? He was able to achieve his heartfelt goal; perhaps his apparent selfishness left no room for remorse or loneliness while he soared the skies. Sea Eagle cares only for himself, yet he also gets what he wants. This Dreaming asks us to suspend our judgment, and focus on the strong, compelling desires that inspire the creation of a new reality.

On this Dreaming card, all we see of Sea Eagle is his head, symbolizing his strong mental powers. The card has equal amounts of sky and sea, as Sea Eagle was focused mentally and emotionally on his goal. His ancestral totem, the Sea Eagle, is also present, in spiritual form, as a cloud-like structure in the sky. The land represents Sea Eagle's origins, his past and present home, and it, too, is a reflection of him. The repetition of these symbols highlights the obsessive focus the young boy Sea Eagle displayed. The predominant color of this Dreaming card is blue, which, in the Western tradition, represents the mind; while white represents spiritual power and will.

Sea Eagle is one of the most powerful of the Dreaming cards. It has similarities with the Tarot "wish card," the Nine of Cups, and the Magician.

Upright

Sea Eagle manifested his desire through the power of visualization, and by actually living that desire. By flapping his arms like his role model, Sea Eagle, the boy imagined and felt the sensation of having wings. This combination of visualization and physical experience forms a magnetic, compelling drive, which seeks manifestation, and propels dreams into reality. You too have as great a potential to achieve what you desire. The practice of visualization and role-playing will certainly help facilitate this. So, believe it, live it and create it; be Sea Eagle and fly free of all which prevents your dream from coming true!

Sea Eagle calls for the consideration of the needs of other people, which must be balanced with your own personal needs. The challenge here is to prevent yourself from being distracted from your goal. Say "no" where it is relevant and appropriate. Be a flying eagle rather than a flying ego; both are powerful, but the former represents a higher perspective, while the latter views everything from the ground, with a limited viewpoint. There may be a tendency towards obsessiveness with the appearance of this card, especially if it is drawn out of balance, that is, pointing towards the left or right.

If **Barramundi** also appears, your quarry is in sight and, if you act promptly, you will achieve your objective. Sea Eagle may appear to be about to swoop on the delicious Barramundi. If so, anticipate the nourishment and fulfillment of your dream. If Sea Eagle is flying away from the fish, or looking in another direction, be careful not to miss any opportunities!

Reversed

Our brother Sea Eagle reversed can indicate obsessiveness. Just as if Sea Eagle were flying upside-down, you feel an urgent need to right yourself. In this position, it is important to resolve your situation or issue before you plummet to the ground. At this point, the needs of other people may be less important, or you may feel unbalanced and disoriented.

Undivided attention on your goal could leave you feeling lonely and isolated, unless you are too obsessed to notice. Possibly, you could make more effort to rejoin your brothers and sisters. This would widen your horizons, and put you more in touch with your humanity, and its connection with other human beings. **Frilled-neck Lizard**, or any other group card, will emphasize the need for a more socially-oriented approach.

If Sea Eagle is reversed, the energies of the ocean, and its association with the emotions, are predominant influences in your issue. Your emotions may be the driving force, which could mean that there is not enough thought and planning to propel you into actualizing your dream. It is a good idea to place this card where you will see it often, to remind you that the strengths of the mind, when combined with the emotions, have the power to make your dreams come true.

Kobong

Sea Eagle soars into the skies, using the wind currents to attain greater heights. The sea eagle is a very powerful bird, one of beauty and majesty. Sea Eagle spies his prey, then plummets with speed and directness onto his victim. Once Sea Eagle begins to plunge from the skies, there is no stopping him.

Sea Eagle is a symbol of the ego, and, as kobong, denotes much power, great respect and social esteem. The challenge of this card is to be a flying Sea Eagle, rather than a flying ego. If this card is drawn reversed, or out of balance, an exaggerated ego may be about to plummet down to earth, and back to reality.

A Sea Eagle person may be the focused businessperson or achiever. Drawn out of balance, this card may indicate obsession, and, therefore, little concern for other people. On a happier note, Sea Eagles carry with them a strong sense of purpose, or destiny. They sense they are meant to achieve something great, even if they are unaware what that might be. They also tend to be loners, which can leave them very set in their ways and views.

As kobong, an inner sense of "going somewhere" affects your situation positively. Knowing the results you want to achieve, you can go ahead with the sureness and power of our brother Sea Eagle. As kobong, this card bodes well for manifesting the best possible outcome in the issue queried. It is the wish card, so, go ahead, and make your dream come true!

33 · Willy Wagtail

COMMUNICATION · MESSAGES · GOSSIP

" *Jitta Jitta the Willy Wagtail was treated with respect, especially in Victoria. The people didn't trust him because he was a trouble maker. They sometimes called him the "bird of death." If he was seen, he was chased away. It was believed that killing him would bring very bad luck, or perhaps even death. If he appeared at an important meeting, all talk would cease, because it was believed that he could eavesdrop and spread tales. Because of this reputation as a gossipmonger, he was not permitted to listen to any conversations.*

In the Northern Territory, it was believed that Willy Wagtail brought the spirits of unborn children to their mothers, so he was seen as a symbol of forthcoming pregnancy. Generally, he was welcomed, unless, of course, a child was unwanted because food was short or there was a drought. The people also believed that, if he was angered, he might bring destructive storms (just as the Frilled-neck Lizard could do if he was angered by human actions.)

Some Aboriginal people of certain tribes (particularly those in southern Australia and the regions around Victoria and the Murray River, as well as in northern Australia) believe this bird is a special messenger for the Great Spirit. Whenever he made an appearance, it was thought he could be bringing an important message, especially if he looked one in the eye, made a noise as if talking, or flew in front of one's path. This message would come, shortly afterwards, in the form of a dream, an unannounced visitor, or an omen in the bush. These omens came in many forms, such as a creature belonging to someone's totem behaving oddly, or a certain formation in nature (smoke, patterns in clouds, or leaves falling upon the ground) making a specific shape which had a symbolic meaning.

Jitta Jitta the Willy Wagtail is an important bird in the Aboriginal Dreaming. In some Dreamings, he brings the first fire, for the people to cook their food. In other Dreamings, he releases fire from other people who refuse to share. The Willy Wagtail's courage is well-known and admired. "

Imagery

Jitta Jitta is the card of communication. The willy wagtail is a cheeky, cocky character, much loved by today's Australians. If anyone comes too close to his nesting spot, he makes a clicking sound and flies close to the intruder, trying to lure the danger away. His courageous tactics enable him to raise his chicks successfully.

Upright

Within a reading, this card highlights anything to do with communication. Jitta Jitta could be asking you to communicate more openly and honestly, or perhaps asking you to take heed of the messages you are receiving. This includes conversations (as well as overheard snippets), radio, television, mail, and so on. The information you need will be evident, as if in black and white!

This bird will bring an increase in all types of communication in your life, from the spiritual to the mundane. So you must remain aware, especially about the issue you are querying.

Are there any delays, confrontations, or broken promises clouding your issue, bringing frustration? It may be time for some order in your life. Be reliable, punctual, and keep your word. Loose ends and disorder can keep you "stuck" in one place. The universe will certainly reflect confusion and loose ends in your issue if you have been lax and undisciplined. If there is a pattern of putting things off, changing this pattern could result in a breakthrough in your issue.

If this card is drawn almost reversed, the energies of communication may be out of balance. The gossipmonger may bring some bad news or juicy tidbits your way. There may be a tendency to speak without thinking, perhaps revealing more than you intended. Or, something you wished kept secret will be revealed to others. Discretion is the key with this card out of balance.

Your gift of communication can be used to help others, whatever your field. The work of the politician, singer, counselor and social worker, and any area associated with speech, comes under Jitta Jitta's influence.

If **Moon** also appears in your reading, be aware of the energies of fertility expressing themselves. This may not necessarily indicate the birth of a child; it could just as easily refer to a new project or a burst of creative energy. The presence of **Dolphin** also indicates new projects.

Like Jitta Jitta, **Crocodile** also carries a lot of respect. The Willy Wagtail is often seen hopping into Crocodile's mouth to catch small insects. His courage, and certainty of safety, bring the energies of protection into your issue. There may also be a strong level of cooperation with other people whom you respect.

Reversed

Jitta Jitta reversed emphasizes a blockage in communication. This breakdown could be in speaking or listening. True communication is a balance of these two. Instead of blaming others, be aware of your own ability to listen and understand, as well as to speak and be understood. Judgments have a tendency to block the expression of higher truth. Truth has difficulty being recognized when one's perspective is limited by fixed views. Such views acknowledge only the reality that suits their own desires, rather than the reality that is for the highest good of all. Finding truth, and being aligned with divine will, requires you to abandon limitations, and drop the word "impossible" from your vocabulary.

We are all capable of empathizing, but this ability can be blocked by a judgmental attitude, and by our expectations. To understand what is really happening, look at other people's views and "try them on for size." With your consequently expanded understanding, you may realize that any communication difficulties are self-created. Breakdowns in understanding, or in being understood, could help you to be more open, expressive, and expansive in your dealings with other people.

Kobong

You are truly a communicator! As kobong, this card highlights the need for open communication. If you feel incapable of expressing your feelings, with practice, you will be able to develop the ability to do so. It is a talent worth developing, especially in the issue you are querying. Sincere communication will not only facilitate progress in the issue questioned, it will also be a valuable tool in your life.

A simple word can change another person's limited ideas, opening up for them unexpected possibilities. The power of the spoken word can move realms of rigid thinking and limitations, delivering insight, wisdom, and understanding. Or, it can close doors, create misunderstanding and resentment, and create barriers. Calling upon the highest and best within yourself, as well as in the other person, can lead to rich interactions from which self-realization can flow.

On a personality level, you enjoy socializing. You have an eye for detail, and relish a good yarn. With Willy Wagtail as kobong, you may need to quell a tendency to speak before thinking, and practice discernment. There may be a degree of gullibility, the "wool can be pulled over your eyes." It is also quite likely that you are not an expert at keeping secrets, like our brother Jitta Jitta. In its most positive aspect, this card points to a being who communicates from an infinite source of knowledge and love.

Jitta Jitta the Willy Wagtail influences the other cards in your reading specifically through the issue of communication. The first card drawn in the spread may indicate the source of important news. All messages, from the physical to the spiritual, will be emphasized. The major message of this card is that the knowledge you need will be revealed.

34 • Barramundi

LOVE • UNION • WHOLENESS

In the Dreaming there was a young couple who grew up together. Their love for each other was so great, they made the promise to marry when they became adults. Unknown to them, they were in a kin relationship which meant that marriage between them could not be permitted. And, at birth the girl had been promised in marriage to another man, a wirrunun, who was many years older than her, and carried great respect and power.

When this fact was revealed, the couple secretly plotted to run away. Their dream was to be together for ever, and they were determined that nothing would stop them, even the severe retribution they would both suffer if caught. Their love knew no bounds and even death was preferable to a life apart.

As the day for the girl's marriage to the wirrunun grew nearer, the young couple quietly stole from the camp. However, the wirrunun sensed something was amiss, discovered their disappearance, and alerted the tribe. The men set off in pursuit.

The young couple heard the movements of their pursuers and quickened their pace until they finally reached the sea, where they realized they were trapped. The young man was a very good hunter and, being resourceful, he had carried several spears for their journey. These he threw at his tribespeople, his love for the girl overcoming his love and respect for his kinsmen.

The spears hit their marks, but there were more men than spears, so the girl picked up the rocks and shells at their feet, and quickly attached them to the pieces of wood which also lay upon the ground, using her hair to bind them together to make spears.

Finally, these resources were also finished, and the young couple were powerless against their opponents, with nowhere to run. Escape seemed impossible.

The young girl then offered to return to the tribe and marry the wirrunun, to save the young man from retribution and death. He refused to allow this and beseeched her to follow him into the sea. Rather than face separation, she held his hand and they plunged into the icy waters.

The moment their bodies were immersed in the water, they were transformed by the Great Spirit into two fish, known today as Barramundi. Thus these two lovers are together forever.

Imagery

By preventing the marriage between the girl and the older man, the lovers in this Dreaming were not supporting the older generation, which considered a younger wife a means of surviving into old age. This Dreaming describes the victory of love over an old established way, a victory which proves courage and the strength of conviction. Struggling through adversity, the Barramundi achieve their dream, to be together. They speak of something eternal and enduring, a bond which will last, suggesting infinity.

On the Barramundi card, the lovers, transformed into fish, are moving away. This is the card of the lovers, the archetypal Romeo and Juliet. It represents love, union, and wholeness.

Upright

When the card is in the upright position, the fish appear to be moving directly upwards, as if coming up for air, an action necessary for life. This may point to where love flourishes—is the card heading towards another in your reading? If the card is unbalanced in orientation, that is, turned substantially to the left or right of the upright position, and not moving towards another card, this suggests that any discord or lack of direction is an indication that you are still formulating what you seek in life.

The tails of the fish can point towards energies which may need "updating" in your issue—take notice of any other cards present here.

Barramundi speaks of success in any endeavor you are working towards, although the journey may not be entirely smooth and effortless. As the card of the lovers, Barramundi can refer to the Tao of life, as in ancient Chinese symbology. However, instead of moving in an endless cycle like the yin and yang token, the two fish are moving together as one, making their own, united, destiny. Change is highlighted, entwined with the path of another. Barramundi always suggests sharing a journey with a loved one.

This card bodes well for lovers, and for any commitment, in any sphere of life. It calls for unity and an enduring relationship, and suggests ultimate success. On a mundane level, you may well have met your proverbial "soul mate," especially if the issue is one of love or relationship. This card, like **Platypus**, blends whatever is around in the reading and if both appear, the love of Barramundi is a union on many levels. Barramundi, however, unites with passion and is more emotionally involved than Platypus. The two together can represent balance on most, if not all, levels. And as **Spider** represents sexual desire, Barramundi brings ultimate consummation.

Reversed

With the card reversed, the fish are diving down into the depths, perhaps seeking safety from an overhead hawk. This may indicate a period of "lying low." At these times, things happen beneath the surface and are less obvious to the casual onlooker, or hawk. Safety and protection are assured, but you may be off-track in some way. Is Barramundi diving towards another card? If so, this second card could indicate a "remedy" for any discord in the issue queried.

By diving down, you will end up in the mud and silt of the river, where there is less clarity. Perhaps you are still unclear about your goals, and are searching for something which will fulfill you and create a sense of wholeness. Or, perhaps you are denying something, or someone, you love. The message is: any load may be lightened by the action of love; allow yourself to experience it and you will be on your path. In this situation, Barramundi needs to swim upwards, take a deep breath of fresh air and face any fears which initiated the dive.

Barramundi need fresh, clean water to survive; they die quickly in contaminated waterways. The message from the environment is that our minds and psyche may contain as much garbage as our local waterways. Any garbage will certainly get in the way, so this card calls for a thorough cleanup which will significantly assist in the success of your issue.

Kobong

Barramundi as kobong reveals a sensitive, loving, and caring nature. "True love" is idealized and tested; and, as it is tested, it is made stronger and more enduring. Commitment, balance, and an open heart are keywords here. Barramundi emphasizes the importance of allowing your loving and vulnerable aspects to express themselves, and the need to create love in your life, on any level.

Barramundi can reveal a strong interest in sexuality. Sexuality and spirituality are different expressions of the same energy, and unless this is acknowledged there is the potential for abuse, excess, or avoidance. If Barramundi is moving downwards, this tendency is more obvious, highlighting the astrological link to dreamy, out-of-this world Neptune. Issues around love and sexuality may seem very unclear.

Those individuals who idealize Barramundi and exhibit its positive qualities are sensual, open, and caring people who are in touch with their spirituality and sexuality. They are able to acknowledge their source of power and express it openly, aware of the intimate connection between the universal life force and Self.

Barramundi as kobong, and positively aspected, reveals a strong desire for, and ability to create, a love which is enduring and eternal. The source of this love may be found in the subject of the reading (the first card drawn). As kobong, the two fish (who had the courage to act on their convictions) augur a change in destiny, whereby the forces of love reign supreme over any disruptive forces. Energies are certainly at play, so be especially aware of dreams and where flights of fancy take you.

35 · Crab

SELF-TRANSFORMATION • PREPARATION • SHAPESHIFTING

" *In the beginning, Crab was an old woman. She was speared because she had eaten children of her tribe. After the men had cut her open and taken the children from her belly, she was buried in a hole, face down, as the people did not want her spirit to come back and haunt them. Although the old woman lay in her own blood, her spirit refused to leave her body. Her spirit still lived and the people did not know this.*

In the trees, the spirit of Waan the Crow watched because he knew her spirit still lived. He spoke to her in his harsh, loud voice: "You should die, for you have done wrong!"

The old woman's spirit spoke: "I was hungry and I ate. For this I shall not die. I do not deserve to die!"

"It is right you should die," replied the spirit of Crow. "And when you come out of that hole, I shall kill you myself!"

So the woman stayed in the hole for many days, *and, in the dark of night, began to change into a Crab. She grew a hard shell which covered her so the Crow spirit could not kill her. A long slit remained where the men had cut her open. This she closed tightly by pressing the two halves of the shell together.*

On the final day, Crab crawled slowly out of the hole. But the spirit of Waan the Crow was waiting for her. He reached forward with his sharp beak and, finding her weakness, he plucked out her eyes. Blindly, she searched for her enemy with her claws. The Crow was just about to strike again when Crab called up great powers of magic. She waved her claws and the Crow spirit was instantly struck dead.

And now the people know that Crabs do not die. When they grow old, Crabs find dark holes and go into them, like the old woman did, to renew their shells and become young and strong again. But men will always die, just as the spirit of the Crow died, so long ago in the Dreaming. **"**

Imagery

Crab epitomizes self-transformation through radical change. She represents the great alchemist who achieves physical change and eternal life through powerful magic. Crab was forced to alter her physical body for protection; it was necessary for her survival.

On the card, Crab waits on the sand. The spirit Crow's footprints surround her, revealing his presence. Because he is in spirit form, we do not see his solid body, just his imprint. The yellow of the sand predominates, symbolizing courage.

Upright

Crab in a reading can refer to being propelled into change by outside forces, sometimes for self-preservation. This "shapeshifting" could refer to physical health, location, career, and even attitudes.

The surrounding cards may give a hint as to where this affects you, although, like Crab, you no doubt already know where change is necessary. Is Crab moving towards another card, or away from one? If Crab is scuttling towards another card, the energies of this second card could represent safety in some way regarding your issue, perhaps even the right course of action. What Crab moves away from is the perceived threat.

Our sister Crab scuttles into your reading to teach you how to protect yourself. Crab's personal boundaries and evident strength are defined by her hard shell. Crab could well be asking you to assess what you find acceptable and what is unwanted in your life; define your shell and acknowledge your strengths. Are you justifying and defending your actions or even your existence? Crab may have been a cannibal, but she did not kill more than she needed—can you make a wrong right?

Build your shell, Crab. You have the personal resources of adaptability and change, to keep yourself safe from the Crows of life; because on some level, you create what you seek to protect yourself from! Like Crab, how are you drawing attack? Are your actions out of balance in some way? How can you fill your belly without harming future generations? Crab calls for forethought and proper action in any endeavor.

The ancient Greeks relate the crab to the summer solstice, a time of harvest, of reaping what has been sown previously. This time could also have some influence in your reading.

Crab is also linked to the moon through the sign of Cancer. If the **Moon** card also appears, the cycle is focused more on renewal rather than permanent change. Maybe a pattern which has repeated itself in different forms many times in your life is presenting itself yet again, seeking your acknowledgment so change can occur.

In Native American Indian lore, it is Crow who is the shapeshifter and guardian of divine law, persisting until justice prevails, exactly as Crow did in this Dreaming. If **Crow** also appears in your reading, he can represent an actual person who, in some way, is perceived as a threat in your situation; one in which you are, perhaps inadvertently, doing the wrong thing. This threat is actually a gift, bringing the lesson of justice.

Reversed

How would you feel if a large crab came running towards you, as Crab appears to do when this card is reversed? Would you feel like running away, or staying? With Crab's claws swinging wildly and purposefully around, you could feel unprepared and vulnerable.

Are you ignoring possible dangers in your situation? Attention and groundwork allow you to foresee what is ahead. Is Crab moving towards another card? This will certainly indicate which energies you may need to work upon to shapeshift into your desired outcome regarding the issue queried.

By appearing reversed, Crab is warning you to take stock of your situation, to evaluate your weak points and work on them. It is not time to take things easy. Prepare yourself for any anticipated challenges, especially if Crab appears to be running directly towards another card. These issues will provide the focus for necessary change.

Kobong

Crab people are the magicians of self-transformation; they can readily adapt to situations they encounter. Shapeshifters extraordinaire, they are just as comfortable barefoot and carefree on the sands of life, as they are dining out in style! They are versatile and clever, good judges of character. They are able to discern any potential threats to their well-being, and to extricate themselves from tricky situations. Courage, adaptability, and an independent spirit are Crab attributes.

It may be ultimate justice that Crab, a previous cannibal, is now a popular delicacy! Crab may point to the wheels of fate reversing, so you can experience what you have been giving out. This turnaround may be positive or negative, depending on your previous actions, but, once completed, it will allow you to move on. Afterwards, you may find the whole situation and focus are so different, you will shapeshift again, especially if the first card drawn does not seem to relate to your query.

As kobong, Crab indicates preparation and self-preservation as key motivators. Your ability to adapt and change is being tested in the issues covered by the surrounding cards. There is a lot of change around you.

Crab people need to be aware that their strong shell can intimidate others, who will look no further than this barrier, perhaps because it emphasizes their own perceived weaknesses. Yet this strength is a cornerstone of Crab's personality, and, without it, Crab would still be buried under the sands of other people's judgments.

Should **Sea Eagle** make an appearance in your reading, Crab may be vulnerable, regardless of her protective shell. You may need to seek shelter and pause until any perceived threat has gone. If **Crow** appears, bearing in mind his role in spirit form in Crab Dreaming, this may refer to the presence of spiritual energies pouring into your issue. This may be a time for clearing away anything that is out of harmony with your higher purpose, and bringing the focus of your issue from the material, mundane planes into spiritual, more meaningful levels.

36 • Crocodile

RESPECT • HEARTLESSNESS

" In the Dreaming, Pukawi the Crocodile was a man. He was camping on a river, up in the Northern Territory. In those days, many bird people were camped there. They were afraid of Pukawi because he was bad tempered and strong.

The people decided they would like to move to an island. They had only one canoe, so it took a long time to get them all across the water to the island. Only a few were left, when Pukawi asked them if they could take him across the creek. He was told he would have to wait until last because he was so heavy. The truth was, the others knew that Pukawi was not only too heavy for this small canoe, he was also dangerous and could not be trusted. They secretly planned to leave him behind.

Pukawi realized that something was wrong. Increasingly resentful, he began to make a fire. He placed ironwood roots on the flames until gum began to ooze out of them, then molded this gum into a long nose for himself. Then he called together all the goannas. He told them of his plan to revenge himself on

the bird people by overturning the boat and killing them.

"Why don't we try to go under the water?" The spotted goanna was the first to try, but he could not stay under long enough, so he was told to stay on the dry land. Pukawi then asked the rock goanna to try, but he could not dive deep enough, so he was told to live among the rocks. Tree climber also tried, but he could not hold his breath long enough, so he went to live in the trees. Finally, Pukawi asked the water goanna to try, and he was able to stay under the water long enough.

Together, they set off up the creek. Pukawi dived under the canoe that was taking the last people across the creek. His anger exploded as he tipped the canoe into the creek. Before he could harm them, though, they were transformed into various birds, who flew out of his reach.

Pukawi said, "From now on, when I get the chance, when I see any people or birds, I will kill them, so it is better to be a crocodile!" From that time on, everyone had to respect Pukawi the Crocodile. "

Imagery

Crocodile was not respected in this Dreaming, instead, he was feared and disliked. Most Dreamings about Crocodile attribute his fearful nature to some rebuff that he has nurtured as a deep resentment towards humans. This Dreaming also explains the habitats of the different goannas and how each is suited to its particular place.

The people of the Northern Territory respected the crocodiles and believed the larger ones embodied the spirits of important people. Crocodiles have a similar life expectancy to humans, and the old ones were thought to have much wisdom (a belief also held in ancient Egypt). Crocodiles carry stones in their bellies, and some of these stones are still considered extremely sacred by the Aboriginal people in Northern Australia. The Aboriginal people lived in relative harmony with crocodiles, but the white man has killed many of them.

Upright

Crocodile is always a "big man" in the Dreaming; his is the card of respect. His other most common role is as a womanizer, like Gien the Moon Man. Here we see Crocodile, in the water and moving towards what is in view. Is it another card in your reading? If so, this could highlight issues of resentment or the source of any difficulties in your situation. Crocodile might be pointing to where your talents lie, as well as the source of difficulty. Like the pearl in the oyster, irritations may transform into a treasured gem.

Crocodile can lower his heart rate to be the slowest of any animal, to enable him to stay under water for long periods of time. Have you "lost heart" in some way in the issue you are querying? Have you lost respect or belief in someone or something? Or, are you flying into a defensive rage, like the mother crocodile, who is extremely protective of her eggs and young? Can you respect other people's views and outward circumstances, and not take things personally?

The ownership of problems is under the domain of Crocodile. Crocodile attitudes include being easily offended, resentful, and unable to accept another person's reality. If someone else is behaving contrary to your expectations, well, that is their problem, unless their behavior affects you directly or you make their problem yours too. Any difficulties you may be experiencing could well be because you are being easily influenced by the attitudes and expectations of other people. Do they really matter? Look at the broader picture. You could "cross the river" by means other than a canoe, or maybe you could work out a compromise to get what you seek.

If Crocodile appears with **Moon** or **Spider**, there is a need to examine closely beneath the surface of your issue. What you think is a "log," may not be—look closely before diving in and making a commitment. Crocodile will influence surrounding cards through his energies of unpredictability.

Reversed

With the card reversed, Crocodile is diving down, preparing to lie in wait for some careless prey to provide him with a meal! Crocodile is well-known for his cunning. Crocodiles will wait patiently for hours and days until the right opportunity for ensnaring tucker presents itself. They can go for months without food. Most of their energy expenditure is in drowning their prey with their characteristic rolling motion, so an unsuccessful attempt can be weakening. In your reading, timing is crucial. Move too soon and, like Crocodile, you will be too drained to make another attempt.

If you are seeking something in your issue, are you expending too much energy for small gains? Or, are you being too aggressive and forward with your approach? Cunning can be a good quality in certain issues, but is Crocodile well-liked? Can you give out some respect, and accept the same consideration back? This attitude could be a key with Crocodile reversed. Honoring another person, however they may be or act, honors and acknowledges the spirit within that person, a spirit that is quite capable of rising over the petty ways of the ego. You may be surprised at how your situation changes!

Kobong

Crocodile is a powerful kobong. If you are drawn to this card, or if he has crawled onto the "banks" of your reading, it may be time to see where you have been like Crocodile—cunning, aggressive, resentful or heartless. These attitudes are energies that are having a negative effect upon your issue. It is not easy to acknowledge one's shadow side, but once you have opened yourself to the possibility of these energies threading their way through your issue, they can be cleared, and you will be able to move on, with more love and awareness. Forgiveness is a challenge under the domain of Crocodile.

The more these statements "push your buttons," the greater the potential for you to open your heart and embody a loving Crocodile! Do you have to be so formidable? Gentleness and softness need to be expressed too. This can be seen in the mother crocodile, who will gently crack open her unhatched eggs, releasing the young into the water. Her aggression is crucial for her young during the first few weeks of their life, as they are prone to attack by goannas, foxes and other creatures.

Crocodile accepts one creature. He allows Willy Wagtail to hop in and out of his mouth to catch insects and parasites—a mutually beneficial arrangement. Compromise could be filtered into your issue, or your life, especially where small things are concerned. With the big things, your ability to assert yourself and go for what you want is very useful! It influences every other card in your reading. Respect the lessons you may be learning, rather than trying to control and subjugate negative aspects, as this will make your journey easier.

37 · Dolphin

UNCONDITIONAL LOVE • FREEDOM • MOCKERY

" *In the Dreaming, a family of Dolphins lived in the sea. The leader of the Dolphins was very bold, though his wife was timid. On the ocean bed lived some shellfish called bailer shells. The Dolphin wife was a good friend of the bailer shells, and she would often visit them to talk of the sun, and the land nearby.*

The Dolphin leader would tease the bailer shells because they could not move about like the Dolphins. The bailer shells would, in their turn, make rude remarks about the Dolphins. The more the bailer shells were teased, the friendlier the female Dolphin became towards them. She brought them food, and tried to reassure them.

Sometimes Mana the Tiger Shark, the enemy of the Dolphins, would pass by. So, when the Dolphins were teasing the bailer shells, the bailer shells would call out that Mana the Tiger Shark was coming. In no time at all, the Dolphins learnt that this was a trick.

One day, the Dolphins were bored, so they went once more to tease the bailer shells. The female Dolphin, feeling sorry for her friends, tried to protect them. The male, stronger than her, managed to reach the frightened shellfish first. They cried out that Mana the Shark was approaching. Of course, the male Dolphin ignored this, thinking it was another trick.

However, this time it was the truth. Before the Dolphins could flee, Mana attacked them ferociously, so that the water turned red with blood. He killed the Dolphin leader. The female Dolphin, now in grave danger, was helped by her shellfish friends, who sheltered her from the shark, under their shells.

When it was all over, the female Dolphin grieved for her dead mate. Her friends, the shellfish, tried to make her feel better by saying he had now become a human and walked upon the land.

One night, when the moon was full, she heard the call of Eerin the Gray Owl, ringing out from a paperbark tree. She was overwhelmed by a longing for her mate, so she made her way to the shore, and pulled herself along the wet sand using her strong flippers. At last, the Great Spirit took pity on her, and transformed her into a woman, so that she could step forth to find her mate. "

Imagery

Dolphins are easily the most beloved of our planet's aquatic creatures, representing the child within, playful and joyous. The image of a dolphin leaping over foamy waves conveys a sense of wildness and freedom to many people.

Dolphin Dreaming contains the character of the faithful and devoted wife. She loves her husband unconditionally, even though he harms her friends. She is, however, also a free thinker; she does not join the other Dolphins in the teasing of her friends. She is more empathic than her husband, and able to follow her own beliefs independently.

This Dreaming is also the archetypal "boy crying wolf" story.

Dolphins have been known to save people from drowning and shark attack. They have been used successfully as therapy for disabled people. Women in Russia sometimes give birth with dolphins present, and some have stated that their children are exceptionally gifted, as a result.

There have been many reports of people claiming a telepathic link with dolphins. Ted Gubboo Thomas of the Yuin people (southern New South Wales) remembers his grandfather communicating with dolphins, from the shore, calling them to herd in fish. There are records of such relationships between man and dolphin from the early days of European settlement.

Dolphins fascinate humans, they intrigue us, yet we also cage them in aquariums and teach them to perform. Even the military of some countries are known to train them for specific tasks of warfare. Their home, the ocean, is quickly being polluted and exploited. They are having to bear the brunt of humanity's shadow aspects. What message does this carry for humanity?

Upright

Dolphin calls you to come and play, to leap into the ocean of infinite possibility, but there is also a special reminder, one that is in contrast to this carefree image. Dolphin can represent our shadow side, the side that can cause hurt and pain, to ourselves and to others. Dolphin can also tease and "poke fun," like a child. Dolphins have been filmed tossing a porpoise between them. (Such film shocks many people.)

With the appearance of this card, you are being asked to be more thoughtful of consequences. This can include not taking things so far that other people are hurt, and not being too hard on yourself. The shadow side could automatically be triggered, if you sense you have been wronged or slighted in some way. When it is directed against yourself, it can manifest itself through being too critical and unforgiving of perceived personal faults.

Perhaps you too could practice the Dolphin wife's acceptance and compassion, if there is disharmony in the issue you are questioning. Children are great teachers of this aspect of loving. There is certainly a strong need for the energies of unconditional love to be put into practice in some aspect of your issue.

If this card appears almost reversed, that is, pointing nearer to the bailer shells, you may find something in the issue is calling your bluff. The message here is not to become too complacent.

Reversed

With the card reversed, Dolphin dives down to the depths of the ocean, and carries you with her. There is a danger that you will dive too deeply, and run out of air, so remember to breathe, deeply and totally. Breathing is such a natural function, yet modern man often seems to have forgotten this essential function, which can be seen as a life-enhancing art. The gift of Dolphin reversed is the present. Breathe deeply, and dive into your experience of who you are now.

Children move and play freely, express their emotions easily, and can let go of any worry or stress. They breathe fully and live totally in the "now." Indigenous people are like this too, in contact with their true nature. Dolphin reversed is the child within us all, diving deep into life's experiences, to explore and learn. Remember to breathe, and connect yourself with your life force, as often as you can. This is an antidote for any negative or stressful experience you may encounter—try it!

Dolphin reversed also brings a message about divided loyalty. Dolphin glides down to join the bailer shells (although they now appear at the top), against the wishes of her husband. This could be an indication of divided loyalties, or a "man in the middle" situation, especially if **Platypus** also appears.

Kobong

Many people feel drawn to this card, or express delight when it appears as kobong, because it brings sun-blessed joy, games and fun. Dolphin as kobong is a message to enjoy yourself, and "splash in the effervescent bubbles of life."

Dolphin can swim around any difficult situation. So, play around with all the possible alternatives open to you in your issue. Make your approach light-hearted, and use your imagination. If Dolphin appears to be swimming towards the left of your reading, solutions may be found in past experiences related to your issue. If Dolphin is moving towards the right, the predominant need is to focus on possible consequences or future outcomes.

Dolphins in the wild may unintentionally injure people swimming with them, by nudging them too hard in the stomach. A pregnant woman, however, will be left alone. When dolphins give birth, they are assisted by a "midwife" dolphin, and it is these "midwives" who detect pregnancy in humans and ward off the other dolphins.

Dolphin people make good "midwives." They are good at "birthing" new projects, getting things started and seeing them through to completion. What are you birthing in your life?

Dolphin influences your reading through the energies of pleasure and joy. The ocean of infinite possibility awaits your exploration, so dive in, and cruise. (In a literal sense, salt water is very cleansing, and ocean air is full of life-enhancing, invigorating negative ions.) It is certainly the right time to enjoy your body, to relish your physical health and well-being, and to experience the great rhythms and tides of life.

38 • Frog

HUMOR • LAUGHTER • PLAY

" *In the Dreaming, there was a greedy Frog called Tilluk. One hot day, when all the creatures were away hunting, he became very thirsty, so he took a drink at the billabong. He drank and drank, and still his thirst was not quenched. He drank all the water in that billabong, then proceeded to the next billabong. He was so thirsty, he drank all the water there, too. He moved on to the river, and when his thirst was finally quenched, every source of water was dry. There was no water left for the other creatures, not a drop. And, as a result of all the water he had drunk, he was gigantic.*

The other creatures came along. It was a hot day, so their throats were dry and they were thirsty. When they discovered every water source was empty, and that the culprit was the greedy Frog, they asked him to return the water so it could be shared. Tilluk the Frog tried to return the water, but he soon realized he couldn't get it out of his distended stomach. So, the animals decided to make the great Frog laugh. They reasoned that his laughing would push out the water.

So, the Kangaroo hopped around, bouncing on her tail—this was her cleverest trick. Everyone laughed, except Tilluk. The Kookaburra told his funniest stories and jokes. They were so funny, he even laughed himself, and his great cackle rang out. Everyone laughed, except Tilluk. Then, a snake rolled around the Frog in a hoop, biting his own tail and tying himself into intricate knots. The creatures thought this was so funny, they rolled around on the ground, holding their sides; but, still, Tilluk did not even smile.

Finally, an angry eel emerged from the mud of the empty billabong, and furiously gesticulated at the Frog, venting his ire. He jumped up and down, screaming in frustration, in eel language. Finally, the Frog began to laugh.

As Tilluk laughed, deep belly laughs, the water came out in a gushing torrent. As more water came out, the Frog shrank, until he became the size he is today. And, because of all the laughter, Frog is now only able to croak. "

Imagery

This image depicts Tilluk the Frog laughing, all the water is being released. The water symbolizes joy and merriment and everyone is happy. There is success, after some striving and failed attempts. Today, Frog's cheerful, thirsty croak welcomes the rain and the replenishment this brings to the land. This rejoicing is an affirmation of life, as water is a very crucial element in an arid land of searing droughts and deserts.

This Dreaming is very similar to Echidna Dreaming; both creatures drank all the water when others needed it. The greedy Echidna was speared, but Frog's life was not threatened. The elements of fun and joy enabled this great creature to release the water for the other creatures, providing a lesson on the effects of greed at the same time. Frog teaches that there are ways of righting imbalances, without resorting to the negative strategies of pain, suffering, and force.

The earth-colored background of the card represents the dry earth (deprivation, and maybe thoughtless greed, and lack of consideration).

Upright

Joy and merriment are flooding your issue. If the earth appears towards the top, there may be an aspect of your issue which seeks replenishment; something is missing and progress will not be made in your situation until this need is met.

Go on, have a laugh! Tilluk's message is to lighten up, see the funny side of your situation. It is so easy to take life much too seriously. Even those things which seem terribly serious do have a lighter side!

Frog has jumped into your reading, so you can apply humor to your situation, and lighten your load. The need for humor can indicate the presence of too much seriousness. Frog wouldn't laugh at those things that everyone else thought was hilarious. Perhaps he was just too "uptight," unable to relax and experience pure pleasure, as his brothers and sisters could. The element of play can open up many possibilities. Once freed, your intuitive side, which believes all things are possible, could create amazing solutions to any dilemmas facing you. Applying humor and fun may be the answer to your issue, or a means of activating the strong sense of success indicated by the presence of this card.

Allow the child within to express the happiness and buoyancy of youthful glee. "Let your hair down," and allow yourself the pleasure of rolling around, holding your ribs and laughing! Do whatever you can to facilitate this—read a funny book, watch a comedy show, tickle a child—and have fun!

If **Echidna** or **Koala** also appear in your reading, you are definitely holding back in some way. Whether this is the result of greed, fear, or thoughtlessness, the presence of either of these creatures indicates that whatever you are keeping to yourself will be shared, to the benefit of all. Any demands from other people in the issue queried may well be met, whether or not you are willing.

Kookaburra, a predator of Frog, may indicate that work and responsibilities are eating away at your time. If Kookaburra is looking the other way, you may be so engrossed in your responsibilities, you are missing the morsel which could sustain you.

Reversed

Appearing in the reversed position, Frog can indicate a need to cry. Laughter and crying are closely allied. This phenomenon is recognized in babies and young children, who will laugh when frightened, or cry when excited. Frog's croak also sounds hoarse, and hoarseness is often an after-effect of "having a good cry"—or repressing one.

Crying is easily the most repressed function of our modern Western society. By allowing ourselves freedom to express all aspects of our personalities, happy and sad, we can function from a more balanced and open perspective. Crying allows the release of stress hormones (mainly adrenaline). This generates endorphins, which block pain. After crying, we have the feeling that the body is relaxed and the soul lightened.

There is a difference between crying as a form of catharsis, and crying as a means of exploring your emotions. Uncontrolled crying could mean that you are tuning in to unshed tears that have been repressed for years, on a personal and global level. If you can be aware that such emotion is not actually part of you, rather, it is simply moving through you, the emotion can be released much more quickly and painlessly. You may then discover that some other emotion was being masked by the original cause of the tears.

Appearing in the reversed position, Frog is welcoming a downpour of tears. Afterwards, you will be free to laugh again. Perhaps you could do with some healing work, or "time out" alone, to experience consciously any pain in your heart, so that you can let it go.

Kobong

Frog people express a keen sense of humor. They have the ability to lighten any mood or situation, if they wish to use their talent. Laughter can transform any negative condition, as it can create a new perspective. By changing attitudes, and opening ourselves to unexpected alternatives, we can change a situation.

Frog as kobong can indicate you may need to look at your situation more seriously. You may find the triviality around you masks a hidden seriousness. The laughter may hide true feelings, and, perhaps, unacknowledged fears. Alternatively, you may be too serious about an aspect of your issue, and the best thing might be to have a break and enjoy yourself.

Frog affects the other cards in your reading, through the level of the emotions, as symbolized by the water. Is the card drawn on the earth or the water? The earth may reveal that you are thirsting for something, there are needs seeking resolution. On the other hand, the water points to emotions running high, needs being met, and success being celebrated.

Frog can be seen in everyone. He carries the essence of the comic, and the child within, free of inhibitions. Frog people can also express the other side of humor. If you are a serious, solemn, and sensible Frog, you could well find your lost giggle due to a tickle from unexpected quarters!

39 · Platypus

DIPLOMACY · TOLERANCE · UNITY

" *When the Great Spirit Biami created the landscape, he made a tribe of animals, a tribe of birds, and a tribe of fish. The last creature he made, the Platypus, had fur like the animals, laid eggs like the birds, and swam like the fish. The three groups all liked the Platypus. But, sadly, the three groups began to argue.*

Kangaroo spoke: "We animals are the best! I can bound across the plains, and balance on my tail. No bird or fish can do this. Let's ask brother Platypus to join us, for we are the best tribe."

The Platypus, being very wise, said: "I do have fur like you, and I would like to join your tribe. Give me some time to make my decision."

The birds called a meeting. Bunjil the Wedge-tailed Eagle said: "We are the best, for we possess the power of flight. No animal or fish can do this. Let's ask brother Platypus to join us, for we are the best tribe."

The Platypus, said: "I do lay eggs, and eat worms, so, surely, I am one of you. I would like to join your tribe. Give me some time to make my decision."

The fish then called a meeting. The Murray cod leapt into the air, came down with a splash, and said: "We are the best. Not only can we swim better than the others, we can breathe underwater. Let's ask brother Platypus to join us, for we are the best tribe."

The Platypus again said much the same thing: "I swim with you on a daily basis, so, surely, I am one of you. I would like to join your tribe. Give me some time to make my decision."

Some time passed, then the Platypus called the three groups together. "Brothers and sisters, I have come to a decision."

All the creatures leant forward, each group sure that it would be chosen. This is what the little fellow said: "I will not join any of you as an individual group. However, I will join you all, because none of you is any better than the others. "

Imagery

The message Platypus brings is one of unity, through acceptance. He shows us the common link of life unifying everything in the world. According to Dreaming lore, Platypus was the last creature to be created. The Great Spirit was weary by then, so Platypus ended up with a mix of characteristics: webbed feet and bill, egg-laying, fur, spurs on the legs, and the ability to swim.

In this beautiful card, we see Platypus on the edge of the circle, surrounded by his brothers and sisters from the different kingdoms of nature: the fish, birds, and animals. His position is predominant, as he plays the role of mediator between the species.

Upright

As individuals, we are joined by our shared humanity, regardless of race, or belief system. We are the "many in one." By acknowledging this paradox, and putting it into practice, you are practicing Platypus consciousness.

Platypus had no pride, and didn't consider any one group better than the others—they were just different. Platypus is asking you to look at your own attitudes. Is there an area in your life where you could practice more tolerance and understanding? Or are there aspects in your issue which are seeking your time and attention? You may be asked to accept all aspects relating to your query, and to treat them equally.

On some level, Platypus highlights group situations and diplomacy. You may be in need of tact, or may need to play the role of mediator. Or, you could find yourself in a competitive situation, like the animals, birds, and fish. Acknowledging similarities, rather than differences, is a step towards healing any social or personal relationship. Look for the common link, and seek the positive in the negative. Platypus aims to "become one" with any card he appears to be moving towards.

If **Lightning Man**, **Sturt's Desert Pea**, or any other card with lightning as a symbol appears, follow the impulses you receive. Platypus detects underwater shrimp, and other prey, by means of the electrical impulses they emit. In a similar way, you could sense the energy flows in your issue. Listen to your intuition. What do you sense? What does your "gut feeling" suggest regarding action to take or final outcomes? Use this ability to determine your actions.

Bat and **Dolphin** also sense their environment in "different" ways. Their appearance in your reading could signify a new way of sensing the world; the "lifting of a veil," or the removal of something which obscures. With this clarity, new things are perceived. Energy dynamics—emotional, mental or spiritual—will be detected much more easily with the appearance of these cards. Previously unseen relationships, or connections between disparate issues, will become clearer.

Platypus unites whatever cards are around in a reading. For example, if he is moving towards **Butterfly**, this could indicate a meeting with others to study or learn something new. Moving towards **Brolga** signifies the expression of creativity in a group situation. Moving towards **Echidna** or **Kangaroo** could mean joining with other people to help those less fortunate, and so on.

Reversed

In this position, various creatures may appear at the top. If the animals are at the top, they represent the material world. The birds symbolize thought, and the water creatures indicate the emotions. These energies are in need of resolution in your issue, particularly where they affect group situations.

Like our brother, think carefully before you act. You may be being tested about a weak point within your psyche. This could be a chance to grow through the apparent negativity, and learn about yourself, and the other people related to the issue queried. Does Platypus appear to be moving towards another card? If so, its issues may bring testing energies and challenges.

If you are experiencing intolerance, in any form (racism, criticism, gossip, jealousy), look within yourself for the powers of diplomacy. Platypus could be diving down, exploring the silt of his waterhole, searching for sustenance. The murkiness does not deter him, for he knows he can find something there with which to nourish himself.

Kobong

If Platypus is your totem, or you are drawn to this card, you are reminded of your uniqueness and strong individuality. You are able to accept all people, from all walks of life, and differing belief systems. Such gifts need to be used; this is one of the challenges of life. Platypus calls for working with groups of people. This is not the time to be isolated or reclusive. On the other hand, the "challenge" inherent in Platypus energy is the need to practice discernment. Acceptance of all people is not always practical, especially if this infringes upon your personal space.

The male platypus has two poisonous spurs, one on each hind leg, for defense. The energy of Platypus is a unique blending of many creatures. He carries the power to blend into any situation, and the ability to ward off danger. As kobong, these qualities positively influence the issue you have queried. Like Platypus, you can draw from your many different backgrounds and experiences.

If Platypus had not been diplomatic and tactful, there could have been much trouble and jealousy amongst the tribes of animals, birds and fish. Like Platypus, it is by using our gifts that we avert trouble. And your gifts will draw to you situations in which to perfect them! By honoring and using our gifts, we are on our true path, and our hearts are open so that peace and happiness may enter—we are unified with our path, our tribe and our spirit.

As Kobong, Platypus seeks to unite the energies displayed by the other cards in your reading. You may find some of the issues covered are in competition, requiring you to find a balance.

40 • Seal

ENVIRONMENT • RESOURCES • EXPLOITATION

" *In the beginning of creation, as we know it today, Ngurunderi, a great hero of the southern Victoria area of Australia, made many great journeys across the land. He was known by many of the tribes in this area, and there are many Dreamings about his epic travels. On one of his lengthy journeys, he cast four of his spears into the sea. At the place where the spears plunged into the ocean's waters, four rocky islands emerged; and they are there to this day. One of the four islands that Ngurunderi created is known to modern people as Seal Rock.*

Soon after the creation of Seal Rock, the very first Seals came to live there. Before this time, these beautiful, sleek creatures didn't exist, either on the earth, or in its waters. The original Seals on Seal Rock were safe from harm and predators, and food was plentiful, so they flourished. Soon the island had many Seals. The colony swam and played safely in the waters, breeding, and feeding on the plentiful supplies of fish.

Yhi the Sun made numerous journeys across the skies, as did Gien the Moon Man in his endless chase of her, while, below, the descendants of the first Seals frolicked and enjoyed their idyllic lives. For many contented years, they remained undisturbed in their isolated environment, with no awareness of pain, suffering, or sorrow.

However, their life of pleasure and plenty was not to remain. Many generations later, the white man came in his big ships, with his harpoons, guns, and greed. He came upon Seal Rock and saw it as a resource to plunder. He killed each and every Seal, from the old ones to the young pups, for their hides, blubber, and meat. Blood stained the waters, and the island was crimson with pain, as each of the beautiful creatures was thoughtlessly slaughtered. Soon the island was barren of all life, while, above, Yhi the Sun wept at the wanton destruction.

Seals are now extinct at Seal Rock. "

Imagery

Seal Dreaming is ancient, yet today's interpretation draws from a recent source (as does the Sydney Harbor Bridge Dreaming.) Seal represents the impact of Western society on Australia and its inhabitants. Seal Rock is a symbol of the injustices committed by a dominant culture against nature: the slaughter of seals for their fur, the attempted genocide of the Aboriginal race and culture, soil-eroded plains, and polluted oceans.

Aboriginal people were in harmony with the land, in a way which has been espoused by mystics and philosophers alike as the epitome of spiritual enlightenment. This oneness with life entwined the people with each other, the land, its life, and the spiritual dimension. As an attitude and approach, it permeated all aspects of life. Even acknowledging the harshness of conditions and some cultural practices in certain areas of the Australian continent, Aboriginal culture contains much from which we can learn.

On this card, Seal's shape forms an island in the sea, representing the present barrenness of Seal Rock. Seal looks displaced and disoriented, there is nothing to ground him. His inability to escape, his powerlessness and vulnerability are exaggerated by the image of the spears about to strike him.

Upright

Seal swims into your reading, rolling in the waves of your issue. Seal was once unafraid, and without enemies. Now Seal has been exterminated (at Seal Rock) and there are no Seals left there, even to be afraid.

The presence of spears in the artwork could indicate that you have, or need, tools, which could be positive or destructive. Your position could go either way, in terms of its power.

This card asks you to be aware of how your environment (on any level) has been used, or abused. The exploitation of your personal resources could indicate the source of any difficulties you may be experiencing.

Seals are not endangered, although they are now extinct on Seal Rock. Seal in your reading could indicate you are sabotaging the issue questioned. You may be taking positive action, but you are not achieving your objectives. Like the Tower in the Tarot, something is in danger of destruction. Seal brings frustrations and setbacks.

It is time to examine your destructive impulses. Patterns of self-sabotage can be passed down through generations. Seal Rock could represent your childhood, and wounds carried into the present. Seal may be telling you not to hang onto the past. Instead, allow the past to be a stepping stone to freedom in the present.

Seal also indicates that there is fertile ground for rehabilitation. A lesson from the past, the need for limits and protection, could be an issue here. Create some boundaries, with thought for the future. If you have drawn Seal, it could be helpful to focus on limits, guidelines, and forethought.

If Seal appears to be moving towards another card, or, if any of the nearby cards seem to be moving towards Seal, these may indicate the source of any misuse of energy. For example, **Magpies** would indicate being ungrounded; **Sea Eagle**, too headstrong; **Opal**, self-righteous; and **Black Swan**, downtrodden.

Reversed

Seal reversed looks as if he is floating face-down upon the water. Is he still alive? Or, is he about to dive down to escape from the spears? If this is the case, there may be a chance he will find a new home, free from fear.

Seal reversed shows signs of regeneration and regrowth. A oneness with life and the intricate balance of nature, cause and effect, short- and long-term, is developing. Seal in this position is a good indicator of an awakening, or awareness, of one's actions and their repercussions. There is also an interest in something of a global nature. It is time to fill the void, and replace what was taken from nature. Seal is calling for an apology, in the form of actions which will restore balance, peace, and harmony to the environment.

This can be a time of breaking a long-standing pattern or status quo, a time of effective change. To continue the imagery, the Seals would be repopulating Seal Rock: free, safe and fearless.

Kobong

With Seal as kobong, or if you are drawn to this card, you are attuned to your environment. You may be sensitive and empathic towards the plight of animals and nature (seals clubbed, a tree felled, lobsters in a restaurant aquarium, or circus bears performing). Your heart aches for the destruction of our natural heritage. Whether or not you act depends upon the strength of your conviction. The cries and environmental causes of Seal people embrace every aspect of humanity's effect on this planet: vivisection, veganism, Greenpeace battles, recycling, anti-nuclear campaigns, and organic food. And, at varying rates of efficiency, Seal people are consolidating, practical, positive transformers.

Seal as kobong urges you to seek positive reformation; from networking within social circles, letter writing, and petition signing, to public protests. Seal energy will find expression. Your urge to heal the environment probably works on many levels. In this case, its influence is strongest in the issue you are questioning. The surrounding cards could indicate how, and where, this might be so.

Seal people, especially if kobong is reversed, can also be allergic to many aspects of our modern age. Their bodies cannot handle the high level of pollutants in the air, water and food. They could also be those who are open to psychic attack, and negative energy fields.

41 · Turtle

RETREAT · SAFETY · INGENUITY

" *In the Dreaming, Turtle was a man, a well-known storyteller. He traveled to many different tribes, sharing his stories and music. He told the tribes of their beginnings, and the creation of their land by the Ancestor Spirits. Turtle enjoyed being on the move. He became restless whenever he stayed too long in one place.*

One time he visited a tribe who lived on an island, out at sea. Because Turtle could not swim, he was helped to the island by two of the tribe's strongest swimmers.

Turtle stayed for some time. Eventually, he felt it was time to go, but the tribe asked him to stay for a special corroboree. Turtle agreed, on the condition that the tribe would teach him to swim. But, when no one came forth to honor this agreement, Turtle realized he was being tricked. He began to plan his escape.

The following night, at the corroboree, he played music, but he had previously made sure that both of his clapping sticks were broken. The tribe offered him other sticks, but he insisted that they must be made from the wood of a tree which grew only on the mainland. The two strong swimmers were sent to the mainland to float back a log from this tree.

That night, when the tribe was asleep, instead of making the clapsticks, Turtle quietly rolled the log into the water, and began to paddle to the mainland. Suddenly, two tribesmen awoke, sensing something was wrong. They saw the floating log not far from shore. In an instant they grabbed their spears and threw them at the log.

Turtle immediately placed his body under the log for protection. The Great Spirit, feeling sorry for Turtle, turned the log into a shell that covered his body. This protected him, so that he could swim in safety. When he finally reached the shore, he was no longer a man, but a creature we all know, called the Turtle. Although he could no longer tell his stories, he could still travel from place to place, and be safe and free. "

Imagery

Turtle showed ingenuity in his use of the log as a "raft" and a shield, to get him across the water safely. The Great Spirit recognized his cleverness, and although Turtle's shell now traps him, he is free to roam without restraint. Other Dreamings also attribute the presence of Turtle's shell to a need for protection.

Turtle embodies retreat, concealing the quality of protection under the armor of his shell. On the card, he is seen from above, as the Great Spirit viewed him. From this vantage point, we can see how he is able to remain safe from the spears thrown at him. His shell is painted up, symbolizing his abilities as a storyteller, who could "embellish" the flickering flames of the campfire with tales from the Dreaming. Turtle, like Brolga, can highlight the arts, particularly the arts of storytelling, music and entertainment.

Upright

Once transformed, Turtle was safe, free, and happy, even though he was separated from his own kind. The quality of retreat, perhaps from a perceived threat, is influencing your issue in some way.

Does Turtle seem to be moving towards, or perhaps away from, any other cards? These cards could signify the safety towards which he is heading, and the problems he is leaving behind.

Turtle brings up the issue of consent. It could indicate that you need to seek some form of permission before proceeding in your issue. This consent gives automatic protection, like an energetic (or "etheric") "shell." Without it, you could draw to yourself the negative energy, or situation, that you are trying to improve, or avoid. You could even draw to you something else unexpected and unwanted.

In this Dreaming, Turtle achieves his dream of learning to swim, and realizes, in the process, that he did not require tuition. Learning out of necessity, he discovers his capabilities and resourcefulness. In your reading, Turtle may indicate the development of personal talents, which may emerge spontaneously and effortlessly, as required by your situation.

Turtle in a reading implies that you are protecting yourself by retreating. Turtle challenges you to dive into the river of your consciousness, to locate the origin of your fear. In doing so, you will release fear's hold, and swim free, able to explore the new territory you find yourself in. You may also realize that it was perfectly safe to make the dive into the water long before you did.

The appearance of **Gray Owl**, who also embodies the energies of protection, emphasizes the importance of moving forward in your issue. These two cards indicate the positive influence of constructive change and development. Any resistance to this change will result in the situation remaining exactly the same. It is up to you to move forward. All restraints are gone. Should **Brolga** dance her way into your cards, she may well be dancing to Turtle's story and music. When Brolga and Turtle are together, there is a strong emphasis on creativity. **Willy Wagtail** also enhances this focus, his energies being predominantly based on communications.

Reversed

Turtle reversed portrays the opposite quality to retreat. He is now advancing. This turnabout reveals courage born of necessity. It can indicate moving away from a repressive, trapped feeling that exists around the issue queried. This meaning is emphasized if **Black Swan** also appears in your reading. The energies of progression will advance your issue. Turtle brings with him the urge to move forward and work constructively.

Turtle is aware of the protection his shell offers. He now moves forward with confidence. Where is he moving to? Which aspects and energies are now being faced? There may even be a sense of excitement and impatience around the issues these cards portray. Any cards behind Turtle may indicate energies which seem to be holding you back in some way, creating this sense of impatience.

Kobong

If you have Turtle as kobong, or if you are drawn to this card, it reveals a creative, artistic person, who enjoys being on the move. Changes of environment, new people, and new experiences are all very stimulating for this person. Any ties or restrictions tend to send Turtle running!

As kobong, this card indicates retreat from something that appears to be restraining you. The other cards in the reading, particularly the first one drawn, could highlight areas of difficulty. Also, if Turtle appears to be moving towards the left side of your reading, this holding back is the result of a past experience. If he is moving towards the right side, Turtle could be fearful of what the future holds, or he is in the process of creating solutions to perceived difficulties.

With Turtle as kobong, it is definitely time to advance in life, to move forward with courage, and confidence in your ability to handle whatever crosses your path. Reviewing previous accomplishments and successes can help you to focus on present capabilities. You can do it!

Turtle influences every other card through some form of "holding back." This is emphasized if **Koala** appears in your reading. Perhaps you are giving only a part of yourself, and keeping a little bit back, in case things do not succeed. Are you hiding under your shell, assessing the situation before you emerge? Take a risk Turtle, it is time to move forward and face your issue.

With Turtle as kobong appearing reversed, Turtle people are generally shy, reclusive souls who appear to hide behind their shell. Their timidity prevents them from taking risks and experiencing life to the full. Their shells shelter them. To overcome their reservations, Turtle people need to "stick their necks out" and "dive into" life. Turtle was clever enough to use a shield, so he should be able to face life with confidence.

The appearance of **Dingo** is significant, because dingoes are very fond of turtle eggs. And, **Sea Eagle** is fond of turtle hatchlings. The presence of either of these predators could alert you to the possibility that your future goals are vulnerable. These warnings give early notice to secure your future goals, by applying either the independence of Dingo, or the strong focus of Sea Eagle.

42 • Whale & Starfish

STRATEGY • BETRAYAL • SELFISHNESS

" In the Dreaming, before Australia was populated by any living creature, everyone lived in a land far way. This place was overcrowded, so some of the creatures decided to migrate south. Whale had the only canoe that could travel the seas, but he was very selfish, refusing to share his canoe, and guarding it well.

Eventually, the desperate creatures asked Whale for the canoe, in exchange for favors. They pointed out that he would be able to swim to the southern land to retrieve his canoe. Whale refused to share, and was very rude.

The little Starfish felt sorry for the creatures, so he devised a plan to trick Whale. Although he was one of Whale's few friends, he thought Whale was wrong, and so felt that his trickery was justified. Starfish was a popular storyteller. He planned to tell stories to Whale, to distract him, and send him to sleep, so that the other creatures would be able to steal the canoe. Starfish planned to tell Whale afterwards, so that he could then retrieve his canoe. The plan was very dangerous because Whale was bigger and more powerful than any of the other creatures.

So the plan went ahead. During the story, Whale asked about his canoe, and the Starfish replied that it was safe. Starfish would tap together two sticks, saying that it was the canoe he was tapping. As expected, Whale began to sleep, but, suddenly, as if sensing something, he opened his eyes, and saw his canoe was gone. Instantly outraged, and without waiting for explanations, Whale attacked Starfish. Starfish was wounded, and thrown into the water, where he remains to this day. Starfish did manage to throw his spear, which made a hole on the top of Whale's head.

Whale then set off to retrieve his canoe. Koala was paddling with all his might, but Whale caught up with them in no time at all. Whale overturned the canoe savagely, and the creatures were tossed into the sea. Somehow, they managed to make it to shore. They moved away from the coast to avoid Whale, and remain there to this day.

Whale's canoe sank and was transformed into an island. Whale now swims along the coastline, always looking for his canoe. "

Imagery

The theme of betrayal is found in many myths and religions. Whale was betrayed by his friend Starfish, who suffered as a result. On the other hand, Whale was selfish and deserved to be taught a lesson.

On the card, Whale chases Starfish angrily, blowing water through the hole in his head and revealing his anger. Starfish lies towards the bottom of the image, depicting the fact he now lives on the bottom of the ocean.

Upright

Betrayal is an issue if Whale appears. Is betrayal ever justified? The quality of trust is under the spotlight, highlighting any insecurities surrounding this issue.

The experience of betrayal is similar to grief. There are stages, which need to be experienced and worked through, before they can be resolved. Getting "stuck" in one of the stages can prevent emotional growth and healing. This could manifest itself as self-righteous anger, resentment, bitterness, and cynicism. There could also be an inability to trust again. Whale pushed the others away with his lack of trust. His fear that they would steal from him created exactly the situation he was trying to avoid. Understanding how you have created your own situation is a part of the healing process.

You must decide whether or not to make the journey through the stages of betrayal. The potential gift is a deeper understanding of the dynamics of the situation, as well as a stronger sense of self, from a higher level of consciousness. Greater trust is also an unexpected gift.

Learning true forgiveness may be a challenge, but the dividends—a renewed sense of connection with others and with the self—are well worth the effort. It is interesting to note that shattered trust can lead to a deeper sense of trust. From the symbolic death of betrayal emerges renewed hope and healing. The phoenix flies through fire, and Whale flies through oceanic waves.

Whale is seeking something long gone. Will he ever let go of this?

Before he was betrayed, Whale was suspicious and distrustful. He was protective of his canoe and found it difficult to relax. There could be worrying circumstances in your issue. You may need to be careful and guard your assets. Follow your intuition here. Be alert for any danger, but ask yourself whether you are motivated by the fear of losing something to which other people have a valid claim. Whale could have retrieved his canoe, but chose instead to play "power games."

If there is something in the issue queried that you are guarding tenaciously, watch out! This could be something physical, like your home or possessions; or it could be a fixed view, an incorrect idea of how things should be, or an unwillingness to take risks. Be aware of the possibility of holding on to the fear of betrayal, which can draw betrayal into your life.

Whale could refer to feelings of anger. If **Bat, Frilled-neck Lizard,** or **Rainbow Serpent** reversed also appear in the reading, anger is emphasized, and you may be challenged to keep your cool. Perhaps you should dive into the ocean with Whale, and swim around your issue, before having a direct confrontation! The appearance of **Crow** accentuates the theme of betrayal. **Crab** emphasizes the idea of being a victim.

Reversed

Starfish is at the top when this card is drawn reversed. He represents planning, strategy, and acting to achieve goals. Use your mental faculties and knowledge to formulate a plan and take steps towards success.

Starfish can indicate a perceived need to "break the rules." You may feel quite justified in your proposed course of action, even if it involves betraying someone. But is there an alternative? Why couldn't the creatures have built their own boat?

Starfish also questions whether the end justifies the means. Does it really not matter how you play the game, as long as you win? Are there alternative tactics that do not hurt other people? Sometimes our actions inevitably hurt or offend another person. Is this the case for you now? Is there a way in which everybody wins, and no one loses?

The challenge of this Dreaming is to act courageously, and follow your decisions through, against competition if necessary. The creatures achieved their goal, and Whale was punished. However, Starfish was also punished. Do you know what is at stake, and are you prepared to face any consequences?

Kobong

If you have Whale as kobong, or if you are drawn to this card, the issue of trust influences your behavior. Are you trusting or suspicious in the issue queried? Can you believe others at face value, or are "warning bells going off" somewhere deep inside?

How have you experienced betrayal in your life? Did you "go with" the feelings this created, or did you shut them away somewhere within? Whale is still in a state of denial, searching for his non-existent canoe.

Whale as kobong asks you to look at "where you are coming from" in the issue of trust and the issue queried. Following your instincts is important, as long as you make a distinction between being paranoid and being cautious, between naiveté and trust. Whale could indicate it is time to keep your wits about you, just in case! And, perhaps, you could share those things that you used to keep to yourself.

Whales are intelligent, powerful, and awe-inspiring creatures. "Save the Whale" has been a modern catch-phrase, yet these giants are still victims of senseless slaughter. With the pollution of the seas, and nuclear testing, what chance do they have? Whale is still being betrayed . . .

Whale energy is both gentle and powerful. After contact with whales, many people have experienced overwhelming feelings of unconditional love and acceptance. We have betrayed these giants of the sea for centuries, yet they still evoke in us qualities that are the opposite of the treatment they have received from man. Allow Whale to sing to you, and draw you into a world of harmony, peace, and beauty.

With this card as kobong reversed, Starfish indicates a time of planning and mental gymnastics, to solve the dilemma which surrounds your issue. As long as the potential consequences are considered, there is every chance of success.

43 · Ochre

MAGNETISM • COURAGE • ARTISTIC EXPRESSION

" In the Dreaming, when the earth was young and before time existed, as we know it today, there lived a giant lizard that terrified the people of a certain tribe, often killing the unwary or defenseless for food, and sometimes just for the pleasure of expressing his cruelty and strength. Even the strongest and bravest warriors were powerless against its sharp claws and ferocious teeth, and many men were killed in battle against the lizard. The people of this tribe had a hunting dingo that they had raised from a pup. Although the dingo now roamed free, he still had a great affection for the people, so he would often visit the tribe.

One dark and moonless night, while the people of the camp slept, the giant lizard saw his chance and crept closer, hunger spurring him on. The dingo, his presence unknown to the lizard, was resting by the campfire. Seeing the threat, the dingo attacked the awesome lizard. Although he was much smaller than the lizard, the dingo's great courage prepared him to fight to the death to save his people.

For a long time, the battle raged, both creatures roaring in anger as they fought. Then the people watched in amazement as the courageous dingo managed to grab hold of the lizard and tear open his throat. The lizard was so badly wounded that it fell gasping to the ground and died, its blood soaking the earth a vivid red color. In honor of the dingo, and as an eternal reminder of his bravery, the Ancestor Spirits turned the blood of the giant lizard into a soft, powdery rock: red Ochre.

The tribe were overwhelmed by the faithful dingo's courage, loyalty, and persistence. To show their appreciation, they prepared a special corroboree, during which they would reenact the fatal battle. They painted their bodies with special and intricate designs, using the red Ochre mixed with the lizard's fat. Since this time in the Dreaming, the red Ochre has always had a special significance for the Aboriginal people, who consider it sacred. "

Imagery

There are several Dreamings featuring a dingo attacking and killing a giant goanna; and one describes a gecko killing a giant dingo. In each case, the blood lost in the battle turns into red ochre, which is considered sacred.

Ochre was used in sacred ceremonies and corroborees, and, in this context, was interchangeable with blood. It was also used for decorating boomerangs, spears, coolamons (shallow dishes of wood or bark, used for carrying water), caves and rock faces. In northern Australia, many cave and rock surfaces attest to long hours during the wet season with time at hand. Art and ochre were used in ceremony, storytelling and magic.

Red ochre was considered sacred, because it carried within it the properties of blood, or the life force. The red color comes from the mineral iron, which has magnetic properties. Magnetic energy influences many things, from the moving of continents and oceans, and the growth of plants, to the homing instincts of animals.

The Aborigine songlines are said to represent the ley lines, believed by some to be electromagnetic lines on the earth. Aboriginal art depicted its world from above, as if creating a map, using dot work and crosshatching that resembled energy patterns. Artists often depicted the songlines and journeys made by the great ancestral beings. Their hand stencils (patterns created on rock walls using the hand as a stencil to draw around) also conveyed the idea of energy radiating, like a corona or aura.

On the card, the splashes of red, white, gray, and yellow represent the colors of the earth. The hand represents reconciliation, the gesture of acceptance, and reaching out towards another person. It also represents human interaction with the Ochre, with nature. Included in this symbol is the role of humans as custodians of the earth, with the power to manipulate (the hand).

Upright

What color appears at the twelve o'clock position? Red symbolizes blood, life force, energy, power, and vitality. With red in this position, the magnetic qualities of Ochre are more potent. Yellow represents the mind, or intellect, stimulation, and the life-enhancing principles of the Sun. White denotes purity and purification. White is also a color of death, symbolizing the otherworld. Blue-gray brings grounding, and symbolizes the earth, twilight, the astral level, and the emotions and desires.

Ochre symbolizes the forces of magnetism. It asks you to acknowledge what you have drawn to yourself. This could refer to physical environment, experiences, or people. Ochre, like Rainbow Serpent, acknowledges your power to create your life circumstances. As artist in your own life, you must use the Ochre in the best way. If you feel you are a lizard battling a giant dingo, call in the energies of courage and tenacity!

Ochre has the potential to connect you with an invisible field of vital force and energy. The ability to deepen this connection is emphasized if other spiritual cards appear, especially **Rainbow Serpent** and **Uluru**.

If **Dingo** also appears, your courage is being tested. Like the dingo in Ochre Dreaming, you are being challenged to stand strong, and fight for your beliefs. Your opponent may appear bigger and stronger, but your perseverance will conquer!

Reversed

Ochre reversed reveals the hand facing downwards, towards the ground. It would have been very awkward to stencil a hand in this position. Turn your hand down, palm outwards on a vertical surface, like a wall, and try it for yourself. How would you do it? Are you in an impossible situation?

Or maybe, this card could represent a cave which has fallen, which would explain how the hand stencil came to be reversed. Ochre reversed points to a break in energy, a change not unlike a cave or shelter collapsing.

This card tells of difficulties and discomfort, or the breaking down of structures. Results are achieved, but they seem to be turned around. When you achieve what you want, it is no longer wanted. Something that you thought would be easy turns out to be difficult, and vice versa. The opposite of magnetism is repulsion. There could be a desire to get rid of things, push them away.

This card can ask you to initiate some practical action. It could be time to throw away, or recycle, some things that you no longer want, or use. This creates room for what you do want.

This card reversed can indicate the negative effects of electromagnetic energy (EME), especially if the issue of the reading is health and well-being.

Kobong

Ochre drawn as kobong, or if you are attracted by Ochre's magnetic power, indicates courage and strength. You are charismatic, with the ability to create and adapt circumstances to your best advantage. It is quite likely you are very sensitive to your environment, and able to detect the hidden currents in social situations.

Your sensitivity can make you open to the invisible fields of energy around you. You could be empathic, able to pick up thoughts and feelings from others. This can cause confusion. Some environments could quicken your psychic sense, resulting in visions, prophetic dreams, and revelations or insights. You may find that some people drain you, or make you feel "spaced-out," and "off the planet." Psychic self-protection is especially necessary with Ochre reversed as kobong.

This card reveals what you are drawing to yourself in the issue queried. Is the overall energy of the reading positive or negative? Does the hand seem to be reaching towards another card? Are the other cards upright, reversed, or at angles? Do they form a pattern? Other cards facing left, or the hand reaching left, can enhance female, receptive energy. Other cards, or the hand, facing towards the right can exaggerate masculine, active energy. By being aware of the energy dynamics, your situation can be perceived in a different way, enabling greater choice in what one draws, like a magnet!

44 · Reconciliation

This card contains the vision of the Council for Aboriginal Reconciliation: "A united Australia which respects this land of ours; values the Aboriginal and Torres Strait Islander heritage; and provides justice and equity for all."

The design of this card is very different to the rest of the deck, as is its interpretation. There isn't a specific Dreaming, mainly because this card acknowledges the modern Dreaming and the concept that the Dreaming has never ended, it continues into present times. This is why the card has images of introduced species combined with Australian native species. If you journey into the outback of Australia, you will see there kangaroos, and also rabbits.

The theme of reconciliation is predominant on this card, and all symbols around the circle are equal. It is as if all creatures are sitting together, in harmony, having reconciled all their differences. Some of the creatures have caused great destruction of the land and native flora and fauna, so they are considered pests, and agriculture has dramatically altered the landscape. Yet the modern Dreaming acknowledges the life inherent in each living thing and, instead of apportioning blame or guilt, demonstrates how each one offers a valuable lesson on a symbolic level.

The black and red background divided by a yellow circle is the Aboriginal flag to remind us of the Dreaming energies that strive to unify and bring spirituality into all aspects of life. The concept shown here is the process whereby Western intellectualism, materialism, and scientific viewpoint (left-brain dominance) are exchanged for a greater awareness of the "unseen realms" of energy and spirit. This allows a deeper meaning to emerge in daily life (right-brain issues).

On the card of Reconciliation, everything is equal, even if there are obvious differences.

The Reconciliation card begins with the self. Accepting our own faults and inadequacies, as well as our own talents and positive attributes, can, like the ripples in a pond radiating outwards and changing the entire surface of the water, bring the energies of harmony and tolerance into our home, workplace, and, ultimately, the world. This card can put into practice the first step towards "justice and equity for all."

How can you give others what you cannot give yourself? The presence of this card in your reading indicates an issue, within your thought or emotional processes, that needs reconciling. An internal tug of war is having an impact on the issue you are questioning.

There are no upright, reversed, or kobong aspects to

this card. Its interpretation is different each time. Look for the image that appears at the top, at twelve o'clock. There may be one creature at the top, or there could be a conjunction of two creatures. If there are two, the meanings for both influence the reading.

The relevance of each creature is determined by you. The meaning of Kangaroo would be different for a cattle farmer than for someone who had a kangaroo as a pet. The qualities that repel or interest you in the symbol drawn have a special place within the issue queried.

Does the symbol "push any buttons" with you? If it does, great! That means there is a part of you that needs to be reconciled with another part. It may have something to do with your emotions. What do you feel: love, tenderness, anger, dislike, fear, non-acceptance, indifference? The stronger the emotion, the stronger the need for balance and, of course, reconciliation.

Your response may be an opinion, or judgment, of the creature, rather than an emotional reaction. These views can limit the situation and prevent change occurring. You will receive what you expect. Your response could also combine the emotional and judgmental.

You may feel or know nothing about what you have drawn. If this is the case, you may need to find out more about the issue you are questioning. Perhaps, further searching and more facts will reveal what you most need to know. You can quite easily discover for yourself what is happening, and what to do. You will find an answer if you look. You may need to reconcile your limited, mundane awareness, which can only see physical effects and short-term results, with your spiritual, all-knowing being—the part of you that can sense the "bigger picture" behind life's experiences.

Whatever your response, it has relevance in the issue queried, and so does its opposite. Explore this now. What is the opposite response, thought, or action to the one that was experienced when you first drew this card? This may be a difficult process for you—if so, can you allow ease in your life? Any difficulty may be a sign to let go of a struggle and allow "what comes naturally."

Look at the two sides, or qualities, of the symbol drawn to achieve reconciliation. By overcoming any barriers to balance and peace, the two aspects can coexist. The reconciliation of the symbol's associations can enable you to reconcile something important about the issue queried. The symbol's relevance is for you to discover. It holds the key to unlock your situation.

The presence of the European animals represents the destruction of Australia's bush, the exploitation of her natural resources, and the attempted genocide and control of a race of people. The whole ecosystem of the continent of Australia has been changed drastically and irreversibly since European invasion. There is still a need for reconciliation in Australia, as a result of past events, present ignorance, the absence of understanding, and stereotyping. The presence of the white hand and introduced species on this card represent this change in balance.

Modern Dreamings acknowledge the presence of a modern reality which is different to that of the past. Aboriginal people may have a piece of machinery, or clothing, a virus, or any kind of manufactured article as a totem. They have reconciled themselves with modern society, perhaps more so than vice versa. This card is the symbol of the modern Dreaming, and it is illustrated in the spirit of true reconciliation.

Key words

BEE AND FLY: A Dreaming about these two insects states that flies were very lazy and, instead of seeking food, they would take or steal from the industrious bees. So the bees hid in trees so the flies could not find them. As the flies lived for each day (unlike the bees who stored their food away for the future) they were unprepared for the winter months. To this day, flies die away in winter. These two insects highlight aspects of leisure and work, living in the now and preparing for the future, working independently (like fly) or in a group (like bee).

HANDS: The black hand reaches out to the extended white hand. The black hand represents our down-to-earth aspects, in touch with nature and nature's energies. It is familiar with seeking sustenance from the land, creating with ochre and using tools made from stone, wood, or twine. It is a reminder to get back in touch with nature, and reacquaint yourself with your own "Aboriginal" nature. The white hand symbolizes modern Western culture, including the lifestyles that separate us from nature, reminding us to accept and use technology and "sophistication" for our benefit, rather than seeing them as isolated from nature and artificial.

KANGAROO: Like the rabbit, the kangaroo is viewed either favorably (as a symbol of Australia), or negatively (because kangaroos compete with cattle for food). To the Aboriginal people, the kangaroo is one of the most important creatures, as its meat, sinew, and bone can all be utilized. Kangaroos are very intelligent animals and pose a challenge for the traditional hunter. An example of this creature's vigilance is its habit of catching flies and sniffing them—if they smell of human then it is time to move away!

Kangaroo may represent power and intelligence; in the Dreaming she represents consideration, kindness, nurturing. On the other hand, she may represent competition, a potential threat to one's livelihood.

MOSQUITO: Although they play a vital role in the chain of life, many people consider mosquitoes a nuisance: their bites can cause allergic reactions, and they carry disease. So, although small, they can make a big impact on your life! Mosquito may represent annoyances, health issues or the need for protection. As mosquito receives nourishment from your life blood, you may find your energy being drained in some way. Mosquito brings a challenge to accept the unacceptable.

RABBIT: Introduced into Australia by the early colonists for hunting purposes, the first rabbits bred quickly, competing with the native animals for food. Now they are found throughout the continent. Rabbits have recently been the focus of a large eradication program that incorporates a form of biological warfare via the introduction of a virus. This controversial program has triggered fears of cross-species contamination with native creatures, and even humans.

Rabbit can symbolize fertility, or issues of control, perhaps even persecution. Health may be a concern, especially regarding something contagious. For the child at heart, rabbit is the symbol of Easter, rebirth and beginnings. Domesticated rabbits are gentle and, if this is your view the rabbit, the home environment may be a focus in your issue.

SHEEP: Here we see a Merino sheep, bred for the Australian climate. The sheep provides wool and meat. The sheep can represent many things: to a vegetarian it can mean the injustice of eating meat; to another, the sheep may be a livelihood; and to someone else it may bring a warning not to be "one of the sheep," but to express one's individuality.

SNAKE: Australia contains the highest number of venomous snakes of any country. To the Aboriginal people, the male or female serpent was the Great Creator or ancestral being in control of law. If anyone broke the law (for example, by killing for pleasure or letting greed overcome need), they would be struck down. Universally, the snake represents healing, transformation, and the spiritual energy of life *(kundalini)*.

SYDNEY HARBOR BRIDGE: This symbol appearing at the top represents that which is introduced and artificial to the land, including technology and structure. The Sydney Harbor Bridge supports Western culture; its enduring steel beams can acknowledge a refining of base products so they can be strong and supportive. Alternatively, depending upon your outlook, the Bridge may represent the control of the environment, pollution, and losing touch with the earth energies.

ULURU: The great Rock is a symbol of power and spiritual energy, representing the Aboriginal people's spirituality and connection to the land. Uluru can represent their struggle to be acknowledged as the true custodians of this land. In a reading, it may point to a conflict between rational and intuitive aspects, or fighting for your spiritual expression.

45 · Sydney Harbor Bridge

STRUCTURE • TECHNOLOGY • ACHIEVEMENT

In the Dreaming, in this case the modern Dreaming, there once was a giant kangaroo who lived on the original land of the Eorta people, on the southern shores of what is known today as Sydney Harbor. He fed upon the grasses that grew there, and, in time, he became the largest kangaroo that had ever lived. He was enormous; his fore legs were like the sinuous branches of a sapling tree, and his hind legs were so large, if a man wrapped his arms around them, he would not be able to clasp his two hands together.

One day, this great kangaroo decided that he would go to the northern side of the water, perhaps because the grass looked greener over there, or because there were more shady trees to protect him from the harsh, penetrating sun that was beating relentlessly down. He may have caught the scent of a potential mate, or there may have been a hungry hunter tracking him. Rather than traveling the long way around the edges of the Harbor, which would take some time, he planned to leap across, perhaps thinking this would be quicker and easier. The distance was very great, so it would require a great jump, but he was a big kangaroo. He was confident, sure of himself, his strength and ability. Besides, he may have thought, if he couldn't leap the entire distance, he could always swim the rest of the way.

The possibility of a shark in the waters would have been a good incentive to extend himself and make the leap successfully!

The kangaroo took a huge run-up to reach the speed needed to leap across the Harbor, but, as he ran, he misjudged his jump, and leapt too soon. This great beast became bogged down in the mud on both sides of the Harbor, with his front legs on one side of the water, his hind legs on the other. He was trapped and unable to move. There he died. Today, his bones form the Sydney Harbor Bridge.

Imagery

This modern Dreaming represents a striving to achieve, to go beyond natural limitations. The Sydney Harbor Bridge is possibly the best-known symbol of Australia, more familiar than any of the native flora and fauna. This, in itself, shows how we have become "out of contact" with nature, including our personal nature.

Today, the kangaroo's bones are a "songline" for the humming and roaring of cars, trucks, trains, and other machines. The pollution these vehicles create is another symbol of how unnatural our lives have become.

The kangaroo thought he could make the leap; he had great confidence. He became a memorial to ambition. Today, traffic can cross from one side of the Harbor to the other much more quickly by the Bridge than by land. The kangaroo's plan was to "save time," which he is doing to this day, albeit in the service of others.

The bridge spans the card. The color blue predominates in the sky, symbolizing mental energies, and highlighting the strong mental focus displayed by the giant kangaroo whose belief in himself surpassed his physical limitations. The blue also represents the energies of air—thought, in the traditional Western description of the four elements of nature. The bridge separates this from the water—a symbol of emotions—and, even though it is an artificial construction, it serves as a unifying principle.

Upright

This card may point to the materialization of your goal, but not in the way you expect. You may misjudge the leap. And, really, is the grass greener on the other side?

Yet, the kangaroo's courage and loss provided gains for other people. Failure can be perceived as success, if not directly for oneself. Stories of disability and hardship may inspire courage and inspiration—the gift of this kangaroo is the gift of failure.

The Sydney Harbor Bridge represents the effects of technology. It is a reminder to keep within sight your nature as a living being. By removing the artificial in your life, you will be less inclined to reach beyond your limits. Crossing boundaries may be exhilarating, but keeping within limits tempers judgment and balance.

With the presence of this card, be prepared to "cross a bridge." These structures represent bridging a gap, joining or uniting things. The Sydney Harbor Bridge spans a body of water. Water relates to the emotions, and the Bridge, high above, is obviously not bogged down in them. This card encourages you to "rise above" the emotions. Short-distance travel, and movement in general, are also possible.

This card may appear to join two other cards in a reading. These could highlight energies you wish to link, or control. The left side of the Bridge may represent your present thinking and goals; the right side, your ambitions and dreams. Surrounding cards will influence any planned shortcuts between the two.

If **Kangaroo** also appears in your reading, this indicates that any striving, or "leaps" you make will be motivated by the needs of other people. This selfless approach indicates lasting success in your issue.

Reversed

The kangaroo overestimated his abilities, just as modern man overestimates his ability to conquer nature. When reversed, this card give the impression that the Sydney Harbor Bridge has succumbed to the forces of gravity, and fallen down, with the heaviest part below. However, it still looks like a bridge.

This could indicate that your need to extend yourself is bogging you down, and creating stress in your life. You could feel out of balance, and may need to rest to gather your resources before attempting any great challenges. It may even be wiser to "take the long route," to be assured of success.

If you possess the confidence and ambition that the kangaroo exhibited, examine your abilities and priorities. Are you really able to make the leap? Is there an alternative, safer route, even if it is longer? Can you release your need to prove yourself against the odds, to make room for ease and pleasure? Can you give up the struggle? Or will you attempt the leap?

The Sydney Harbor Bridge hangs down, out of balance yet still performing its function as a bridge. It is still a force representing ambition and structure. How can you "right" these energies so that equilibrium is restored in your issue?

Kobong

The Sydney Harbor Bridge represents the urge to construct, to be orderly, and to integrate structure into life. As kobong, it indicates that you are in the process of building something, or making a leap. This project involves problem solving and preparation, perhaps even physical challenges. The urge to test your abilities and boundaries could be tempered by a careful evaluation of your objectives, and any possible alternatives.

This card influences every other card in your reading, through the need for structure and achievement. You know what you want to achieve, and your goals are directed towards this. Any cards out of balance will require "fixing." You will not be satisfied until everything is perfect and in its rightful place.

As kobong, this card indicates a personality which seeks achievement and instant satisfaction. Such people always seem to be rushing around, as chaotic and busy as the traffic which crosses the Bridge at peak hour. Their minds are very agile; they are able to find solutions quickly. Their creative innovations often have positive, yet unconsidered, benefits, even if they aren't always successful. This speed of thought and action could mean that Sydney Harbor Bridge people are out of touch with their inner selves.

The natural forces of life provide a great antidote to the tensions of a Sydney Harbor Bridge person. Focus on the weeds growing through the cracks in the concrete, the sparrows vying for crumbs, and the free expanse of clouds in the sky. It is important not to lose touch with nature, which provides a balm for the spirit, and is much more attuned to your soul than noisy traffic and the modern, hectic rush of daily life.

PART TWO

Using the Oracle

This part of Oracle of the Dreamtime *is the user's guide, presented as an easy question-and-answer session. This makes it straightforward to use, even if you are using oracle cards for the first time. Many aspects are covered here, including shuffling and dealing the cards; how to decide whether a card is upright, reversed, or kobong; your environment during a reading; and how to give readings for yourself and other people. Several different layouts are described, from a simple one-card spread to more detailed, in-depth readings.*

This section also covers using the Dreamings and the cards with children. The Dreamings stand alone as simple morality tales, and the cards are an excellent teaching tool, for sparking children's imaginations. The cards are also a powerful aid for meditation and visualization.

An unusual feature of Oracle of the Dreamtime *is its potential for bringing even greater self-understanding and self-development, when the cards are used with the Australian Bush Flower Essences. The Aboriginal people recognized the healing power of flowers, and used them often. The Australian Bush Flower Essences bring these natural energies into focus, and make them available to us today. Using the Essences with the oracle may help one address, and further explore, any current issues highlighted by the cards. It is through awareness and personal growth that we are able to become more fully functioning individuals. A handy table is presented as an Appendix for those who wish to explore this use of the Essences with the cards.*

How to Read Oracle of the Dreamtime

The purpose of giving readings is to explore the subconscious issues and themes that are at play in our daily lives. It is through an awareness and understanding of these energies that we become active creators of our destiny. This moves us from a passive, powerless position, where there are few choices, to actively participating with wider options. Our sense of direction is enhanced, and previous problems are viewed as challenges.

The measure of a good reading is not how accurately it reflects your life (or the life of the querant, the person for whom you are doing the reading), or how much "comes true" if you explore the divinatory aspects. The secret resides in such questions as: "What is the key to this reading?" "How can I change my actions or thoughts to gain the most from the situation?" Look for a message that the querant can take home to ponder, and perhaps apply in life. Refer to the sample readings in Interpreting the Spreads for examples.

Why is environment important?

The environment that you have chosen, or adapted, for your reading can set the scene, or impress upon your subconscious mind the fact that you are using the cards to reach a deeper perspective about yourself and your life. The more attention you give to the cards and the reading, the more profound will be your answers. Mood and atmosphere can be enhanced by candles, incense, aromatherapy oils, inspirational music, crystals, or even taking a dose of an Australian Bush Flower Essence.

The resulting state of relaxation and right-brain dominance (the right side of the brain governs our intuitive natures) encourages the higher self to come through in the form of synchronicity, and makes you more "open" to any insights or messages contained within the reading. Each reading, its combinations and placements, is unique, and specific to its issue.

How should I store the cards?

Some people prefer to store the cards in silk, because silk is supposed to offer protection from outside psychic influences and keep the energy of the cards "high." Any fabric, color or pattern you admire should work just as well as silk, given your intention that it should have protective qualities. A deep red would be a particularly good color for the cards, because that is the color of the earth. A scarf with Aboriginal designs could serve to keep the Dreaming in focus, and could be used under the cards when you give a reading.

Should I allow other people to use my cards?

This depends on you—follow your gut feeling! Some people believe that their cards become attuned to their specific energies, and that other people handling them "confuses" the energy and makes readings less reliable.

I believe the cards adapt themselves to whoever touches them. After someone else has been using your cards, it is a good idea to hold the deck between the palms of your hands for a few minutes. I call this "clearing" the cards. The energy radiating from your hands, with your conscious intention, will attune the cards to you. You might even like to blow on them. Many cultures have acknowledged breath as "chi," or life force. Blowing is a way of imprinting the cards with your specific energy. All this aside, the powers of the universe don't really seem to worry too much about who touches the cards.

What should I know about giving readings?

There are a few different ways of doing a reading. You may choose to devise your own method, use traditional Tarot layouts, or follow one of the layouts described in Interpreting the Spreads. These layouts work well because they are specific to *Oracle of the Dreamtime*.

A reading usually consists of asking a question about a specific issue or situation. This question is generally related to some issue in your life that needs more clarity: relationships, home life, career, health, travel, and so on. Before dealing the cards, shuffle them for a few minutes, keeping your question in mind. If any of the cards fall out while shuffling, place them back in the deck the way they fell. A card falling upside-down utilizes the reversed aspect of the interpretations. Due to their circular aspect, the cards do seem to have a life of their own. They will reverse themselves regardless of your intervention!

It is best to limit your readings or questions to a number (or a length of time) that is comfortable for you. Each reading has to be assimilated and too many can be confusing.

After reading the Dreaming stories appropriate to the cards drawn, read the relevant interpretations. You could devise your own interpretations or meanings for the Dreaming; or add your own ideas to the given interpretation. The readings are limited only by your imagination, and you may feel drawn to a different interpretation.

Giving a reading to yourself involves stepping away from yourself and pretending you are giving the reading to a separate person. Forget it's you, in other words!

If you are being given a reading by someone else, or if you are giving the reading for another person, remember to interact. Ask for confirmation, to verify that you are on the right path. There are so many possibilities, levels of meaning, and ways to interpret a spread. Signposts, in the form of feedback and questions from the querant, can prevent you from going down the back alleys instead of the main roads where it's all happening!

Readings are not a "guessing game." This two-way flow can actually enhance the reading in a way that encourages a new approach to, or view of, a situation. A good sign is the "Ah ha!" response. When you hear that, you know that the reading is "hitting home," and that there may well be an important message for the querant to take home.

Giving a reading to another person can also be a bit scary. We have to communicate what we sense, and risk our interpretation being totally inapplicable. Generally, it is when we are most afraid of "going out on a limb" that the limb supports us. This can teach us to trust our judgment, to communicate openly, and nurture our faith in, not only ourselves, but our concept of a higher power or guiding force (God).

It is important to suspend any doubts, and approach all readings with an open mind. You may return to your skepticism afterwards.

What questions should I ask the cards?

Asking a question is like programming a computer; the more specific the question, the more specific the answer. Questions that open up options are best, such as: "What can I learn from ... situation?" "What course of action can I take with ... situation?" or "What do I most need to know about ... issue?" Make sure your question or query is clear and simple.

On the subject of romance, a favorite topic, a specific question such as "Will Andy and I live happily ever after?" cannot be answered. However, the cards might indicate which issues should be worked on to encourage this to happen, or even those things that are hindering the situation. Remember, the future is in your hands. The cards are but a tool.

Sometimes, it seems, we are just not meant to know the answer. Or the time chosen may not be a good time for a reading. Everything has its own cycle of growth and stasis, ease and difficulty. Sometimes, we seem to be really "in tune" with the cards, and, at other times, they (or we) seem to be "out of synch." Sometimes, pushing the issue can break through this resistance, but it is often best to try again another time.

Generally, for each new question, or issue, a new spread is dealt. With this method, cards that keep reappearing can emphasize important current issues. This is also a good way of choosing an Australian Bush Flower Essence, if you wish to explore this aspect of the oracle *(see page 152)*.

Do I need permission?

Readings are a wonderful gift for those who are confused or uncertain, but doing a reading for another person without their consent or permission is wrong, no matter how well-intentioned. Even if you have sensed that the other person would find the reading useful, always ask permission first. In some circumstances, it is appropriate to use dowsing as a way of asking permission.

It is OK to do a reading on one's personal relationships, but anything about the personal life of someone else just won't make any sense, especially if your intentions are not entirely honest!

How should I cut the deck?

Some people prefer to have a system for cutting the deck, others go by what feels right at the time. One good cutting system is to divide the deck into three from the bottom of the deck, left to right *(see below)*. The top pile on the right represents the future, the middle pile represents the present, and the bottom pile on the left represents the past. The future (top pile) is placed on the past (bottom pile). The present (middle pile) is then placed on top of the other two piles. Then the cards are laid out as determined by the chosen spread. By dividing the deck in this way, you can judge how much the past is influencing the situation, or if there is a lot of meaning invested in future outcomes.

How should I read the circular cards?

The interpretation of the cards relies to a certain extent upon their circular shape and the way they are drawn.

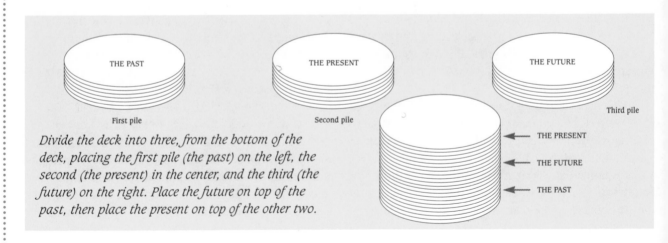

THE PAST

First pile

THE PRESENT

Second pile

THE FUTURE

Third pile

THE PRESENT
THE FUTURE
THE PAST

Divide the deck into three, from the bottom of the deck, placing the first pile (the past) on the left, the second (the present) in the center, and the third (the future) on the right. Place the future on top of the past, then place the present on top of the other two.

In a reading, you might notice that some of the cards seem to be looking towards each other, or one appears to be running away from the others, or one card seems to have its back to another card (or vice versa). Eye contact between the creatures on the cards points to harmonious energy; lack of it can point to difficulties, or an issue that is being avoided.

Sometimes, all of the cards will be looking in one direction or even towards one card. Such dynamics are important and should be noted. They are simple to read just by observation.

In some ways, a reading is like being an observer at a party. Some cards appear to be together as a group, some will snub others, or they could all be scattered, in their own little worlds.

When is a card upright or reversed?

You will see that there is an upright, reversed and kobong interpretation for each card. A hand motif has been placed at the twelve o'clock position of each card, to make it easier to judge how the card is placed. Working clockwise, if the card is drawn with the dot anywhere between nine o'clock and three o'clock, the upright interpretation applies. If the card is drawn with the dot anywhere between three o'clock and nine o'clock, the reversed interpretation applies.

If the card is drawn with the dot exactly at either three o'clock or nine o'clock, this indicates that the situation is swinging between the two interpretations, and therefore there is change in the issue. Exactly on nine o'clock tends to favor the reversed interpretation, whereas exactly on three o'clock highlights the upright interpretation.

Certain symbols, for example a billabong, lightning bolt, or fire, also have relevance if they appear at the top. The meanings for these symbols are outlined in the interpretations.

What is kobong?

"Kobong" is an Aboriginal word. Its nearest meaning in English is "totem," though this does not fully explain the kobong concept. A card becomes kobong by a particular placement in a reading, or a card can become a person's kobong if that person is particularly and consistently drawn to that card. The kobong concept has similarities with the signs of the Zodiac in astrology. Your kobong applies to your own actions and personality, and how you directly influence the course of the situation you are querying in a reading.

The Aboriginal Dreaming describes common traits relevant to all of humanity, which have much to teach us about ourselves and others. These archetypal forces are portrayed in the oracle as kobong, and their influence may be felt in a way that is similar to the influence of the Zodiac symbols of astrology.

The kobong can show us how we are influencing our lives, positively and negatively. Sometimes the cards, and in particular the kobong, can reveal something which seems incredibly obvious, though we had not noticed it previously. In this way, it can be likened to Western or Chinese astrology, relating directly to personality, motivation, and actions.

If the kobong appears reversed, this could refer to an aspect of yourself that requires expression, but which has been repressed. Reading the reversed interpretation may make its meaning clearer.

Are there any time factors, and what do the numbers on the cards mean?

Some cards include a timing aspect. If such a card appears in the recent past *(see pages 157–8)*, it may indicate an event that has influenced the situation. If it appears in the near future, or result, it can indicate the timing of future changes in the situation questioned.

Uluru has a sense of timelessness. Lightning Man

refers to an instant in time (or the wet season of December to February). The Sydney Harbor Bridge relates to modern or recent time. The Moon can relate to a month.

The numbers on each card (as well as helping you find your way around the book) could relate to days, weeks, months, or years, depending on the query. This aspect is for lighthearted fun. The more entertaining your approach, the better your chance of accuracy. Have a guess and see what happens!

Why should I record the readings?

Sometimes a reading may have relevance much later, so it is important to record all readings. Write them down, or record them on tape. Otherwise, it is easy to forget the details, when so much information is imparted. Rather than seeing this as a chore, you could view it as a way of honoring any messages you may receive by recording them in a concrete way.

The interpretations are generally written in the present tense. They also apply to the past and future positions in a spread.

We all have special talents and qualities, and the cards can point us in the direction of how to use them. The cards spark understanding, and inspire solutions to dilemmas, but sometimes the insights come later. This is when a written record is invaluable.

How do I deal with "impossible" readings?

Occasionally, a reading seems confusing and off target. In this situation, you could redraw, taking notice of any recurring cards. If it doesn't make any sense at the time, it may later, if you have a record.

If we have a "vested interest" in the reading "working out," because we want to prove the accuracy of the cards, or because we want to impress someone, this can create the opposite effect.

Also, ask yourself how clear was your question?

How do I use the Australian Bush Flower Essences?

The Australian Bush Flower Essences give the oracle an added dimension. They enable further exploration of, and work with, the issues in the Dreamings, beyond the time frame of a reading. Using them introduces a process of self-exploration and healing, which is well worthwhile. The Appendix gives further information, and a Table of cards with appropriate Essences.

The Aboriginal people were familiar with the healing potential of flowers and would sip the dew from blossoms in the early morning. They were also aware of the qualities of the different flowers, on a physiological as well as spiritual level.

Each card has a relevant Essence, sometimes more than one. To choose an Essence, ask yourself if you feel particularly drawn to a certain card or issue. Some cards crop up regularly in readings, giving a good indication of certain issues that could be explored further. You may find yourself encountering some of the creatures in your life—in reality, or through dreams, meditation, the media, or conversation.

Another way to determine an Essence is through "radionics" or dowsing, using a pendulum. Ian White outlines this and other techniques in his book about the Australian Bush Flower Essences *(see Bibliography)*. This book also describes the Essences in detail, including case studies.

How can I use the cards with children?

My five-year-old daughter and three-year-old son enjoy picking a card at random, and I have found the same response with other children. I first choose several relevant cards, for example, Butterfly, Frilled-neck Lizard, Frog, Kangaroo, Lyrebird, Opal, Platypus and Wombat. Then, I ask the child to make a choice, and I tell the Dreaming belonging to whichever card has been chosen. This can be accompanied by painting or drawing in sand, making cutout puppets, or even an impromptu dance or play. Sharing the Dreamings with children is great for bringing out the inner child within adults—try it for yourself!

Some of the Dreamings (Frog, Kangaroo and Wombat) particularly capture the imagination of the young. The lessons around greed, anger, repentance, and kindness certainly leave their impression. Greedy Tilluk and Echidna teach sharing; the kind Kangaroo teaches consideration; and Wombat teaches the negative effects of resentment, aggression, and anger.

How can the oracle help meditation and visualization?

Oracle of the Dreamtime can be combined powerfully with meditation. The archetypes embodied by the Dreamings live today, within our psyches, just as they did centuries ago. In conjunction with a structured guide to meditation, such as *The Inner Guide Meditation* by Edwin C. Steinbrecher *(see Bibliography)*, it can create possibilities for personal growth and insight which are exhilarating and profound.

Internal dialogues with Waan the Crow about mental patterns, or with Jitai the Spider about desires and sexuality, or with the Seven Sisters about initiation and the tests of life, all contribute to understanding ourselves, our thoughts, actions, and goals. Many new insights can be accessed this way.

Also, the cards carry the energy of each creature and quality they portray. Placing the Magpies card or even a Magpie feather, for example, where you can see it regularly, can heighten your awareness and bring it into your life. This process is similar to visualization, or a manifestation board. It impresses upon your subconscious and conscious minds the qualities portrayed. Uluru can center you, and the Seven Sisters can give you strength and endurance. Butterfly or Lyrebird are good for students taking exams; they remind us of the qualities of learning and its process of growth.

Interpreting the Spreads

What creatures have you noticed around you lately? Perhaps a butterfly flew close by, entrancing you with her grace, or maybe a bat has swooped past you in the night? Or perhaps you received a postcard with a koala on it, or saw an emu or frog on television. You might open a newspaper, magazine, or book and see a picture of an opal, or the moon, or one of the other "characters" of the Dreamings. If you open your eyes and look around you, you will notice that many of the card symbols appear daily. Bogong Moth might appear as a moth, or Koala as a bear, for example. It is quite intriguing to witness the synchronicity of their appearances with their Dreaming messages, and the events in one's life.

The indigenous people of Australia believed that, if an animal or bird behaved strangely, or if an animal of your totem looked you in the eye, then you had to be alert for a special message. The creatures of the bush were essentially living omens.

Some readings will deal with mundane events, such as career changes and romance. Others will be more spiritual or enigmatic. This isn't just the luck of the draw. The readings reflect those things that you most need to know, on a level which goes beyond anything you could interpret or wish for at the time.

The Kingdoms

The cards are grouped into five kingdoms, each category representing the different levels of nature: Nature, Earth, Air, Water and Humankind. Each kingdom can have a specific influence, so it is useful to take into account the different characteristics of these groups when interpreting a spread. Note that the kingdoms and the card numbers and names are repeated at the top of the pages in Part One: The Dreamings, to help you find your way quickly to the Dreaming interpretations.

Nature

Cards in the Nature kingdom relate to a higher power, or God, connection to the earth and spirituality, cycles of life, shadow aspects (facing fear, loss, learning to trust), sensing, and omens.

Nature cards in your reading will bring to the fore your personal concepts of a God or higher power. There may seem to be a hidden direction in your situation, a motivating force which propels you into certain areas or actions. These cards indicate the importance of connecting to the divine in all things, whether through meditation or dream symbols, creative expression, getting in touch with nature or defining your purpose in life.

Earth

Cards in the Earth kingdom relate to social interaction, interpersonal dynamics and self in community.

A predominance of Earth cards emphasizes your role in the community. Issues relating to the consideration of other people, relationships, and self-esteem will be influencing your situation. Any action needs to be considered with regard to its effect on other people in your life, and even in your community.

Air

Cards in the Air kingdom relate to thoughts, willpower, self-expression, communication issues, change, learning, and self within self (personal thoughts, direction, incentives, goals, how you are within your self).

A strong presence of Air cards highlights your ability to control the course of your situation through how you think. Your actions and their results will reflect any mind sets, fixed views, or inspirational impulses. Air cards are a sign that there are opportunities to express your creativity, that there is divine support, and powerful forces are at work within your situation—it's up to you how you use them.

Water

Cards in the Water kingdom relate to emotions, planning and strategy, independence (including going against social norms), differences, and action.

Water cards often indicate your actions will be unexpected, or there will be a strong element of surprise. Water cards emphasize the need to ensure your situation is "watertight." Like water, you are adaptable, able to flow into whatever situation or action best suits your issue.

Humankind

Cards in the Humankind kingdom relate to issues of control and direction, patterns, laws of cause and effect, our ability to affect and change ourselves and our environment, and our role as creators.

Should two or all three of these cards appear in your reading, you are being asked to examine closely your intentions, your motivations behind the actions you are taking, or what you expect should happen. These cards point to your ability to create what you want through initiating change and action. If Opal, Rainbow Serpent or Sea Eagle also appear in the spread, your ability to create what you want may be stronger than you expect. You will need to be certain that you do want what you are seeking in your issue, for you will certainly create it.

Nature	Earth	Air	Water	Humankind
• Spirituality	• Social interaction	• Thoughts	• Emotions	• Control
• Cycles of life	• Interpersonal	• Willpower	• Planning	• Direction
• Shadow aspects	dynamics	• Self-expression	• Independence	• Patterns
• Sensing	• Relationships	• Communication	• Differences	• Cause and effect
• Omens	• Self in community	• Change	• Action	• Ability to change
1 Gymea Lily	12 Dingo	20 Bat	34 Barramundi	43 Ochre
2 Lightning Man	13 Echidna	21 Black Swan	35 Crab	44 Reconciliation
3 Moon	14 Emu	22 Bogong Moth	36 Crocodile	45 Sydney Harbor
4 Opal	15 Frilled-neck	23 Brolga	37 Dolphin	Bridge
5 Rainbow Serpent	Lizard	24 Brush Turkey	38 Frog	
6 Seven Sisters	16 Kangaroo	25 Butterfly	39 Platypus	
7 Southern Cross	17 Koala	26 Crow	40 Seal	
8 Sturt's Desert Pea	18 Spider	27 Gray Owl	41 Turtle	
9 Sun	19 Wombat	28 Kookaburra	42 Whale & Starfish	
10 Uluru		29 Lyrebird		
11 Waratah		30 Magpies		
		31 Rainbow Lorikeet		
		32 Sea Eagle		
		33 Willy Wagtail		

One- and Two-card Spreads

ONE-CARD SPREAD

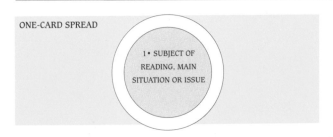

1 • SUBJECT OF
READING, MAIN
SITUATION OR ISSUE

For a one-card spread, shuffle the cards, all the time thinking of the issue or question which is being queried. Draw a card at random. Read the card's Dreaming story and the interpretation. Try to apply the interpretation to your situation. See this as a challenge. If you cannot see any relevance, draw again.

For a two-card spread, follow the method for the one-card spread. Then draw a second card. Apply the kobong concept to this second card, and see it as representing you, your desires, and your actions that are influencing the situation directly.

Sample Reading: One-card Spread

In this sample reading, the querant asks what he most needs to know about his relationship with his partner.

Lightning Man brings a warning. In some way the querant's actions were incorrect, he was going about things the wrong way. **Lightning Man** suggests a need to look at alternative approaches or ways of communicating. This card does not point to the end of the relationship, rather, it is a signal to change something which is not quite working. By following **Lightning Man's** warning, the situation can be improved.

Sample Reading: Two-card Spread

The querant, who was single, asked what she most needed to know about her relationship situation.

Turtle revealed that, in any potential relationship, she retreats. This card was drawn facing to the left, representing the past. She may wish for a past love to be recreated, but, with **Waratah**, this is unlikely. **Waratah** shows that she is frightened of separation, perhaps as a result of a previous relationship breakup, so she puts up her "shell."

The key for her is to be aware of her tendency to retreat emotionally to protect her heart. Overcoming this will allow the situation to blossom. Otherwise, she could sabotage it (by retreating) through her fear of potential loss. Turtle could also indicate a fear of intimacy, a running away from **Waratah's** devotion.

SAMPLE READING
ONE-CARD SPREAD

• Lightning Man

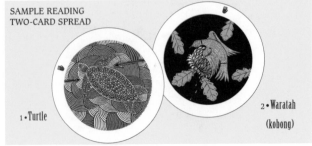

SAMPLE READING
TWO-CARD SPREAD

1 • Turtle

2 • Waratah
(kobong)

Three- and Four-card Spreads

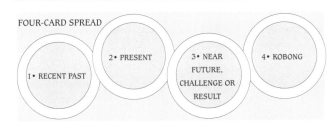

FOUR-CARD SPREAD

1 • RECENT PAST

2 • PRESENT

3 • NEAR FUTURE, CHALLENGE OR RESULT

4 • KOBONG

In the three-card spread, the first card represents the recent past, the second card represents the present, and the third card represents the near future, challenge or result.

The four-card spread is the same, with the addition of a fourth card, which can be interpreted using the kobong section. This highlights where you yourself are affecting the dynamics of your situation. It also influences the other cards. *(See Kobong, page 151)*

Another option for the three- and four-card spreads is to select the card or cards you feel most drawn to, or that you like the most.

Sample Readings: Three- and Four-card Spreads

In this sample reading, the query is: What do I most need to know about moving house?

Emu points to the recent events which have prompted the query. Emu is all about social competition, so the querant needs to look at motives—why is he or she considering moving? What need does it fulfill, and can this need be met in other ways?

Gymea Lily as the present card indicates an increase of personal responsibilities generating change—these will affect the querant whether or not the decision is made to move.

Rainbow Serpent reversed, as the future card, suggests the need to resolve something from the past to make it possible to move forward. Alternatively, the move could be to somewhere relevant to the past, such as a place near a childhood home, or a place similar to a previous home.

In the four-card spread, a fourth card (Frilled-neck Lizard) is drawn, and this card indicates the kobong. Frilled-neck Lizard indicates that the querant is definitely "in control," and perhaps acting against other people's expectations.

The querant will be certain that he or she knows the right course of action, but perhaps there is a need to communicate more with other people, to gain a broader view of the implications of moving, and make the best decision.

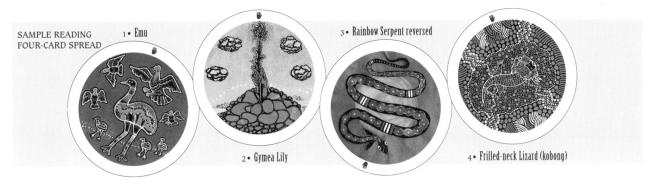

SAMPLE READING FOUR-CARD SPREAD

1 • Emu

2 • Gymea Lily

3 • Rainbow Serpent reversed

4 • Frilled-neck Lizard (kobong)

Southern Cross Spread

This spread is ideal where the situation queried is specific. It may be used when there is a choice to be made (should I change vocation or place of residence?), or when you seek more information about a particular issue (what do I most need to know about my relationship with my mother?), or a specific experience in life. This spread will cover issues from the past as well as challenges in the future. It is a good one for developing your concepts about a situation, and it encourages deeper thought and problem solving through the issues raised by the cards that are drawn.

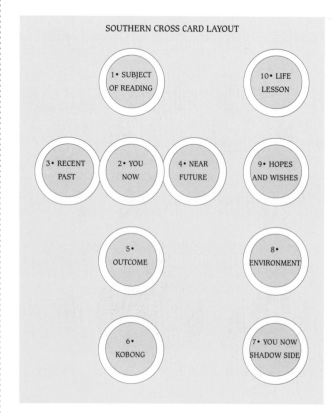

SOUTHERN CROSS CARD LAYOUT

1 • SUBJECT OF READING

10 • LIFE LESSON

3 • RECENT PAST

2 • YOU NOW

4 • NEAR FUTURE

9 • HOPES AND WISHES

5 • OUTCOME

8 • ENVIRONMENT

6 • KOBONG

7 • YOU NOW SHADOW SIDE

1 • The first card, the topic, represents the situation being queried. It will reveal what is really on your mind regarding the issue questioned, or it could show a perspective you haven't considered. It is what the issue is "all about."

2 • This card indicates where you are, right now, in the situation. You can see that this card is central to the reading. From here, you can look behind you to position number three, and ahead to number four. This card is the "man in the middle." It shows what you are dealing with now, what you have learnt from the past, and what you are creating for your future. Take notice if this card faces, or looks away from, another card.

3 • The third card shows your recent past, where you are coming from regarding your issue. It can highlight mental attitudes, a physical event, or other influences which are reaching into the present, and affecting your current situation.

4 • This Dreaming card reveals the short-term results of your situation, and directs you to the near future, the situation that is "just around the corner." This card could challenge you to apply the messages of the previous cards, by offering a solution, or action to be taken. It could also refer to emotional issues that are influencing the issue and need to be overcome.

5 • The fifth position reveals the outcome. Remember, this outcome is a result of heeding the messages of the cards and reading in general. The outcome is not fixed. You are in charge of your destiny! This card could also hold a key to your situation, offering positive action that you could apply to the dynamics.

6• The sixth card utilizes the kobong or totem aspect. This relates to aspects of your personality that are affecting the situation. The kobong could be in your way, and blocking your progress (especially if reversed), or it could be helping you. Try to relate this card to your actions and thoughts around the issue. It can be quite revealing. (I see the card on the very bottom of the deck as a "message from spirit." It's like a postscript to the reading. This card can reinforce the reading, or contain useful advice.)

Advanced Southern Cross Spread

You may wish to draw additional cards for more clarity or depth. These cards give further information about the cards they are situated near.

7• This card is similar to the first one drawn. It shows where you are now in the issue, and it is influenced by the first. It can indicate your shadow, that is, where you are hindering the issue, or repressing certain aspects.

8• The eighth card will outline your environment. This card may indicate supportive or disruptive forces in your situation. Does the card appear to face another? This could indicate a direction you wish to move in, or change. The card it faces may also be influencing your environment directly.

9• This card will highlight your hopes, wishes, and dreams, including fears around the issue queried. Is it a positive card, or does it tend to focus on those aspects of yourself that need work?

10• As the fifth card reveals the outcome, this card will either reinforce or contradict it. The two are directly linked: the fifth card highlights results, while the final card reveals the life lesson. The final card reveals the potential gains in your situation, and, with the first card drawn, the purpose of your situation. As life is a journey of learning, *Oracle of the Dreamtime* can be a focus for these lessons, highlighting their energies in the issue you are querying.

Sample Reading: Southern Cross Spread

The querant asked what she most needed to know at that time.

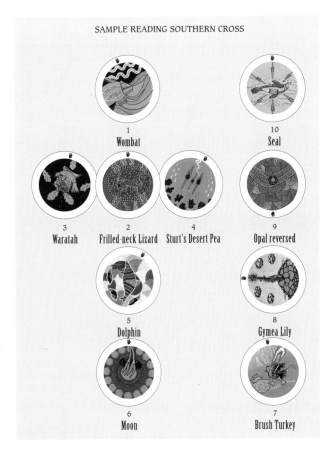

SAMPLE READING SOUTHERN CROSS

1 Wombat

10 Seal

3 Waratah

2 Frilled-neck Lizard

4 Sturt's Desert Pea

9 Opal reversed

5 Dolphin

8 Gymea Lily

6 Moon

7 Brush Turkey

1 • **Wombat** shows that the reading is about personal relationships, most likely a family member.

2 • **Kendi (Frilled-neck Lizard)** places her in a position of personal power (with the potential of abuse) regarding the surrounding cards, though, because he is facing Waratah, the cause is pain, and perhaps a loss. Frilled-neck Lizard shows she is in a position of power, and is quite able to use the hurt and pain of Waratah against Wombat, the person this reading is about.

3 • **Waratah** shows the situation has recently been one of hurt, pain, and potential loss. The near future could indicate pain, or even the end of a relationship. Waratah urges the querant to follow her feelings. There are many emotions to be worked through. The reading indicates a plunging to the depths to release this negative energy. It is important for her to acknowledge her intuition.

4 • **Sturt's Desert Pea** also suggests emotional pain in the near future.

5 • **Dolphin** as outcome asks that she integrate play into the relationship (I suggested that she and her partner do together things they enjoy, to relax and be at ease), and be aware of unconditional love being a test. Dolphin brings the reminder not to carry things too far, for example, any anger, however justified.

6 • **Moon** as kobong reveals her desire to start afresh, to see things from a new perspective, to change the energy, and bring new potential.

I later found out that the querant had indeed been going through a crisis with her husband. Dolphin was the key to this reading, making sense to her and allowing her to view the dynamics of the situation from a less emotional perspective. Waratah would be the appropriate Bush Flower Essence, as it carries the cause of the rift, and would assist in dealing with her pain. Her husband could also take it, to help them work on the issues together. Sturt's Desert Pea would be useful, as it also deals with emotional pain, a focus of the reading.

This reading was quite "negative," so I had to push through my "people pleasing" aspects to convey the pain and suffering I saw. In pushing through my limitations, I actually offered a gift to my friend, a validation and deeper understanding of the difficult journey she was making. In another reading, the querant, a woman unknown to me, burst into tears because the acknowledgment she received moved her so much.

This example shows the potential in the cards for healing deep emotions through validation of one's personal experience. For this woman, the reading was a "coming home," an acknowledgment of and confrontation with events in her life. The reading helped her to sense a higher purpose, a greater power guiding us all.

Sample Reading: Advanced Southern Cross Spread

To the above reading, four more cards are drawn to give a broader perspective of the issues being faced.

7 • **Brush Turkey** brings forward issues of self esteem, indicating that the querant is questioning herself, and making negative judgments. This card is influenced by the first card, Wombat—perhaps she is blaming her home life. (Brush Turkey is centered in the home.) A negative viewpoint may be hindering the positive resolution of the issue queried.

8 • **Gymea Lily** is the third grief card drawn, pointing to a strong emotional current in the situation. Fear of loss is perhaps dominating the querant's thoughts, prevent-

ing a true blossoming of the relationship. This may influence her environment with negativity. The card points towards the left, to Dolphin, indicating that the energies of unconditional love and leisure could be more consciously embraced.

9• **Opal reversed** points to the querant's strong desire for peace and harmony. She may be blaming herself for her problems. The demand for perfection may be behind her current distress. She needs to look closely at her personal ideals and how she reacts when reality falls below expectations.

10• **Seal** suggests that the negativity the querant is experiencing may be causing her to exploit something in the relationship. On some level, there is a misuse of resources. Perhaps she is using guilt, or her pain, to obtain what she wants. She needs to resolve this issue before what is left of the relationship is "used up." The lesson is to think more of possible consequences, resisting the impulse to exploit, and concentrating on the unconditional love represented by Dolphin, the earlier outcome card. Although negative issues are raised, Seal represents an opportunity for the relationship to flourish and prosper.

Rainbow Serpent Chakra Spread

This seven-card spread is dealt in a vertical line, with the first card at the bottom. It is not (like the Southern Cross Spread) for specific queries, but is better for an overall view of where you are in all levels of your life.

7• **CROWN:** How does this card represent my spiritual seeking? How am I like/not like this symbol? What do I like/not like about it? What can it teach me? Where would it lead me? Does it reveal a pattern in my life?

6• **THIRD EYE:** How could this card represent my dreams, visions? How does it show how I wish things to be? How does this symbol represent my connection to my intuition? How could this symbol guide me? How could this symbol represent the mask I put on for others?

5• **THROAT:** What does this card say about communication issues in my life? How does it represent my personal truth? What would this symbol say to me if it could talk? What truth do I need to speak out about? What have I kept quiet about?

4• **HEART:** How does this symbol show how I express love and the state of my heart? How do I love myself? Am I open to giving and receiving love?

3• **SOLAR PLEXUS:** How does this card reflect my rational mind and sense of personal power? Does it show I feel in control of my life, or reveal my negative self-judgments? How does this card represent what I really enjoy doing? Does this card indicate my gifts and talents?

2• **SACRAL:** How does this card reflect my emotions and how I express them? Do I accept and love myself, or does it reveal what I reject? What kind of feelings do I get when I think of this symbol? What does it reveal about my attitudes towards sexuality?

1• **BASE:** How does this card reflect my basic survival instincts? How does it reflect the way I handle my resources (e.g. money, health, time)? How does it represent my physical world and sensations, my environment? What is the main quality of this symbol?

Sample Reading: Rainbow Chakra Spread

In this sample reading, I have drawn the cards to improve my understanding of where I am now in my life, what issues are at play, and what challenges I am facing.

7 • CROWN: Platypus Spiritually, I seek to unite different groups, I can see this in my writing and designing the oracle, and in my book on native symbols which focuses on reconciliation between black and white. I am like this symbol. I am diplomatic and accepting of others, regardless of their belief systems, or who they are. I like Platypus's approach, and his consideration of others. There isn't anything I really dislike about this card, except perhaps the fact that, in another version of this Dreaming, Platypus doesn't join any group and goes off alone. He seems to be alienating himself, yet I see this reflected within myself, as I tend to be a hermit socially. Platypus can teach me to practice more consideration and forethought before I act. He leads me to a united humanity; and the pattern he shows me is my ability to unite the common threads in disparate belief systems.

6 • THIRD EYE: Rainbow Lorikeet (reversed) The bird is flying downwards, and this is how I feel, having completed the oracle. It represents my feelings of coming down to earth and seeking the impetus to fly with another writing project. As to my wishes, it shows me that it is timely to be going downwards, perhaps I need to be grounded for a while, though there is always the possibility of a crash with this card! It shows my connection to my intuition is linked with my perceived disabilities, and finding creative solutions to them—perhaps this is limiting my awareness, and this is why the bird is flying downwards? Rainbow Lorikeet could guide me back, through her conviction that she can find solutions. She repre-

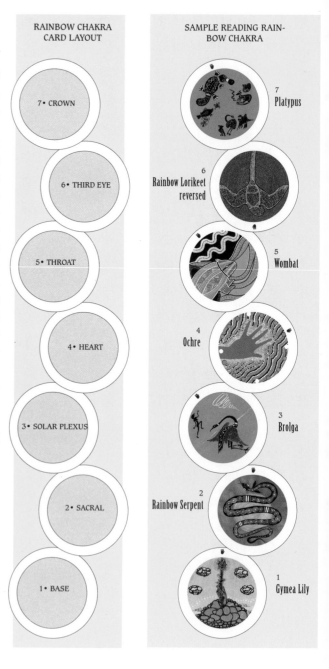

RAINBOW CHAKRA CARD LAYOUT

7 • CROWN

6 • THIRD EYE

5 • THROAT

4 • HEART

3 • SOLAR PLEXUS

2 • SACRAL

1 • BASE

SAMPLE READING RAINBOW CHAKRA

7 Platypus

6 Rainbow Lorikeet reversed

5 Wombat

4 Ochre

3 Brolga

2 Rainbow Serpent

1 Gymea Lily

sents my mask—beneath the bright, glorious colors is someone disabled by her own fear of not being perfect.

5 • **THROAT:** Wombat This card shows that the main communication issues are around my home, which makes sense, as I have young children. It represents my personal truth because I believe parenting is one of the most important things in life. Wombat would tell me to be content with where I am, that there is a time to be in one's burrow, and a time to emerge. I need to acknowledge my feelings about being so home-oriented; the positive as well as the negative. I've kept quiet about the positives more than the negatives, I guess!

4 • **HEART:** Ochre The hand reaching out, towards the right, shows how I am reaching into the future with my love (my love of writing and my love of my children) to create a positive future. Ochre shows I express love through my hands, through writing and art, as well as nurturing and healing. The hand is open, and this is something I try to be: open with my feelings, giving and receiving, though this can be very difficult for me. How do I love myself? Perhaps I am more oriented towards the future, than to loving myself in the present. This card shows my heart is open, especially when I am in "creative mode." I also have the ability to draw love to me, as a magnet.

3 • **SOLAR PLEXUS:** Brolga Brolga has the whirlwind at the top. In this position Brolga shows me as being swept up in some winds of change. Perhaps a new opportunity to express myself will emerge. My personal power is not directed, perhaps the outer turmoil is concealing an inner truth, and afterwards I will be able to "dance" again. I am definitely not in control, and I am consciously awaiting inspiration to write or focus on one project, instead of thinking about several. This card also shows

that I really enjoy being creative, and that I can sustain myself with this. My gifts and talents are reflected in Brolga's love of dance; providing an affirmation that I should continue doing what I love to do.

2 • **SACRAL:** Rainbow Serpent The powerful Rainbow Serpent runs straight upwards, and I see this as creative, spiritual energy threading its way through the issues covered by the reading. It reveals that my emotions are strongly linked to my spirituality. I am more balanced and "together" when there is some spiritual practice in my life, such as meditation. Rainbow Serpent also reveals that I am more accepting of myself when I am in touch with my spirituality. I think of power, creation and transformation when I see this symbol; and, as it has a strong link with sexuality, it reflects my own opinion that sexuality and spirituality are different expressions of the same energy.

1 • **BASE:** Gymea Lily This card highlights my responsibilities, especially with Wombat also in the reading. It reveals that I am capable of providing for others, and that I can be diligent and disciplined. It shows that I handle my resources in the light of my responsibilities, and until now I have not recognized this. To me, the most significant aspect of this card is the emergence of the blossom after the struggle, which is an affirmation of ultimate accomplishment.

This reading gave me the opportunity to evaluate where I am emotionally, mentally, physically, and spiritually. It clarified issues and helped me understand why I seem to be unsure of which project to work on now. It also reaffirmed my role as a parent based at home. It reminded me to trust, to have faith. Inspiration will come, and, if I continue with what I love to do, I will stand as tall and proud as the Gymea Lily, the base of the reading.

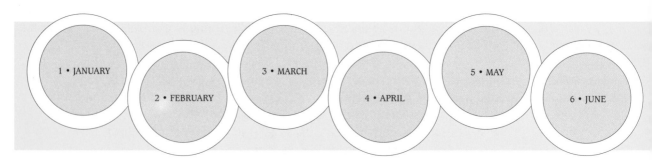

Twelve-month Spread

The twelve-month spread can give an interpretation for every month of the year.
The reading is necessarily more general than with other spreads, as it is not appropriate
to ask a specific question. Draw twelve cards, each one representing a month.

Sample Reading: Twelve-month Spread

JANUARY: Echidna

With Echidna drawn for January, at that time you will need to deal with issues around give and take, sharing, and possessions.

FEBRUARY: Bogong Moth

In February, Bogong Moth brings travel, curiosity, searching for answers, and acting against the advice of other people.

MARCH: Seven Sisters

In March, Seven Sisters brings a testing challenge.

APRIL: Wombat reversed

Wombat turns the focus on to home issues in April, perhaps even a move.

MAY: Opal

Opal brings a spiritual focus in May, bringing issues around "the Law," receiving what you have been "dealing out," and trying to live up to ideals.

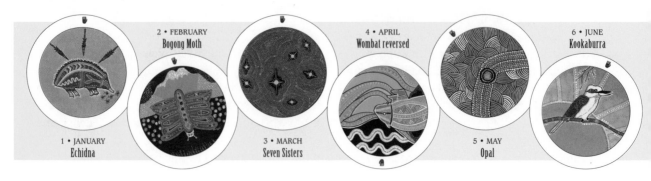

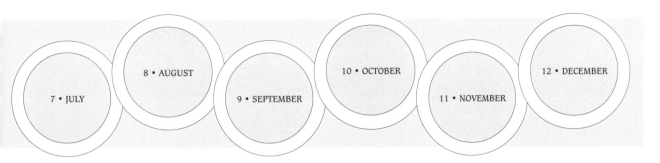

7 • JULY   8 • AUGUST   9 • SEPTEMBER   10 • OCTOBER   11 • NOVEMBER   12 • DECEMBER

JUNE: Kookaburra

Kookaburra brings a work focus, perhaps a promotion, or, at least, an increase in responsibility. Kookaburra suggests a positive influx of energy, laughter, and joy.

JULY: Barramundi reversed

In July, Barramundi suggests issues around love. At that time, the querant needs to be aware of a tendency to avoid this issue, and make a conscious effort to face it.

AUGUST: Waratah

In August, Waratah signifies the need to face fears of loss. Feelings of panic may surface and need to be worked with, perhaps reflecting the previous month's focus.

SEPTEMBER: Koala reversed

Koala reversed suggests the feeling of being "out of your tree," and a need to reflect and share some secrets.

OCTOBER: Crab

Crab suggests a change in the situation in October. Things will shift into another focus. This will be another month of karma, with the results of past actions crystallizing into present life.

NOVEMBER: Black Swan

In November, Black Swan brings feelings of being victimized or "hard done by," along with a chance to rise above any negativity, and acknowledge personal power and choice.

DECEMBER: Uluru reversed

Uluru reversed is a very disorienting card, and one which brings to the surface feelings of loss and alienation. December could be a time to embrace the centering energies of Uluru and reconnect yourself with your spirituality.

7 • JULY — Barramundi reversed   8 • AUGUST — Waratah   9 • SEPTEMBER — Koala reversed   10 • OCTOBER — Crab   11 • NOVEMBER — Black Swan   12 • DECEMBER — Uluru reversed

Appendix: The Australian Bush Flower Essences

The Australian Bush Flower Essences were developed by naturopath Ian White. As catalysts to help unlock potential and resolve negative beliefs, they work well with *Oracle of the Dreamtime*, because they too address issues which confront us in our daily lives.

Flower remedies are not new. The Australian Aboriginal people used flowers to heal the emotions, as did the ancient Egyptians. Flower remedies were popular in the Middle Ages, and Dr Edward Bach rediscovered their healing potential sixty years ago. The Australian Bush Flower Essences, however, work with issues relevant to the modern era of radical change.

Ian White is a fifth-generation herbalist who has been practicing successfully as a naturopath and homeopath for over eighteen years. He has spent a great deal of time traveling throughout Australia, researching and developing his range of sixty-two specific remedies using native flowers. These remedies are used by naturopathic practitioners, medical doctors, pharmacists, and ordinary people to assist in healing the emotions. Ian's informative and color-illustrated book is available worldwide. Ian also conducts workshops throughout Australia, North America, South America, Asia, Europe and the UK.

There are distributors of Australian Bush Flower Essences in: Argentina, Austria, Brazil, England, France, Germany, Hong Kong, Italy, New Zealand, Norway, Poland, Singapore, Scotland, South Africa, Spain, Switzerland, the Netherlands, and the USA.

For further information, contact the Australian Flower Remedy Society, P.O. Box 531, Spit Junction, NSW 2088, Australia; or visit their Web site on the Internet: *www.ausflowers.com.au*

Administering the Essences

You may find a card in the oracle appears often in readings, or you may be particularly drawn to a certain card, or its image. If you wish to understand its meaning in your life more fully, the Australian Bush Flower Essences can facilitate this. Taking them will help you to face and understand the relevant issues, and resolve your situation more quickly.

To use the table opposite, once you have chosen the card that seems most relevant, look up the Essence which best relates to that card. If there are a couple of Essences listed for that card, pick the one which covers your issue the best; or take them all. Be aware of what happens in your life; how you think, feel, and act; and relate these to the card and its issues. By being aware of how you are, and any changes within your self and your life, you will be able to develop a deeper understanding of your situation.

The remedies should be used for a maximum of two weeks at a time. If, at the end of this period, it appears that the issue is not resolved, take a week's break, then repeat, or use another Essence to address the issue. Take seven drops morning and night (on rising and retiring).

Gymea Lily	Alpine Mint Bush (looking after others, feeling depleted), Gymea Lily (strength), Waratah (courage)
Reversed	*Wedding Bush*
Lightning Man	Isopogen (learning from mistakes), Bauhinia (open to change), Emergency Essence (shock), Angelsword (listening to your higher self, protection)
Moon	She Oak, Bottlebrush (change)
Opal	Yellow Cowslip Orchid
Rainbow Serpent	Southern Cross (power creating what you want, control over destiny), Silver Princess (sense of direction)
Seven Sisters	Mint Bush (burns the dross, spiritual initiation)
Reversed	*Jacaranda (scattered, side-tracked)*
Southern Cross	Bottlebrush
Sturt's Desert Pea	Sturt's Desert Pea, Bush Fuchsia (intuition)
Sun	Red Lily (awakening), Boab (patterns)
Reversed	*Yellow Cowslip Orchid (seeing bigger picture), Boab (subconscious)*
Uluru	Sundew (personal), Red Lily (spiritual)
Reversed	*Tall Yellow Top*
Waratah	Waratah (acute), Sturt's Desert Pea (loss, sadness)
Dingo	Morton Waratah
Reversed	*Flannel Flower*
Echidna	Bluebell (sharing), Sturt's Desert Rose (asking, being true to self)
Emu	Mountain Devil
Frilled-neck Lizard	Gymea Lily
Kangaroo	Kangaroo Paw
Koala	Angelsword
Reversed	*Sundew*
Spider	Bush Iris (seduced by the senses)
Reversed	*Hibbertia*
Wombat	Tall Mulla Mulla (own space)
Bat	Hibbertia
Black Swan	Southern Cross
Bogong Moth	Paw Paw
Brolga	Turkey Bush
Reversed	*Sundew (procrastination), Jacaranda (dabbler)*

Brush Turkey	Five Corners
Reversed	*Tall Mulla Mulla (easily led)*
Butterfly	Bush Iris
Crow	Rough Bluebell
Gray Owl	Fringed Violet, Bottlebrush
Kookaburra	Wedding Bush, Sturt's Desert Rose (integrity)
Reversed	*Kapok Bush (perseverance)*
Lyrebird	Isopogen (learn from past experiences), Kangaroo Paw (guidance, teaching by example)
Magpies	Red Lily
Reversed	*Waratah*
Rainbow Lorikeet	Bottlebrush
Reversed	*Wild Potato Bush*
Sea Eagle	Boronia
Willy Wagtail	Bush Fuchsia (clarity), Flannel Flower (expressing feelings)
Reversed	*Kangaroo Paw*
Barramundi	Bush Gardenia, Wedding Bush (spiritual sexuality)
Reversed	*Bluebell, Pink Mulla Mulla (fear of emotional hurt)*
Crab	Fringed Violet (protection), Bauhinia (open to change)
Reversed	*Flannel Flower*
Crocodile	Gymea Lily (strength), Dagger Hakea (resentment), Five Corners (self-esteem, bully)
Dolphin	Little Flannel Flower (play), Rough Bluebell
Frog	Little Flannel Flower
Platypus	Slender Rice Flower
Seal	Red Helmet (respect, nurturing of planet)
Turtle	Kangaroo Paw (with others), Dog Rose (fear)
Whale & Starfish	Kapok Bush
Ochre	Gymea Lily (charismatic), Waratah (courage), Turkey Bush (creativity)
Reversed	*Mint Bush (change in belief systems, major upheaval), Bottlebrush (change), Mulla Mulla (E.M.E.)*
Reconciliation	Bush Fuchsia (integration of duality), Paw Paw (for choices), Mint Bush (confusion, perturbation, for clarity)
Sydney Harbor Bridge	Black-eyed Susan (stress), Kapok Bush (how it works)

GLOSSARY

Bailer shell shell of a tropical mollusc *(Voluta aethiopia)*. These shells, also known as melon shells, were used by Aboriginal people as water carriers, and to bail the water out of their canoes.

Barramundi popular edible fish of northern Australia. There are several species, coastal and freshwater (belonging to the Centropomidae and Osteoglossidae families) The barramundi may change sex during its life, if there is a shortage of male or female fish.

Billabong waterhole. The billabong was known as a common resting place of the Rainbow Serpent.

Black swan *Cygnus atratus*, the state emblem of Western Australia. Its first sighting by white men caused a stir in Europe, as the existence of black swans was previously considered impossible.

Bogong (bugong) moth popular staple food of the Aboriginal people. Great ceremonies and social activities were held at the time of the bogong moth's annual migration, especially in the Snowy Mountains region of New South Wales and Victoria.

Bottlebrush any of the various Australian trees or shrubs of the genera *Callistemon* or *Melaleuca*, also called callistemon, tea trees or meleleucas. The twenty callistemons have large red flowers, with protruding, brushlike stamens.

Brolga Australia's only endemic crane *(Grus rubicinda)*, sometimes known as the native companion. Found mainly on the inland grass plains, brolgas have a stately dance, which has fascinated humans for centuries.

Brush turkey large black Australian bird *(Alectura lathami)*, with a prominent tail, also known as wild or scrub turkey. It lives mainly in coastal areas on the eastern side of Australia.

Bush tucker native Australian food.

Chakra Indian term referring to the energy vortexes, or centers of spiritual power, in the human body.

Clapsticks rhythm sticks carved from wood and often decorated with ochre. They are used in corroboree.

Claypans layer of hard, impervious clay that holds water after rain.

Coolamon shallow dish of wood or bark, used by Aboriginal people for carrying water or food, and, by some tribes, for carrying newborn babies.

Corroboree Aboriginal ceremonies that include music, drumming, chanting, dance, and "painting up." There are several types of corroboree: some reenact the day's adventures, for play; others are strictly for men or women only, and have a spiritual purpose.

Didgeridoo deep-toned Aboriginal wind instrument, said to be the world's oldest instrument, made from a log hollowed out by termites. The didgeridoo originated in northern Australia and is now played throughout the continent. It is traditionally a man's instrument; women are believed to miscarry, or give birth to deformed children, if they play it. The didgeridoo is played in corroboree, and for pleasure, and healing.

Dingo Australia's only native dog *(Canis familiaris)*, which may have been introduced from Asia thousands of years ago.

Eaglehawk the wedge-tailed eagle *(Aquila audax)*.

Echidna Australian spine-covered mammal *(Tachyglossus aculeatus)*, also known as the spiny anteater, similar in appearance to the European porcupine. It has a long snout and claws, for hunting ants and termites. The echidna and the platypus are the only egg-laying mammals in the world.

Emu Australia's largest bird *(Dromaius novae-hollandiae)*, similar to the ostrich, but with three-toed feet. The flightless emu features on the Australian coat of arms.

Eorta people the original inhabitants of the earliest area of Australia to be colonized, around Sydney. Most of these people were killed, or died as a result of introduced western diseases.

Frilled-neck lizard Australian lizard *(Chlamydosaurus kingi)*, that has an erectile hood on the neck which raises when the lizard is intimidated.

Goanna any of the various Australian

monitor lizards. "Goanna" is possibly an adaptation from the word "iguana." Goannas were a popular staple food of the Aboriginal people, and goanna fat was often used for its healing properties.

Gymea lily indigenous Australian flower, with a large, pink blossom on the end of a tall spike. It is common in New South Wales.

Gunya(h) *see* Humpy.

Hand stencils Aboriginal painted motifs, common in the Northern Territory. A hand stencil was created (by children and adults) by blowing mouthfuls of ochre, mixed with saliva and animal fats, over the outstretched hand, generally on a cave wall.

Humpy small, circular-shaped hut made by Aboriginal people for shelter. The humpy was made from branches, sheets of bark, leaves, and mud, held together by twine made from grasses. The inside walls of a humpy provided a popular surface for artistic expression. Also known as a gunya(h).

Kangaroo well-known Australian marsupial *(Macropus giganteus)*. The kangaroo's long tail gives it its unusual leaping gait. A popular food source of the Aboriginal people, it was a challenge to hunt.

Katajuta Aboriginal name for the Olgas, an impressive series of monolithic rock formations, near Uluru.

Koala well-known Australian marsupial *(Phascolarctus cinereus)*, often misrepresented as a bear. The word "koala" is from a southern Aboriginal dialect, and is said to mean "no drink." The koala's water requirements are met through the eucalyptus leaves

it eats, and dew or rain which collects upon them. Koalas were hunted extensively by white men for their fur (which is the most insulating of the marsupial furs), which is why they are very low in numbers today. The koala was highly respected by the Aboriginal people.

Kookaburra large Australian kingfisher *(Dacelo gigas)*, with keen eyesight to detect prey: insects, reptiles, baby birds, and fish. The kookaburra's loud, ringing laugh is famous.

Koori an Aboriginal person. The term is said to come from the Ku-ringgai people. "Koori" can refer specifically to the Aboriginal people of New South Wales, or to all Aboriginal people. *See also* Murrie.

Murrie an Aboriginal person. "Murrie" can refer specifically to Queensland Aboriginal people, or to those who live along the banks of the Murray River in Victoria, or to all Aboriginal people.

Nullarbor Plain vast low plateau of southern Australia, without surface water or trees.

Olgas *see* Katajuta.

Outback inner regions of Australia, where "the crow flies backwards," or where someone "goes bush." The term covers several different environments: wild, desolate desert areas; wetlands of great beauty; and rugged mulga-scrub-cloaked plains.

Palmer River a river of the north-eastern area of Australia.

Paperbark tree tree *(Melaleuca quinquenervia)* of swampy regions, having spear

shaped leaves and a papery bark that peels off in layers. The bark of the paperbark tree was traditionally used during childbirth and menstruation.

Pitjantjatjara one of the two tribal groups that "belong" to Uluru.

Platypus amphibious, egg-laying Australian mammal, known as the duck-billed platypus *(Ornithorhyncus anatinus)*, having dense fur, a broad bill and tail, and webbed feet.

Rainbow lorikeet swift, brightly-colored bird *(Trichoglossus moluccanus)*, its tongue having a brush-like tip specially adapted for extracting the nectar from seasonal flowers, such as eucalyptus.

Songlines trails of songs or stories left by the Aboriginal totemic ancestors as they traveled the land. These songlines were entrusted to the Aboriginal people to be passed on to the next generation. A songline, or cycle of songs, may cover thousands of miles and several language and tribal groups. A songline connects people in the Dreaming.

Southern Cross small, but conspicuous, and well-known constellation of stars in the southern hemisphere.

Sturt's desert pea Australian plant *(Clianthus formosus)*, one of the first to flower after rain, named after the explorer Charles Sturt, who collected samples while on expedition. It is the state emblem for South Australia.

Sugarbag honey from the trigona, native bee. This bee is much smaller than the domestic bee, and it does not have a sting, though it does bite. The honey is very sweet and much sought-after. It is not produced in sufficient quantity to make it commercially viable, so it has remained strictly bush tucker.

Turwan "big man," any power, or entity that carries power, for example, the sun and the Rainbow Serpent. The word comes from the Kalkadoon people, from the area around Mount Isa, in central northern Queensland.

Uluru Aboriginal name for Ayers Rock.

Walking your talk Native American term for living up to your expressed ideals, or not being a hypocrite.

Waratah Australian flowering shrub *(Telopea speciosissima)*. It grows in New South Wales, and its large red flower is the state's emblem. The name is Aboriginal, said to mean "seen from afar," from the flower's vibrant coloring.

Wattle Australian native tree of the acacia family, having spikes of small, ball-shaped yellow-colored flowers, which mass together. The flexible branches were used by Aboriginal people and early settlers in constructing humpies, or buildings, and fences.

Wirrunun medicine man. Amongst his spiritual duties, a wirrinun may heal, work "love magic," or wreak revenge. The wirrunun may "point the bone," to make someone mortally ill. The wirrunun is highly respected for his powers and wisdom. In some cases, he may be evil and greatly feared.

Wombat burrowing Australian marsupial *(Vombatus ursinus* or *Lasiorhinus latifrons)*. A solitary, vegetarian, nocturnal creature, the wombat has short limbs, a heavy body, and coarse fur.

Wonga pigeon stately, slate-colored pigeon *(Leucosarcia melanoleuca)*, which lives in the rain forests, wet eucalyptus forests, timbered gullies and drier woodlands of the east coast of Australia.

Woomera notched stick used as a spear thrower by Aboriginal people, to gain increased leverage and propulsion.

Yankuntjatjara one of the two tribal groups that "belong" to Uluru.

REFERENCES: The Dreamings

Gymea Lily This Dreaming is retold from Roberts & Roberts, *Shadows in the Mist.*

Lightning Man The Lightning Man is a prominent feature of northern Australian Dreamings. This Dreaming is retold by Francis Firebrace and found in Allen, *Time Before Morning.* Information is also contained in Mountford, *The Dreamtime;* Isaacs, *Australian Dreaming;* and Mudrooroo, *Aboriginal Mythology.*

Moon This is retold by Francis Firebrace and found in Mathews, *The Opal That Turned Into Fire.* Other Moon Dreamings can be found in Isaacs, *Australian Dreaming;* Reed, *Aboriginal Myths, Legends and Fables;* Mudrooroo, *Aboriginal Mythology;* and Ramsay

Smith, *Myths and Legends of the Australian Aboriginals.*

Opal This Dreaming, from the Andamooka area, is found in Roberts & Roberts, *Shadows in the Mist;* with additional information in Mudrooroo, *Aboriginal Mythology.*

Rainbow Serpent This Dreaming is told by Francis Firebrace. Its origins are unknown. Another beautiful Dreaming, similar to this one, is found in Noonuccal and Noonuccal, *The Rainbow Serpent.*

Seven Sisters I have retold this Dreaming from the version by Francis Firebrace. It is found in Reed, *Myths and Legends of Australia.*

Southern Cross This Dreaming is well-known and can be found in Parker, *Australian Legendary Tales;* Reed, *Aboriginal Myths, Legends and Fables;* and Mudrooroo, *Aboriginal Mythology.* The last states it is from a story told by Oodgeroo Noonuccal of Stradbroke Island, Queensland. I have also read that it is from New South Wales.

Sturt's Desert Pea This Dreaming has many similarities with Barramundi Dreaming. It is retold from the version told by Francis Firebrace, and is found in Mountford, *The Dreamtime;* and White, *Australian Bush Flower Essences.*

Sun Sun Dreamings and information are found in Isaacs, *Australian Dreaming;*

Mountford, *Before Time Began*, *The First Sunrise*, *The Dreamtime*, and *The Dawn of Time*; Mudrooroo, *Aboriginal Mythology*; and Reed, *Aboriginal Myths, Legends and Fables*.

Uluru Information is found in Burnum Burnum, *Burnum Burnum's Aboriginal Australia—A Traveller's Guide*; Layton, *Uluru—An Aboriginal History of Ayers Rock*; Isaacs, *Australian Dreaming*; and Mudrooroo, *Aboriginal Mythology*.

Waratah This Dreaming was retold by Francis Firebrace. It comes from New South Wales, as well as other areas, in various forms, and is found in Burnum Burnum, *Burnum Burnum's Aboriginal Australia—A Traveller's Guide*; Mountford, *The First Sunrise*; Reed, *Aboriginal Myths, Legends and Fables*; and Mudrooroo, *Aboriginal Mythology*.

Dingo This Dreaming is from the Kalkadoon people of Mt Isa. It is included by courtesy of George Apps, previously Manager of Kalkadoon Aboriginal Sobriety House (KASH). It was told by the late Charlie Ah Wing.

Echidna This Dreaming is retold by Francis Firebrace and found in Trezise, *Dream Road*. A similar Dreaming is found in Reed, *Aboriginal Myths, Legends and Fables*; and Mudrooroo, *Aboriginal Mythology*.

Emu This Dreaming is very well-known and popular with children, as it carries an important message. There are several similar versions in print and multimedia, including Cox, *Fables of the Aborigines*; Isaacs, *Australian Dreaming*; Mountford, *Before Time Began* and *The First Sunrise*; and Mudrooroo, *Aboriginal Mythology*.

Frilled-neck Lizard This Dreaming, from the Northern Territory, and retold by Francis Firebrace, is found in Roberts & Roberts, *Shadows in the Mist*.

Kangaroo This Dreaming, like the Frog, has become a children's classic, and is retold from the version by Francis Firebrace.

Koala This is a Kurnai Dreaming from New South Wales, or Kulin, Victoria. There are several similar versions in print, including those in Isaacs, *Australian Dreaming*; Lee & Martin, *The Koala*; Mountford, *The Dreamtime* and *Before Time Began*; and Reed, *Aboriginal Myths, Legends and Fables*.

Spider This story, from the Murinbata people of northern Australia, is retold by Francis Firebrace, and found in Allen, *Time Before Morning*.

Wombat This Dreaming is very well known as a children's story. It is found in Mountford, *The Dreamtime*.

Bat Francis Firebrace retells this Dreaming. It is found in many books, including Mountford, *The First Sunrise*, and appears in different forms in New South Wales and Queensland.

Black Swan This Dreaming is retold by Francis Firebrace. Another version is in Mountford, *The First Sunrise* and *The Dawn of Time*; Roberts & Roberts, *Shadows in the Mist*; and Reed, *Aboriginal Myths, Legends and Fables*.

Bogong Moth Francis Firebrace retells this Dreaming. It is found in Roberts & Roberts, *Shadows in the Mist*.

Brolga Francis Firebrace tells this well-known Dreaming. Versions are found in many books and multimedia, including Mountford, *The Dawn of Time*.

Brush Turkey This Dreaming is very well-known and popular with children, as it carries an important message. There are several similar versions in print and multimedia. I have retold it from Francis Firebrace's version. It is found in Reed, *Aboriginal Myths, Legends and Fables*; and Mountford, *The First Sunrise* and *Before Time Began*.

Butterfly This Dreaming, from a tribe who lived on the banks of the Murray River, is retold by Francis Firebrace. There are many versions in print. Similar ones are found in Ramsay Smith, *Myths and Legends of the Australian Aboriginals*; and Ellis, *This Is the Dreaming*.

Crow Francis Firebrace retells this Dreaming, of which there are many versions. It is found in Mountford, *The First Sunrise*; and Mudrooroo, *Aboriginal Mythology*. A similar version is in Isaacs, *Australian Dreaming*.

Gray Owl This Dreaming is told by Francis Firebrace and is found in Roberts & Roberts, *Shadows in the Mist*; and Parker, *Australian Legendary Tales*.

Kookaburra This story is said to come from south-west New South Wales, near Cobar, but it has also been attributed to other areas. It is found in Cox, *Fables of the Aborigines*; Ellis, *This is the Dreaming*; Mountford, *The Dawn of Time*; and Reed, *Aboriginal Myths, Legends and Fables*. Wattle Dreaming is found in Ramsay Smith, *Myths and Legends of the Australian Aboriginals*.

Lyrebird This Dreaming, said to be from the Blue Mountains area, is retold by Francis Firebrace. One version is found in Ramsay Smith, *Myths and Legends of the Australian Aboriginals*; and Reed, *Myths and Legends of Australia*.

Magpies This Dreaming is found in Mountford, *The Dawn of Time*; and Reed, *Aboriginal Myths, Legends and Fables*.

Rainbow Lorikeet This story, from the Bilbulmun people of Western Australia, is retold by Francis Firebrace. A version is found in Bennell and Thomas, *Aboriginal Legends from the Bilbulmun Tribe*.

Sea Eagle This story is retold by Francis Firebrace. It is found in Allen, *Time Before Morning*, which states that it comes from Manggalilji country in northern Australia.

Willy Wagtail This Dreaming information is provided by Francis Firebrace and several other Aboriginal people, from different parts of Australia. Similar information is found in Mountford, *The Dreamtime*; Mathews, *The Opal That Turned Into Fire*; Isaacs, *Australian Dreaming*; and Ellis, *This is the Dreaming*.

Barramundi This Dreaming, from a version by Francis Firebrace, is found in Bozic and Marshall, *Aboriginal Myths*; and Gulpilil, *Gulpilil's Stories of the Dreamtime* (sound recording).

Crab This Dreaming, from the Murinbata people of northern Australia, is retold by Francis Firebrace, and found in Allen, *Time Before Morning*.

Crocodile This Dreaming, from the Maung people of Goulburn Island, Northern Territory, is retold by Francis Firebrace, and found in Berndt and Berndt, *The Speaking Land*. Other Crocodile Dreamings are found in Reed, *Aboriginal Myths, Legends and Fables*.

Dolphin This story, retold by Francis Firebrace, is found in Allen, *Time Before Morning*, which states that it comes from the Wanungamulangwa people of Groote Eylandt, whose earliest ancestors were the dolphins or indjebena. *See also* Mountford, *The Dreamtime*; and Mudrooroo, *Aboriginal Mythology*.

Frog This Dreaming, a classic of children's literature, is retold from the version by Francis Firebrace. It is found in several books, including Mountford, *The Dreamtime*; Cox, *Fables of the Aborigines*; and Mudrooroo, *Aboriginal Mythology*.

Platypus Another children's classic, from Grafton in New South Wales, this Dreaming is retold by Francis Firebrace. There is a similar Dreaming from the Murray River area of Victoria.

Seal This Dreaming comes from Lake Alexandrina, at the mouth of the Murray River, Victoria; its setting is Rosetta Head, or The Bluff. The Dreaming is retold from Roberts & Roberts, *Shadows in the Mist*. Other Seal Dreamings are found in Reed, *Aboriginal Myths, Legends and Fables*; and Isaacs, *Australian Dreaming*.

Turtle This Dreaming is retold by Francis Firebrace, and found in Bozic and Marshall, *Aboriginal Myths*; and Ellis, *This is the Dreaming*.

Whale & Starfish This Dreaming has been retold many times. It has been attributed to different areas of New South Wales, and appears with little variation in the different versions. It is found in Reed, *Aboriginal Myths, Legends and Fables*; Isaacs, *Australian Dreaming*; Marshall, *People of the Dreamtime*; Mountford, *The Dawn of Time* and *The Dreamtime*; and Ellis, *This is the Dreaming*.

Ochre This Dreaming, said to come from the Flinders Ranges, central and South Australia, is retold by Francis Firebrace. There are several versions, known to many tribes, all describing a dingo or a gecko attacking a giant beast. Ochre Dreaming is found in Isaacs, *Australian Dreaming*; Ellis, *This Is the Dreaming*; and Mudrooroo, *Aboriginal Mythology*.

Sydney Harbor Bridge This modern Dreaming, said to be from La Perouse in Sydney, is retold from the version told by Brendan Kerin Japantardi.

Bibliography

The Aboriginal Children's History of Australia, Australia, Rigby, 1977

Kwork Kwork the Green Frog and other Tales from the Spirit Time, Canberra, Australian National University Press, 1977

Allen, Louis A. *Time Before Morning*, Australia, Rigby, 1976

Baglin, Douglas & Mullins, Barbara, *Aboriginals of Australia*, Sydney, A. H. & A. W. Reed, 1976

Bennell, E. and Thomas, A. *Aboriginal Legends from the Bibulmun Tribe*, Australia, Rigby, 1981

Berndt, R. M. and C. H. *The Speaking Land*, Australia, Penguin, 1989

Berndt, R. M. and C. H. (ed.) *Aboriginal Man in Australia*, Sydney, Angus & Robertson, 1965

Bettelheim, Bruno, *The Uses of Enchantment – The Meaning and Importance of Fairy Tales*, England, Penguin Books, 1979

Bozic, Sreten and Marshall, Alan, *Aboriginal Myths*, Victoria, Gold Star Publications, 1972

Breckwoldt, Roland & Steer, Gary, "Dingo!" *GEO, Australasia's Geographical Magazine*, 1986, vol. 8, number 2

Burnum Burnum, *Burnum Burnum's Aboriginal Australia – A Traveller's Guide*, Sydney, Angus & Robertson, 1988

Cairns, Sylvia (told by), *Uncle Willie Mackenzie's Legends of the Goundirs*, Australia, Jacaranda Press, 1967

Chapman, Graeme, *Common Australian Birds*, Australia, Lansdowne Press, 1970

Cowan, James, *Mysteries of the Dream-Time*, revised edn, UK/Sydney, Prism/Unity, 1992

Cox, Peter (selected and retold by), *Fables of the Aborigines*, Sydney, Antipodes Design, 1991

Cronin, Leonard, *Key Guide to Australian Mammals*, Australia, Reed, 1991

DeJose, John, *Australian Coastal Birds in Colour*, Australia, Treasure Press, 1989

Ellis, Jean A. *This Is the Dreaming*, Victoria, Collins Dove, 1994

Estes, Clarissa Pinkola, *Women Who Run With the Wolves*, Australia, Random House, 1995

Fontana, David, *The Secret Language of Symbols*, UK, Pavilion Books, 1993

Frazer, J. G. *The Golden Bough*, UK, Macmillan, 1922

Gulpilil, *Gulpilil's Stories of the Dreamtime*, sound recording, Sound Information Pty. Ltd, 1983

Huxley, Francis, *The Way of the Sacred*, London, Aldus Books, 1974

Isaacs, Jennifer (ed.), *Australian Dreaming*, Sydney, Lansdowne Press, 1980

Jung, Carl Gustav, *Man and His Symbols*, Garden City, NY, Doubleday, 1964

Lawlor, Robert, *Voices of the First Day*, Vermont, USA, Inner Traditions International, 1991

Layton, Robert, *Uluru – An Aboriginal History of Ayers Rock*, Canberra, Aboriginal Studies Press, 1986

Lee, Anthony & Martin, Roger, *The Koala*, Australia, New South Wales University Press, 1988

Lester, Yami, *Pages From an Aboriginal Book – History and the Land*, Alice Springs, Institute for Aboriginal Development, 1984

Marshall, Alan, *People of the Dreamtime*, Melbourne, Hyland House Publishing, 1952

Massola, Aldo, *Bunjil's Cave*, Australia, Lansdowne Press, 1968

Mathews, Janet (compiled by), *The Opal That Turned Into Fire*, Broome, Western Australia, Magabala Books Aboriginal Corporation, 1994

Morris, Ramona and Desmond, *Men and Snakes*, London, Sphere Books, 1965

Mountford, Charles P. *The Dreamtime*, Australia, Rigby, 1965
——. *The Dawn of Time*, Australia, Rigby, 1969
——. *The First Sunrise*, Australia, Rigby, 1971
——. *Before Time Began*, Melbourne, Thomas Nelson, 1976
——. *Aboriginal Conception Beliefs*, Melbourne, Australia, Hyland House Publishing, 1981

Mowaljarlai, David and Malnic, Jutta, *Yorro Yorro*, Broome, Western Australia, Magabala Books Aboriginal Corporation, 1993

Mudrooroo, *Aboriginal Mythology*, London, Aquarian, 1994

Nangan, J. & Edwards, H. *Joe Nangan's Dreaming*, Australia, Nelson, 1976

Noonuccal, Oodgeroo and Noonuccal, Kabul Oodgeroo, *The Rainbow Serpent*, Canberra, Australian Government Publishing Service, 1988

Parker, K. Langloh, *Australian Legendary Tales*, London, David Nutt, 1957

Ramsay Smith, W. *Myths and Legends of the Australian Aboriginals*, USA, Harrap, 1930

Reed, A. W. *Aboriginal Myths, Legends and Fables*, Australia, A. H. and A. W. Reed, 1982

___. *An Illustrated Encyclopedia of Aboriginal Life*, Australia, Literary Productions Ltd, 1974

___. *Myths and Legends of Australia*, Australia, A. H. and A. W. Reed, 1965

Roberts, Ainslie & Roberts, Dale, *Legends of the Dreamtime*, South Australia, Art Australia, 1975

___. *Shadows in the Mist*, Art Australia, 1989

Robinson, Roland, *The Man Who Sold His Dreaming*, Australia, Currawong, 1965

Robinson, Roland (selected by), *Aboriginal Myths and Legends*, Australia, Hamlyn Publishing, 1969

Roman, Sanaya, *Personal Power through Awareness*, California, H. J. Kramer Inc. Publishers, 1986

Steinbrecher, Edwin C. *The Inner Guide Meditation*, 6th edn, USA, Samuel Weiser Inc., 1988

Trezise, Percy & Roughsby, D. *The Quinkins*, Australia, Collins, 1978

Trezise, Percy, *Dream Road*, Australia, Allen & Unwin, 1993

Underhill, David, *Australia's Dangerous Creatures*, Reader's Digest (Australia), 1993

Wells, Anne E. *This Their Dreaming*, Australia, University of Queensland Press, 1971

White, Ian, *Australian Bush Flower Essences*, Australia, Transworld, 1991

Acknowledgments

First of all, gratitude to Spirit for the inspiration for this journey and the confirmations that supported its writing.

Many people and organizations have assisted me. My thanks to all who have helped me (including those that there was not space to include!), especially the Department of Aboriginal and Torres Strait Islander Arts, the NSW Aboriginal Educational Consultancy Group, the Aboriginal Council for Reconciliation and the Kalkadoon Aboriginal Sobriety House. Also, my gratitude to Andrew Powell; Sally Anne Brown; Jo Buchanan; Ian White; Carolyn Adams; Jannise Beecroft; Brendan Japantardi Kerin; Francis Firebrace; Danny and Pam Eastwood; Carolinda Witt, John and Liz Gilbert-Grant of "Freedom Potentials;" George Apps; Sandy Tutty; Len Sorbello of Wizz Cards BBS, Townsville; my sister Cathy and my Dad, Denis; and encouragement from Linda Tsdao; Angelo Cicada Catalano; Lizbeth Pulman, Maggie Hamilton and Peter Garrett. I would like to acknowledge the support of the late Burnum Burnum. Also my thanks to the artists and to Eddison Sadd Editions who have supported this project and helped me towards the realization of a dream, especially Sarah Howerd.

EDDISON • SADD EDITIONS

Editorial Director — Ian Jackson
Project Editor — Vivienne Wells
Proofreader — Russell Walton

Senior Art Editor — Sarah Howerd
Mac Designer — Brazzle Atkins
Production — Karyn Claridge and Charles James

CARDS PAINTED BY EACH ARTIST
DANNY EASTWOOD Gymea Lily, Lightning Man, Dingo, Emu, Koala, Brush Turkey, Black Swan, Crow, Magpies, Reconciliation (with Jamie)
JAMIE EASTWOOD Uluru, Echidna, Wombat, Bat, Kookaburra, Willy Wagtail, Seal
FRANCIS FIREBRACE Rainbow Serpent, Waratah, Brolga, Lyrebird, Platypus
LEAH DAWN PRIOR Moon, Seven Sisters, Sun, Kangaroo, Spider, Gray Owl, Rainbow Lorikeet
ROCKY D. SAVAGE Opal, Frilled-neck Lizard, Barramundi, Crab, Crocodile, Dolphin, Turtle, Whale & Starfish, Turtle Dreamtime (front of pack)
IAN BUNDELUK WATSON Southern Cross, Sturt's Desert Pea, Bogong Moth, Butterfly, Sea Eagle, Frog, Ochre, Sydney Harbor Bridge

The Author

Donni Hakanson

Donni Hakanson, shown here against a wall mural painted by Leah Dawn Prior (photo by Kirstin Heritage)

DONNI HAKANSON grew up in the outback of Queensland, Australia, and has since lived in Sydney and Townsville. This oracle is the result of a dream in early 1993. Her concept of the oracle as "a collection of contemporary Aboriginal art" as well as a representation of the ancient Dreaming in a modern form, brings together the culture and work of Aboriginal people today. The Dreamings were researched with Aboriginal storyteller Francis Firebrace. As a white person interpreting the Dreamings, she found the project a challenge but hopes it will help understanding of native tradition and contribute to Aboriginal reconciliation.

Donni has worked as a radio announcer, in film, in a bookshop, and as a street busker. She was also the agent for an Aboriginal performing troupe and her articles have appeared in national magazines. She is a trained bodyworker (Holistic Pulsing) and Reiki channel. Donni has self-published a book, *Native Symbols: A Guide to the Energies of the Australian Bush*, and gives readings with *Oracle of the Dreamtime*. She can be contacted by writing to PO Box HP366, Hermit Park, Queensland 4814, Australia (include SAE or IMO for return post) or email Brogla@hotmail.com.

Pauline E. MᶜLeod (Foreword)

Pauline is a highly respected and well-known storyteller, in the Aboriginal tradition, with an extensive repertoire of both traditional and original stories. She relates her stories with a clarity and simplicity that can only come from a deep understanding of, and empathy with, their intrinsic values. Pauline has developed a kind, gentle, yet graphic storytelling style that she has made her own.

Although Pauline became active as a storyteller, writer, and performer in 1988, since then, she has certainly made her mark. Working throughout NSW, as a teacher of Aboriginal culture, she has combined this work with that of a performing artist deeply committed to promoting a wider awareness and appreciation of the riches to be found in the Aboriginal cultural heritage.

Her undoubted ability and dedication have enabled her to win several awards and scholarships through the Australian Council of Arts. She has utilized these grants to further her research into Dreaming stories of the western regions of NSW. As a Writer-in-Residence, Pauline has researched and written a number of original stories, thus reinforcing the relevance of a continuously evolving storytelling tradition to contemporary Aboriginal culture.

More recently, Pauline has been involved in ABC TV productions (including "Playschool") as a writer and storyteller, and has accepted frequent invitations to weave her own special brand of storytelling and magic at the Australian Museum, the Powerhouse Museum, the Sydney Opera House, and the Museum of Contemporary Art in Sydney.

The Artists

DANNY EASTWOOD was named Aboriginal Artist of the Year by the New South Wales Aborigines and Islanders' Day Observance Committee in 1988. White dots are a prominent feature of his work, as they are in much Aboriginal art, both contemporary and traditional. He maintains that this is a form of impressionism and is useful for blending color. Danny spends much time in schools, promoting to children a better understanding of Aboriginal culture through arts and crafts.

JAMIE EASTWOOD, son of Danny, recently won the same award and is now a student on a three-year Visual and Performing Arts course at the University of Western Sydney. He intends his work to reflect his sensitivity and hope for a peaceful and harmonious relationship for the future of both black and white Australians. For him, displaying his respect for the land comes naturally, having descended from a culture where regeneration has been successful for more than 40,000 years.

FRANCIS FIREBRACE is one of Australia's best known Aboriginal storytellers and artists. His father was a member of the Yorta Yorta people in Victoria, Southern Australia. His performances include a traditional dance troupe and didgeridoo players, and he enjoys teaching dance and telling the Dreaming stories to help educate and mend bridges between white and Aboriginal Australia. His work is now recognized in North America and in Europe. Francis is father of Donni Hakanson's two children.

LEAH DAWN PRIOR, an artist since childhood, works closely with the Aboriginal community in Townsville, and has an Associate Diploma of Arts. Her grandmother was a "stolen child" from the Kanju tribe in far north Queensland. Her grandfather was of the Birri-Gubba people just south of Townsville (Bowen). Leah views her art as an important way of expressing her identity and culture as an Aboriginal person. She also sees it as a way of sharing her culture with others.

ROCKY D. SAVAGE is a Thursday Island Aborigine who has been painting for ten years. He comes from a large family which has no other artists, though he hopes to encourage other family members to take up art. He paints from his own inspiration, and from feelings deep within, prompted by childhood memories of the sea stories told by his father and uncle. His work features a number of different styles, and depicts colorful representations of the marine life that is familiar to coastal and island peoples.

IAN BUNDELUK WATSON is descended from the Boorooberongal and Warmuli clans, two of the 29 clans of the Darug nation whose traditional lands are now occupied by metropolitan Sydney. He is involved in Native Title land claims on behalf of his people, and is deeply committed to the preservation of his traditional culture. He is a prolific artist whose work is in demand throughout Australia and overseas, and he is also active in organizing Aboriginal art workshops and personal tours of Darug sites.